Exploring the Religions of Our World

Teacher's Manual

Nancy Clemmons, SNJM

ave maria press ● notre dame, indiana

Founded in 1865, Ave Maria Press is a ministry of the Indiana Province of Holy Cross.

www.avemariapress.com

ISBN-10 1-59471-126-7   ISBN-13 978-1-59471-126-8

Cover design by Katherine Robinson Coleman.

Text Design by Andy Wagoner.

Project Coordinator: Catherine M. Odell.

Printed and bound in the United States of America.

Contents

Introduction

Survey courses on the world's religions have grown in popularity over the past two decades. With the global village getting smaller, the rise in immigration, particularly from Asia and Latin America, and the fall of Communism in eastern and central Europe in the 1980s and 1990s, our awareness of religion as a driving force in the world's many cultures has increased. During this same period of time the number of ecumenical and interreligious dialogue groups has multiplied. The late Pope John Paul II contributed much to the increase in the relationships between Catholics and people from various religious traditions during his twenty-six year papacy. The chapter "Why So Many Religions?" in John Paul's book *Crossing the Threshold of Hope* is essentially a commentary on *Nostra Aetate*, the Vatican Council II document *Declaration on the Relation of the Church with non-Christian Religions*. Pope Benedict XVI continued this enthusiastic ecumenical outreach, making overtures in his first years as pope to the Jewish, Greek Orthodox, and Muslim communities.

Likewise, this course responds to the document *Nostra Aetate* (*In Our Time*). In this milestone document the Council called for a mutual understanding between Catholics and other religious traditions:

> The Church therefore, exhorts her sons, that through dialogue and collaboration with the followers of other religions carried out with prudence and love and in witness to the Christian faith and life, they recognize, preserve and promote the good things, spiritual and moral, as well as the socio-cultural values found among these men. (3)

To this end, all efforts to engage students in "dialogue and collaboration" with people of other religions are encouraged. For students to engage in dialogue and collaboration, it is important that they begin with some knowledge of other religious traditions for their efforts to be fruitful. *Exploring the Religions of Our World* strives to be as balanced as possible, asking the reader to hear the voices of those from other faiths. In addition, the separate features and the various activities attempt to bring each religious tradition more to life for the students.

These activities and learning challenges are based on the eight multiple intelligences: bodily/kinesthetic intelligence; interpersonal/relational intelligence; intrapersonal/introspective intelligence; logical/mathematical intelligence; musical/rhythmic intelligence; naturalistic intelligence; verbal/linguistic intelligence; and visual/spatial intelligence. Though people learn using all eight learning styles, each person has preferred ways of acquiring and processing information. The best overall learning takes place for a group when a variety of learning style options are provided for individuals in the group.

A course on the world's religions is different from any other course in a Catholic high school religion curriculum. In this revised edition, a new feature, "Through a Catholic Lens," has been added to each chapter to help students see similarities between other religious traditions and Catholicism. On the other hand, in this course, students are not primarily engaged in learning about the Catholic faith tradition, but about other religious traditions. For many students this is the first time they have sustained exposure to other religious traditions, especially those of the East. An open mind and heart as well as respect for the "other" is very important for each student to have as they strive to learn as much as they can from this course.

Student Preparation

This course is primarily for high school students in the eleventh and twelfth grades. There are some assumptions as to the typical student enrolled in this class. It is assumed that the student has some knowledge of the following:

- the Bible
- the biblical period of Jewish history
- Christian beliefs and practices
- Western history

How the Teacher's Manual Is Organized

The Teacher's Manual is prepared with the Catholic high school teacher in mind. However, both this manual and the student textbook can be used in parish programming and in other parochial, private, and public school settings.

How the Student Textbook Is Organized

The student textbook is organized into nine chapters. Chapter 1 is an introductory chapter to the study of the world's religions. Chapters 2 through 8 are in-depth studies of various religious traditions. The Appendix is a very brief survey of religious traditions with Christian roots founded in the United States.

The format of chapters 2 through 8 is a similar one:

Introduction: Historical Overview of the Religion
    Section Summary
    Section Review Questions
Section I: A Brief History of the Religion
    Sections on Historical Eras in the Life of this Religion up to the Modern Period
    Section Summary
    Section Review Questions
Section II: Sacred Stories and Sacred Scriptures
    Section Summary
    Section Review Questions
Section III: Beliefs and Practices
    Section Summary
    Section Review Questions
Section IV: Sacred Times
    Section Summary
    Section Review Questions
Section V: Sacred Places and Sacred Spaces
    Section Summary
    Section Review Questions
Section VI: The Religion Seen Through a Catholic Lens

The Purpose of the Student Textbook

It is well known that students learn best when they are interested in the topic. This textbook is intended to describe and explain in an appealing way some major elements of the world's religions. This textbook does not pretend to be exhaustive and does not claim to cover every or even a majority of the world's religions. Rather, it is intended to inform students on those religious traditions they are most likely to encounter. In addition, it is highly likely that not all students enrolled in this course are Catholic. Thus, the people students meet in class, at school, in sports, in neighborhoods, in places of employment, and in the media are likely to be represented in this book.

Since it is assumed that the starting point for students is some knowledge of biblical Judaism and Christianity, it is best to begin there. After an introductory chapter, students study Judaism, followed by Christianity and Islam. Each of these religious traditions began in the Near or Middle East and espouse belief in the one God of Abraham. After studying religious traditions other than their own, but which have some familiar roots, the textbook moves to Hinduism in Chapter 5 and its offshoot Buddhism in Chapter 6. Chapters 7 and 8 move from the subcontinent of India to the continent of Asia, where Buddhism continued to spread and where it encountered the indigenous religions of China and Japan.

The Epilogue (Religions with Christian and American Roots) can be used in conjunction with Chapter 3 (Christianity). The Epilogue briefly surveys five religions that have some Christian roots that students may have encountered or even espouse—the Church of Jesus Christ of Latter-day Saints; Church of Christ, Scientist; Seventh-day Adventist; Jehovah's Witness; and Unitarian Universalist.

It is emphasized that this is a survey course, but students are encouraged to go beyond what they learn in the textbook. Various student activities are suggested to bring to life the religious traditions of others.

Two different testing instruments are provided for each chapter—a multiple choice test and a short answer test. Using both of these tests allows students to show their cognitive comprehension of much of the material presented in these chapters. Reflection questions, class discussions, written and oral reports, and the wide variety of enrichment activities offered in Research and Activities allows other ways to assess your students' affective learning.

Engaging Minds, Hearts, and Hands is a multi-faceted educational mission statement for high school religious education texts published by Ave Maria Press that promises to educate the whole student. "An education that is complete is one in which the hands and heart are engaged as much as the mind," wrote Fr. Basil Moreau (1799–1873), founder of the Congregation of Holy Cross. "We want to let our students try their learning in the world and so make prayers of their education." Throughout this text, there are many opportunities for students to explore the religions of the world, through learning experiences that engage their own minds, hearts, and hands.

Student Activities

Students learn through a variety of modes. The running text within a chapter presents information about these religious traditions in a very direct way. Section Review Questions and Chapter Review Questions offer objective checkpoints for testing the student's knowledge of the material. Many features are included to enrich and bring life to the text. In addition, photos depicting adherents of the various religious traditions, sacred places, and the actual practice of devotions or worship are also presented to enhance the written information.

Text Reflection Questions

Besides reading, reflection questions are suggested to personalize the students' reflections and understanding. Reflection questions in the text may be approached in several manners. Whatever mode is chosen, it is strongly suggested that students be given time to really reflect before there is any concrete movement. Writing down the question, followed by an opportunity for students to jot down their thoughts helps them to keep focused on the task at hand. The following are suggested modes of approach. Choose the one most appropriate for the particular question asked and for student needs.

Journal Writing

Have the students write down the question and then respond. Their responses should reflect both their thoughts and feelings. Of course, you may use this exercise in other ways—not simply to have students respond to reflection questions in the text.

Decide ahead of time whether journal writing will be part of a student's formal course evaluation. Let the students know your decision from the start. Emphasize that this information is confidential between the individual student and the teacher. Admittedly, the evaluation of journal writing is subjective. The grade should not be based on *what* students write, but on whether the students were *thoughtful* about the assignment.

Writing Assignments

Students may also address the reflection questions as a more formal written assignment. This can be accomplished by individuals or by small groups. It can be done as an in-class activity or as a homework assignment. If done with a small group, the students should first discuss the question. Then, one paper can be presented to represent the group with the names of each participant included. The same grade goes to all whose names are on the paper.

Discussions

Discussion of a reflection question can take several forms:

Class Discussion: The entire class is engaged in the discussion of the question. The desire is to hear from as many students as possible. Make efforts to hear from others—not just the same few who are comfortable speaking in a large group.

Fishbowl Discussion: This engages a small group of students in the discussion of the topic while others observe. The name "fishbowl" comes from the configuration of the activity. A small group of students, perhaps six or seven in number, sit in a circle and discuss the question at hand. The rest of the class sits around the outside of the circle and observes the discussion. Only those within the circle talk. It is often desirable to have more than one fishbowl activity on the same question. They would not be conducted simultaneously, but consecutively.

Small Groups Discussion: This activity enables all students to participate in the discussion. Often students who are not comfortable sharing in a large group contribute in a small group setting. Students whose ideas are affirmed in a small group tend to feel freer to share when class is reconvened to the large group.

Dyad or Triad Discussion: Before having a class discussion it is sometimes helpful to have students discuss the question at hand with one or two other students. As with a small group, some students will feel freer to share in the large group after their peers have validated their ideas.

Inviting Adherents of a Religious Tradition to Share Their Faith

There is no doubt that students can learn much from engaging in conversation with practitioners of a particular religious tradition. However, it must be recognized that those who espouse a religious tradition do not speak for the entire tradition. Rather, they speak about their experience as one individual practitioner of that tradition. For example, a Buddhist from Sri Lanka would have a very different experience than a Buddhist from Korea. In like manner, a Catholic from Los Angeles would have a very different experience than a Catholic from Kenya. Yet, listening to an adherent from a particular religious tradition brings life to the written pages of a textbook. Unless you live in a very religiously pluralistic region of the country, it is doubtful you would be able to get guest speakers for every religious tradition studied in this course. However, there are indirect ways to learn from people of various persuasions. For example:

Guest Speakers: It is very effective in a course on the world's religions to invite people who are practitioners of a religious tradition to share their beliefs with students. Start close to home. If you have students, either in the class or in the school, who are from the religious tradition being presented, invite them to share something about their religious tradition. If students have parents or relatives who are adherents of the religious tradition under study, invite them to speak. If students practice the religious tradition being studied, perhaps their religious leader would be willing to be a guest speaker. You can also contact a local ecumenical and/or interreligious affairs office for suggestions.

It is important that any speakers should be adept at speaking with teenagers. These people should also be empathetic toward the whole interreligious dialogue endeavor. Prepare the speaker by allowing him or her to review the text material related to his or her religion, telling this person how many students are in the class and your time constraints. Find out about this speaker's openness to a question and answer period. Invite speakers to bring any objects important to their religious tradition.

Field Trips: A good way to learn through many senses at once is to go on a field trip to various places of worship. There, students will be able to hear from one or more practitioners of a religious tradition in their own setting. Students will also be able to see religious objects in their proper context, feel, and perhaps even smell that which is sacred to adherents of that religious tradition.

It is important to prepare both the speaker(s) and the students for this event. Besides what you believe to be important for preparation, ask the speaker(s) what *they* believe is important for students to know ahead of time.

Interviews: If it is difficult to take an entire class on a field trip, assign students the project of interviewing a person from a religious tradition that is under study. Students may want to work with a video camera or even with a cassette tape recorder. Suggestions for interview questions:

- In what ways is this religious tradition a driving force in your life?
- What part of this tradition do you find most difficult?
- Why do people in your religious tradition believe _____?
- How does one become an adherent to your religious tradition?
- How does this religious tradition relate to other religious traditions?
- What do you think is the greatest contribution this religious tradition makes to humankind?

It is suggested that students conclude their written or oral report on the interview with their reaction to the interview process. Was the interview a positive experience? What did they learn? What was helpful? What was not helpful?

Audio-visual Presentation: If having a speaker from this religious tradition is not possible, watching all or segments of a video or DVD about a particular religious tradition is also quite effective. Though it is a monologue rather than a dialogue, audio-visual presentations often have several people speaking on behalf of what they believe. In this way students hear a variety of experiences within the same religious tradition. Some videos or DVDs come with a teacher's guide to assist the teacher.

Computer Technology: Students can now learn about various religious traditions through the Internet and through computer software. More and more religious traditions are using the World Wide Web to share who they are, what they believe, what their activities are, and the like. However, it is important to guide students to accurate and authoritative sources on the Web.

Individual religious traditions also produce computer software that is helpful in learning about at least one aspect of that tradition. In addition, software containing information about a variety of religious traditions can also be found on the market.

Newspaper and Magazine Clippings: With the growing interest in the topics of religion and spirituality, students are more apt to find newspaper and magazine articles about activities of various religious traditions. Besides a growing interest in spiritual concerns, religion also plays an important role in many of the world's conflicts. A number of newspapers and news magazines have a religion section, at least periodically.

Encourage students to keep a scrapbook of clippings. Then when a particular religious tradition is studied, what was recently in the news can be discussed with more background information.

Content and Scope

The content of this text includes an introductory chapter and then seven chapters about the major religions of the world: Judaism, Christianity, Islam, Hinduism, Buddhism, Chinese Religions, and Japanese Religions. The Appendix surveys five smaller religious traditions indigenous to the United States that students may have already encountered. These smaller religious groups are: the Church of the Latter-day Saints; the Church of Christ, Scientist; Seventh-day Adventist; Jehovah's Witness; and Unitarian Universalists.

As with most textbooks, *Exploring the Religions of the World* provides an abundance of material for the cognitive domain of learning. After completing the course, students should have a working knowledge of the major religions of the world, as well as familiarity with religious vocabulary linked to each religious tradition. However, the exercises and reflection questions and many of the Research and Activities projects can move students to the higher levels of learning such as application, analysis, synthesis, and evaluation.

As noted previously, each chapter also offers students the option to look at each religious tradition through "the lens of Catholicism." This feature examines the core differences between the featured religion and Catholicism. This Catholic theological touchstone at the end of each chapter enables students to look again at each world religion. It encourages students to analyze that religion in the spirit of ecumenism and with a renewed understanding of their own Catholic tradition.

Chapter outlines for *Exploring the Religions of the World* follow:

1. **Beginning the Journey**
   - Setting the Stage
   - What Is Religion?
   - Why Study the World's Religions?
   - A Different Religion Class
   - Setting the Context of Catholics in Dialogue

- Some Elements or Patterns of Religion
  - Sacred Stories and Sacred Scriptures
  - Beliefs and Practices
  - Sacred Time
  - Sacred Places and Sacred Spaces
- Research and Activities
- Prayer—The Peace Prayer of St. Francis

2. **Judaism**
   - Living Religion
   - A Brief History of Judaism
   - Sacred Stories and Sacred Scriptures
   - Beliefs and Practices
   - Sacred Time
   - Sacred Places and Sacred Spaces
   - Judaism through a Catholic Lens
   - Conclusion
   - Research and Activities
   - Prayer—Aleinu

3. **Christianity**
   - Followers of the Nazarene
   - A Brief History of Christianity
   - Sacred Stories and Sacred Scriptures
   - Beliefs and Practices
   - Sacred Time
   - Sacred Places and Sacred Spaces
   - Other Denominations through a Catholic Lens
   - Conclusion
   - Research and Activities
   - Prayer—The Lord's Prayer

4. **Islam**
   - Overcoming Stereotypes
   - A Brief History of Islam
   - Sacred Stories and Sacred Scriptures
   - Beliefs and Practices
   - Sacred Time
   - Sacred Places and Sacred Spaces
   - Islam through a Catholic Lens
   - Conclusion
   - Research and Activities
   - Prayer—The Fattiha

- Japanese Religions through a Catholic Lens
- Conclusion
- Research and Activities
- Prayer—Shinto Prayer for Peace

9. **Epilogue**
    - Close to Home
    - Church of Jesus Christ of Latter-day Saints
    - Seventh-day Adventists
    - Watchtower Bible and Tract Society
    - The Church of Christ, Scientist
    - Unitarian Universalists
    - Research and Activities

Appendix

Catholic Handbook for Faith

Glossary

Additional Activities

Using both the right brain and the left brain expands student learning. Create projects in which students can explore the art, architecture, music, and literature (including poetry and plays) of the various religious traditions. This can be done on an individual or small group basis. They can be in-class projects or projects that are presented to the class. Consider showing at least one or two full-length videos during the semester.

Chapter 1: Beginning the Journey

Introduction

This first chapter sets the context for studying the world's religions. Students have typically had a number of courses covering many aspects of Catholic Christianity. This course is an opportunity to explore religious traditions other than Catholic Christianity, as well as one response to the Church's call to respect what is true and holy in other religious traditions. Additionally, a new chapter feature, *Through a Catholic Lens*, highlights similarities—and differences—between Catholicism and other religions.

There are many religions in our world and most are represented in North America. There is no one religious tradition in any given region of the United States.

In this chapter, students will:

- survey religious diversity;
- learn a definition of "religion" and reasons for studying the world's religions;
- reflect on why they are taking this course;
- gain attitudes of empathy and respect towards those who think and worship differently;
- discover some common elements and patterns found in religious traditions.

Resources for Chapter 1

Books

Carmody, Denise Lardner, and T. L. Brink. *Ways to the Center: An Introduction to World Religions.* 6th ed. Belmont, CA: Wadsworth Publishing, 2006.

Cassidy, Edward Idris. *Ecumenism and Interreligious Dialogue: Unitatis Redintegratio, Nostra Aetate.* New York: Paulist Press, 2005.

Confessing Christian Faith in a Pluralistic Society. Collegeville, MN: Institute for Ecumenical and Cultural Research, 1995.

Earhart, H. Byron. *Religious Traditions of the World: A Journey Through Africa, Mesoamerica, North America, Judaism, Christianity, Islam, Hinduism, Buddhism, China, and Japan.* San Francisco: HarperSanFrancisco, 1993.

Eliade, Mircea. *The Sacred and the Profane.* New York: Harcourt, Brace, 1959.

Flannery, O.P., Austin. *Vatican Council II: The Conciliar and Post Conciliar Documents.* Northport, NY: Costello Company, 1975.

Ludwig, Theodore M. *The Sacred Paths: Understanding the Religions of the World.* 4th ed. Upper Saddle River, NJ: Prentice Hall, 2005.

Noss, David S. *A History of the World's Religions.* 12th ed. Upper Saddle River, NJ: Prentice Hall, 2007.

Novak, Philip. *The World's Wisdom: Sacred Texts of the World's Religions*. San Francisco: HarperSanFrancisco, 1994.

Richard, Lucien. *What are They Saying About Christ and World Religions?* New York: Paulist Press, 1981.

Sharma, Arvind. *Our Religions*. San Francisco: HarperSanFrancisco, 1993.

Smart, Ninian, and Richard D. Hecht. *Sacred Texts of the World: A Universal Anthology*. New York: Crossroad, 1982.

————. *Dimensions of the Sacred: An Anatomy of the World's Beliefs*. Berkeley: University of California Press, 1996.

————. *The World's Religions*. 2nd ed. New York: Cambridge University Press, 1998.

————. *Worldviews: Crosscultural Explorations of Human Beliefs*. 3rd ed. Upper Saddle River, N.J.: Prentice Hall, 2000.

Smith, Jonathan Z., William Scott Green, and Jorunn Jacobsen Buckley. *The HarperCollins Dictionary of Religion*. San Francisco: HarperSanFrancisco, 1995.

Audio-visual Resources

Essentials of Faith. Films Media Group, 2006. A seven-part series in which five are relevant to this course: *Judaism, Christianity, Islam, Hinduism,* and *Buddhism*. 24 minutes each.

Religion as a Window on Culture. Films Media Group, 1998. A six-part series that includes *Introduction and Sacred Space; Sacred Rituals, Sacred Spaces; Sacred Time; Sacred Memory; Sacred Text and Stories;* and *Sacred Journey and Conclusion*. 17–23 minutes each.

Religions of the World Video Series. Schlessinger Media, 1996. A thirteen-part series, each part 50 minutes in length. Of interest are the following: *Judaism, Orthodox and Roman Catholic Christianity, Islam, Hinduism, Buddhism, Confucianism and Taoism,* and *Shinto*. A teacher's guide for each is available at www.libraryvideo.com.

The Long Search Video Series. DVD/VHS. (Ambrose Video Publishing, 2001) A thirteen-part series with the British television drama writer, Ronald Eyre, who spent three years investigating various religious traditions of the world. The original broadcast was on the BBC in 1978, but much is still relevant today.

Internet Resources

Creating Interfaith Communities— http://gbgm-umc.org/missionstudies/interfaith/o-faith.html

Monastic Interreligious Dialogue— www.monasticdialog.com

Phan, Peter C. *Evangelization in a Culture of Pluralism: Challenges and Opportunities*. A pdf from the United States Conference of Catholic Bishops' website, www.usccb.org/evangelization/Phan.rtf.

Pontifical Council for Interreligious Dialogue— www.vatican.va/roman_curia/pontifical_councils/ interelg/documents/rc_pc_interelg_pro_20051996_en.html

Religion and Ethics. Public Broadcasting Services— www.pbs.org/wnet/religionandethics/index_flash. html

Speaking of Faith. American Public Media— www.speakingoffaith.publicradio.org

United States Catholic Conference of Bishops Department of Ecumenical and Interreligious Affairs— www.usccb.org/seia

www.beliefnet.com

Setting the Stage (pages 7–9)

Preview

A course on the world's religions is a distinctively different course than any other religion course students have thus far taken. In this course students will explore a number of religious traditions. Beliefs and practices may seem very foreign and even strange to your students. However, it's important to remind students that all people—no matter what their religion—are created by the one loving God.

Warm Up

Give the class ten to twelve minutes to look through the textbook to familiarize themselves with it in a general way. Ask students to tell what they personally know about the religious traditions represented in photos and in the chapter titles throughout the book.

Conduct some quick straw polls. "How many of you know Muslims?" "How many have met a Hindu?" "Who has been to a Jewish synagogue?" "Which religions do you and your peers know little or nothing about?"

Using the Text

- Give students several minutes to read this section, "Setting the Stage," on their own.

  Break the class into dyads or triads to discuss in their groups: "What is it about religion that can motivate people to move to a foreign land or even die for their beliefs?"

  Allow fifteen minutes for these small group discussions before reconvening the class as a whole. Call on students from each small group to share their perceptions and ideas about the impact of religion.

- For the Reflection Question about local religious diversity on page 9, list the various religious traditions in your area on the board. Circle the ones they will be learning in the course of the next few months. You may want to have a map of your region and indicate locations of the various places of worship in your town or region.

What Is Religion? (page 9)

Objective

In this section the students will:

- learn that the word "religion," like "wisdom" and "beauty," is difficult to define, but that the Latin root, "religio," means "to bind."
- understand that religious beliefs and practice were once much less separated from the rhythm of life for people.

Preview

Though illusive and hard to define, the students will see later in this chapter that there are some elements, patterns, or what Professor Ninian Smart calls "dimensions," that help in categorizing whether or not something is a religious tradition. The term "religion" comes from the Latin word "religio" which means "to bind." Those who embrace a religion "bind" themselves to certain beliefs and practices because they hold certain things sacred, and therefore worthy of reverence and respect.

Using the Text

- Ask the students to write in their notebooks a definition of "religion" in their own words. Go around the room asking students to read their definition. As they do, jot down the main phrase on the board or a flipchart. Put checks next to those that are repeated.
- Generally, students come up with definitions that relate to beliefs, ethics, the meaning of life, etc. In a concrete way, students will see that defining religion is "all over the board." Save this list to use for a later discussion on the common elements and patterns of various religious traditions.

Extending the Text

- After having students read this section, assign the first Research and Activities project on page 24 of the student text as an in-class or school library research assignment. This activity asks students to use four different English dictionaries to locate and write down definitions of the word "religion." As a wrap-up activity, students should write their own definitions of the word in light of what they have learned in this section.

Why Study the World's Religions? (pages 9–10)

Objective

In this section the students will:

- learn seven reasons to study the world's religions;
- identify elements that would be useful in any systematic study of religion.

Preview

On their own, students will probably be able to articulate one or two common reasons for studying the world's religions. This section offers seven of the most common reasons. Elaborate on these reasons in light of current events and in terms of the religious diversity of your own area, which students have already discussed.

Using the Text

- After students have read this section, "Why Study the World's Religions?", initiate a discussion about the reasons for studying religion listed in their book. Which reason do students think would be the strongest?

- Have students answer the Reflection Question about why they are studying the world's religions on page 10 in their notebooks or journals. This reflection question gives students an opportunity to set a goal. For example, if a student responds that he or she is studying the world's religions "to gain a better understanding of the present world," that could be a goal for this course.

- Let students know that the reason they choose could constitute a personal goal they could adopt for the course. As the course proceeds, schedule a periodic journal assignment in which students note how what they are learning has helped them "gain a better understanding of the present world" (or whichever of the seven reasons they noted).

A Different Religion Class (pages 10–12)

Studying with a New Attitude

Objective

In this section the students will:

- learn why the study of the world's religions is different from any other religion class;
- appreciate the need to adopt an attitude of empathy to understand the religious framework and attitude of others;
- recognize that the study of religion requires learning in both the head and heart.

Preview

At the beginning of this chapter, the text states that studying the world's religions is different from any other religion class. This section answers *why* it is different. Previous religion classes have addressed such issues as God, creation, the human condition, living a moral life, and salvation as understood by Catholic Christianity. A study in the world's religions addresses these and other issues, but looks at how other religious traditions understand and interpret them.

Remind students that empathy toward other religions is an important attitude for those taking this course to adopt. Treating the religious beliefs and practices of others as inferior or superior makes it difficult to study and encounter other religions with objectivity and respect. Neither is it helpful—or valid—to adopt a relativistic approach. Relativism erroneously advises us that "what is true for you is true, and what is true for me is true." Different religious traditions ask different questions, so comparing truth statements is not helpful.

Empathy is the best attitude, for it assumes that practitioners of other religious traditions have something to teach us. In addition, empathy calls us to respect persons of other faiths as fellow human beings, regardless of their religious tradition. And, as Pope John Paul II noted in 1990 in his encyclical letter *Redemptoris Missio* (The Mission of the Redeemer), "dialogue can enrich each side."

Warm Up

Divide the class into five groups. Assign one of the issues mentioned in the previous section—God, creation, the human condition, living a moral life, or salvation—to each group. Distribute markers and large sheets of newsprint to each group. Have the groups discuss and then write down what Catholic Christianity teaches about their topic.

Using the Text

- Compare and discuss the newsprint posters. Hang them around the room so that others can comment and add to the response.
- Engage students in a discussion about the need for empathy in friendships and in all relationships. Ask students what they think of the Navaho proverb which asks us to "walk a mile in the moccasins of another."
- Show a fifteen to twenty minute film segment of one of the films listed as a resource to give students an overview of basic information and cultural knowledge about Judaism, Christianity, Islam, Hinduism, or Buddhism.

Extending the Text

- Read aloud the quotation from Pope Benedict XVI about "equality."
- Reinforce the Holy Father's point. This study of the religions of the world does not teach that all religions are *equally* inspired by God or *equally* valid. Equality in interreligious dialogue refers to the equal and personal dignity of each person in the dialogue.
- Remind students that in a broader way, this study will reaffirm the unique and sacred dignity of all people, particularly in the context of their chosen religious tradition.

Setting the Context of Catholics in Dialogue (pages 12–16)

Benefits of the Council and *Ecumenical Dialogue Is a Duty of All Catholics*

Objective

In this section the students will:

- learn of the ecumenical efforts of Pope John XXIII during his brief pontificate, 1958–1963;
- recognize that ecumenism is an ongoing effort by the Catholic Church to engage in dialogue *with* other churches, rather than setting itself *against* them;
- gain a fuller understanding of the term **liturgy,** the public worship of the Church;
- appreciate that the ecumenical efforts of the Catholic Church continue up to our present day;
- become familiar with the three Vatican II documents that address ecumenical dialogue and religious freedom for other Christians and also for non-Christians;
- explore modern Catholic understandings of the vocabulary terms **evangelization** and **witnessing.**

Preview

When Cardinal Angelo Roncalli became pope, he was already committed to ecumenical outreach. He had ministered side by side with Greek Orthodox and Muslim religious leaders in Turkey and had helped Jews pursued by the Nazis before and during World War II. As John XXIII, Roncalli continued to work towards Christian unity and active dialogue with non-Christian religions. Additionally, this pope had language offensive to Jews removed from the Good Friday liturgy. It was also Pope John who called for an Ecumenical Council in 1962, making sure that it included not only Catholic bishops from around the world but Protestant, Eastern Orthodox and Jewish leaders as well.

Using the Text

- Present the ecumenical initiative and outreach of the Catholic Church as a continuing and growing story—from Vatican Council II (1962–1965) to the present. Every pope since Pope John XXIII, who called the council, has followed in his footsteps. Pope Paul VI, Pope John Paul II, and Pope Benedict XVI have all made great efforts to meet with non-Catholic religious leaders in their own lands and churches. Fostering and supporting ecumenical dialogue has rebuilt a spirit of respect and collaboration among many of the churches of the world. All Catholics are called to evangelize the world. This mandate includes young people and high school students who live in a nation and world that is more religiously diverse than ever before. Integrating the values of loving tolerance and respect and learning to dialogue through actions as well as words should be the focus of discussion as students read and reflect on this section.
- Ask: "What's needed for constructive dialogue between people with different points of view?"
- Invite students to discreetly share reconciliation experiences in their own lives or families.
- Share several examples of reconciliation brought about through dialogue.

- Build on the definition of **liturgy** presented in the text. As the official public worship of the Church, liturgy is also the perfect context for reconciliation, for prayer for those of other faiths, and for peace among all peoples.

Extending the Text

- If possible, pass around several copies of the published documents of the Second Vatican Council. Bookmark documents that focus on interfaith dialogue, and have students briefly page through them.
- Show pictures of the gathering of religious leaders at Vatican Council II, 1962–1965.
- Create a historical context for this event. Share easily researched facts that students could identify with about what life was like in the U.S in 1962. John F. Kennedy was President of the United States. A first class stamp cost 4¢. Lt. Col. John Glenn was the first American to orbit earth. In October, the Cuban Missile Crisis brought the nation close to war with the U.S.S.R. The U.S. population was 186 million, etc.
- Referring to the Reflection Question on page 16, engage students in a discussion on what "evangelization" means and "looks like."
- Provide seven or eight basic facts about the creeds and practices of Judaism, Islam, Buddhism, and Hinduism. Have students break down into small groups of three or four to create skits showing how they could respectfully "evangelize" with students from other religious traditions.

Some Common Elements or Patterns (pages 17–21)

Sacred Stories and Sacred Scriptures and *Beliefs and Practices* and *Sacred Time* and *Sacred Places and Sacred Spaces*

Objective
In this section the students will:
- survey the four aspects of religious tradition found in most religions—Sacred Stories and Sacred Scriptures; Beliefs and Practices; Sacred Time; and Sacred Places and Sacred Spaces;
- discuss the vocabulary term **myths** as it relates to Sacred Stories;
- gain a broad overview of the meaning of the four aspects of religion in the major faith traditions.

Preview
One dictionary calls religion "a specific fundamental set of beliefs and practices generally agreed upon by a number of persons or sects." Refer to the definitions of "religion" that students have already written. Then explain what's meant by the text which states that students will study "what a religion is" rather than "what is religion." Those elements of religion addressed in the next section, "Some Common Elements or Patterns of Religion," are Sacred Stories and Sacred Scriptures, Beliefs and Practices, Sacred Time, and Sacred Places and Sacred Spaces.

Using the Text
- Give students ten to fifteen minutes to carefully read this section.
- Gather copies of the sacred books (Sacred Stories and Sacred Scriptures) from Judaism, Anglicanism, (or another Protestant denomination), Islam, Buddhism, etc. to show students.
- Assign the second activity in Research and Activities on page 24 on the common elements of religion. This can be done in class either in small groups or by students working on their own. The following is a sample.

Catholicism
  Sacred Stories
    Creation of Adam and Eve
    The birth of Jesus
    The many stories about Mary and the saints
  Sacred Scripture
    The Bible
  Community
    Church
    People of God
    Body of Christ
  Beliefs
    One God
    God created all things and they were good
    Trinity

Jesus is both human and divine

Communion of saints

Resurrection of the body

There is eternal reward or eternal punishment

God forgives all sin

Actions

Love God above all things

Love your neighbor as yourself

Sacred Spaces

Churches

Chapels

Shrines

Holy Land

Sacred Times

Prayer

Sacramental moments

Liturgical seasons

Benediction

Personal devotions

Extending the Text

- Recap each of the four sections on the elements of religion and summarize the major points.
- Call on students to respond to the Review Questions throughout this section, especially the questions on pages 19 and 21 that focus on prayer, sacred time, and sacred places and spaces.

Through a Catholic Lens (pages 22–23)

Other Elements or Patterns

Objective

In this section the students will:

- be reminded that this course will study other religions by identifying common elements they share with Catholicism. These religions will then be examined in the light of Catholicism;
- recognize that all religions feature the search for God and a desire for salvation;
- realize that the mission of the Catholic Church is to preach the Gospel to all, and then to share first its common elements, and then the fullness of the Gospel, with other religions.

Preview

The Catholic Church recognizes that there is a genuine and holy search for God and salvation in all other religions. Nonetheless, it is commissioned by Christ to preach the Gospel to all peoples of the world. "Go and teach all nations," Jesus Christ told his apostles. Seeing itself as successors of Peter and the apostles, the Church believes that it has a fuller teaching and truth to share with the world. Catholicism respectfully maintains that its teaching goes beyond the teaching of other religions. Sharing its own unique teaching through an **apologetic** outreach is a continuing mission of the Church. This section not only summarizes the working principles that will guide this course of study, it also challenges students in a wonderful way. They can fully engage themselves in the academic study of the world's religions. They are also encouraged, however, to look for opportunities to engage in dialogues with people of other religious traditions and perhaps even visit their places of worship.

Using the Text

- Have students flip through the book to locate the *Through A Catholic Lens* feature near the end of each chapter.
- Remind students that looking at other major religions through the Catholic "lens" or point of view can strengthen their own sense of identity as Catholics and also build their understanding and appreciation for people of other faiths. On the other hand, students should commit themselves to a respectful and open-minded attitude in this study of different systems of thought, worship, and lifestyle.

Extending the Text

- Call on students to find out how comfortable they are in immersing themselves in the study of cultures and belief systems that will be very different than their own.
- Ask students if they think they will find any special difficulties in using the basic tools of study in this exploration of major religions of the world.
- Inform students of the date set for this first chapter test. Then, spend twenty to thirty minutes reviewing with the students. Conclude the review and direct students to *The Peace Prayer of St. Francis* on page 25 of the student text. Recite the prayer together. Then point out the universal appeal of this prayer.

Chapter 1 Review Questions and Answers

1. Briefly describe the religious diversity in our world today.

   We live in a global village. Religious diversity abounds in the world, especially in large cities such as London, Montreal, Johannesburg, and Bombay. In each of these cities, you could find Christians, Buddhists, Muslims, Jews, Hindus, and many others. Even among Christians, there are many different denominations and rites.

2. Why use the term "world's religions" rather than "world religions" in studying the various religious traditions?

   We use the phrase "world's religions" rather than "world religions" because we are studying religions that are in our world, but are not necessarily worldwide religions.

3. Where did the word "religion" originate? Why do you think it is so difficult to define "religion"?

   The word "religion" is derived from the Latin word religio meaning "to bind." (Answers will vary on second part of question.)

4. What attitude is asked of us in studying some of the world's religions? Explain.

   In studying the world's religions, we must be non-judgmental and maintain an attitude of empathy. This means that we should try to identify and understand the situation of another. It is also important to remain humble, open, and respectful towards those who belong to a different religious tradition.

5. What makes a class on the world's religions different from other religion classes?

   A class on the world's religions is different from other religion classes in that in every other religion class we learn about many aspects of the Catholic Christian religion. In a class on the world's religions we learn about other religions, too.

6. What are some reasons for studying the world's religions?

   Some reasons for studying the world's religions are: to assist a person in being more open and accepting of people who, on the surface, seem different; to dispel fears and misunderstandings relating to persons of other religious traditions; to gain a better insight into human beings by understanding their religious activities; to gain a better understanding of the history of humankind's various civilizations, since religion is almost always an important factor; to gain a better understanding of the various cultures around the globe today; to learn from some of the world's great sources of wisdom.

7. Relate some of the ways in which Popes John XXIII, Paul VI, John Paul II, and Benedict XVI broke ground in the Catholic Church's relationship with other religious traditions.

   Pope John XXIII had been a diplomat in Turkey during World War II and had worked closely with Greek Orthodox and Muslim religious leaders. He profoundly believed in ecumenism. During his short papacy, he reached out to other Christians, to Muslims, and to the Jewish people. Pope Paul VI continued an ecumenical outreach and met with the Patriarch of Constantinople as well as the Anglican bishops of England. Pope John Paul II was the first pope since Peter to enter a synagogue.

He tirelessly pursued ecumenical dialogue with other faiths. Pope Benedict XVI has continued to dialogue with Muslims and those from other religions of the world.

8. Why is interreligious dialogue a duty of all Catholic Christians? In what way can a Catholic fulfill this duty?

    All people baptized in Christ are called to evangelize. Even though we live in a world of great religious diversity, Catholics should feel free to witness to their faith without necessarily trying to convert those who are equally committed to their religious traditions. We must respectfully share the gift of our Catholic faith with others.

9. What are the common elements or patterns we will be using in studying the world's religions?

    The four common elements or patterns we will be using in our study of the world's religions are: 1) sacred story and sacred scriptures; 2) beliefs and practices; 3) sacred time; and 4) sacred places and sacred spaces.

Chapter 1 Test Answers

Multiple Choice (3 points each)

1. b, 2. c, 3. a, 4. b, 5. d, 6. b, 7. d, 8. a, 9. a, 10. c

Short Answer (20 points)

1. The four common elements or patterns we will be using in our study of the world's religions are: 1) sacred story and sacred scriptures; 2) beliefs and practices; 3) sacred time; and 4) sacred places and sacred spaces (examples will vary).

Note:

All subsequent Chapter Tests are graded on a 100 point scale. The Chapter 1 test, due to the shorter length of the chapter, is more like a quiz and is graded on a 50 point scale.

Chapter 1 Test

Name _____

Multiple Choice. *Write the letter of the best choice in the space provided.* (3 points each)

_____ 1. The major reason for the expansion in religious diversity in the United States is
    a. a growing interest in religion.
    b. an increase in immigration from Asia and Latin America.
    c. the United States Constitution was revised.
    d. a decrease in Christianity.

_____ 2. The major reason a class on the world's religions is distinct from other religion classes is
    a. a world's religions class deals only with facts and not beliefs.
    b. a world's religions class does not include Christianity.
    c. a world's religions class explores many religious traditions, not just one.
    d. none of the above.

_____ 3. It is difficult to define religion because
    a. there are so many definitions scholars cannot decide which one is best.
    b. every religion has its own definition.
    c. the word cannot be found in the Bible.
    d. none of the above.

_____ 4. We are asked to come to the study of the world's religions with an attitude of empathy because
    a. Jesus demonstrated empathy.
    b. empathy allows us to accept the beliefs and practices of other people on their own terms.
    c. empathy is better than sympathy.
    d. none of the above.

_____ 5. A myth
    a. is a true story.
    b. is a false story.
    c. is a legend.
    d. points to a spiritual truth.

_____ 6. With regard to the world's religions, the Catholic Church teaches that those who believe in one God
    a. are the true religions.
    b. share a fundamental belief called monotheism.
    c. are true and holy while others are not.
    d. are superior while others are inferior.

_____ 7. The term **religion** traditionally means
    a. to pray constantly.
    b. to be a peacemaker.
    c. to search for God.
    d. to bind one's self to God or to something else beyond.

_____ 8. When the Catholic Church talks about **evangelization**, it means

    a. witnessing to one's faith without trying to get others to convert to Catholicism.

    b. ignoring all religious differences.

    c. insisting that everyone should be a Catholic.

    d. pretending that all religions are equally valid.

_____ 9. Two of the common elements seen in every religious tradition are

    a. beliefs and practices.

    b. prayer postures and sacred space.

    c. scripture verses that must be said daily.

    d. extensive training for priesthood or ministry.

_____ 10. The only reason that is *not* a valid one for studying the world's religions is

    a. to gain a better understanding of the present world.

    b. to gain a better understanding of your own faith.

    c. to learn how to win religious arguments.

    d. to discover what is universal among all the world's cultures.

Short Answer. *Answer the following question using what you have learned in this chapter. Add examples from your own experience with people from other religious traditions.* (20 points)

1. List the four elements or patterns found in religious traditions and give one example of each.

Chapter 2: Judaism

Introduction

We begin our study in specific religious traditions with Judaism. Judaism is the religion of Jesus. Because of their previous studies in Catholic Christianity, high school students have some familiarity with Judaism. This background along with some familiarity of the Hebrew Bible is a natural jumping off point for a more focused study in Judaism.

The essence of Judaism is God, Torah, and Israel. (Israel refers to both a people and a nation.) These three components interact in a dynamic way to make Judaism a truly living religion. God gave the Torah to Israel. The Torah instructs Israel on the nature of God, the human condition, and how to live a holy life. Both changing geography and changing times place Jews in situations not mentioned in the Torah. These new situations gave rise to the need to interpret the Torah anew, keeping in mind that the interpretations must always reflect on how God would act.

As a historical religion, Judaism remembers its history and the God who acts within it through personal observances, communal festivals, and rites of passage. For example, the Pesach, or Passover ritual, memorializes the saving power of God to not only liberate the Hebrew people from Egyptian slavery, but to give all Jews true freedom through a covenant with God.

Resources for Chapter 2

Books

The Bible, the Jews, and the Death of Jesus: A Collection of Catholic Documents. Washington, D.C.: United States Conference of Catholic Bishops Publishing, 2004.

Catholics Remember the Holocaust. Washington, D.C.: United States Conference of Catholic Bishops Publishing, 1998.

Catholic Teaching on the Shoah. Washington, D.C.: United States Conference of Catholic Bishops Publishing, 2001.

De Lange, N. R. M. *An Introduction to Judaism.* New York: Cambridge University Press, 2000.

Encyclopedia Judaica. 2nd ed. 22 vols. New York: MacMillan, 2006.

Finkelstein, Louis. *The Jews: Their History, Culture, and Religion.* Westport, CT: Greenwood Press, 1979.

Fishbane, Michael A. *Judaism: Revelation and Traditions.* San Francisco: Harper and Row, 1987.

Hammer, Reuven. *Entering Jewish Prayer: A Guide to Personal Devotion and the Worship Service.* New York: Schocken Books, 1994.

Heschel, Abraham Joshua. *The Sabbath: Its Meaning for Modern Man.* Boston: Shambhala, 2003.

Jacobs, Louis. *The Book of Jewish Practice.* West Orange, NJ: Behrman House, 1987.

JPS Hebrew-English TANAKH: Student Edition. Philadelphia: Jewish Publication Society of America, 2000.

Neusner, Jacob. *An Introduction to Judaism: A Textbook and Reader*. Louisville: Westminster/John Knox Press, 1991.

———. *The Way of Torah: An Introduction to Judaism*. 7th ed. Belmont, CA: Wadsworth Publishing, 2004.

Pope John Paul II. *On Jews and Judaism*. Washington, D.C.: United States Conference of Catholic Bishops Publishing, 1987.

Scholem, Gershom Gerhard. *The Messianic Idea in Judaism and Other Essays on Jewish Spirituality*. New York: Schocken Books, 1995.

Steinsaltz, Adin. *The Essential Talmud*. 30th Anniversary Edition. New York: Basic Books, 2006.

Telushkin, Joseph. *Jewish Literacy: The Most Important Things to Know About the Jewish Religion, Its People, and Its History*. New York: William Morrow, 1991.

Waskow, Arthur Ocean. *Seasons of Our Joy: A Modern Guide to the Jewish Holidays*. Boston: Beacon Press, 1990.

Werblowsky, R. J. Zwi, and Geoffrey Wigoder. *The Oxford Dictionary of the Jewish Religion*. New York: Oxford University Press, 1997.

Audio-visual Resources

Heritage: Civilization and the Jews. DVD/VHS. (Home Vision Entertainment, 1984, 540 minutes)

The Holocaust: A Teenager's Experience. DVD/VHS. (United Learning, 1991, 30 minutes) Includes teacher's guide.

Jerusalem: Within These Walls. VHS. (National Geographic Video, 1987, 60 minutes)

Jewish Holidays Video Guide. VHS. (Sisu Home Entertainment, 1994, 90 minutes)

Judaism. Essentials of Faith Series. DVD/VHS. (Films Media Group, 2006, 24 minutes)

Judaism. Religions of the World Video Series. DVD/VHS. (Schlessinger Media, 1996, 50 minutes)

Judaism: The Chosen People. The Long Search Video Series. DVD/VHS. (Ambrose Video Publishing, 2001, 60 minutes) Study Guide available for separate purchase.

A Passover Seder: A Video for the Family. DVD/VHS. (Warner Vision, 1994, 180 minutes) Made with Holocaust survivor Elie Weisel.

Schindler's List. DVD/VHS. (Universal Studios, 1993, 196 minutes) An Academy Award-winning film by Steven Spielberg, based on a true story about a Gentile businessman who saves 1,300 Jews from Nazi atrocities. Since this film is rated R, teachers can preview the film to find segments that are appropriate for students. A Study Guide is available for purchase as an e-document from www.amazon.com.

A Stranger Among Us. DVD/VHS. (Walt Disney Video, 1992, 109 minutes) Commercially released film about a crime within a Hasidic community in New York.

Walking God's Paths: Christians and Jews in Candid Conversation. DVD/VHS. (United States Conference of Catholic Bishops Publishing, 2004, 90 minutes)

Internet Resources

Boston College Center for Jewish Learning— www.bc.edu/research/cjl

Commission of the Holy See for Religious Relations with the Jews— www.vatican.va/roman_curia/pontifical_councils/chrstuni/sub-index/index_relations-jews.htm

Hebrew College Online— www.shamash.org

Jewish-Christian Relations (multi-lingual)— www.jcrelations.net

www.MyJewishLearning.com

Sacred Heart University Center for Christian-Jewish Understanding— www.sacredheart.edu/pages/122_center_for_christian_jewish_understanding.cfm

A Living Religion (pages 27–29)

Using the Text

- Give students ten to fifteen minutes to read this first section, "A Living Religion." This material can help students build on their understanding of Judaism as the religion of Jesus and of the Hebrew Bible. This is excellent preparation for gaining new insights into Judaism as a living religion.

- A confusion many people have about Jews is the difference between Jewishness as an ethnic group and as a religion. The opening paragraphs in the text address this confusion in order to make clear that this chapter addresses the religious tradition of Judaism.

- Call on individual students to ask what they would like to learn from Judaism. Take notes and write their suggestions on the board. Record this information for review at the end of the chapter to see how many of their interests were addressed. If some were not, they could be made topics for research projects.

- Unfortunately there are still prejudices and misunderstandings about Judaism and Jews, and high school students are not immune. It is important to take quality class time to create a safe environment for students to articulate any prejudices they might have and for teachers to address them before continuing on in the chapter. If students have had any previous diversity education, this is the time to review it.

Extending the Text

- Even if students don't raise this issue, be proactive and address the potential charge of religious "hypocrisy." Point out that people do seem to be happiest when they live their lives in conformity with a freely embraced religious tradition—"when they walk the walk" and "talk the talk."

- Direct student attention now to the sidebar feature on page 29 that features dates in the history of Judaism. Let them know that *BCE* stands for "Before the Common Era," though it was once commonly understood to stand for "Before the Christian Era" or "Before Christ." Most theologians and religious historians believe that the approximate birth date of Yeshua of Nazareth (Jesus) was in the fall, sometime between 7 and 4 BCE, although we have seen estimates as late as 4 CE and as early as the second century BCE. *CE* stands for "Common Era," and it is expected to eventually replace *AD*. The latter is an abbreviation for "*Anno Domini*" in Latin or "the year of our Lord" in English. The latter refers to the approximate birth year of Yeshua of Nazareth (a.k.a. Jesus Christ). CE and AD have the same value, so 2008 CE = 2008 AD. Of course, one can always interpret the letter "C" in CE and BCE as referring to "Christian" or "Christ's." The *Abbreviations Dictionary* does this.

- Point out—as the timeline indicates—that the history of Judaism spans more than four thousand years and touches many nations. As students undoubtedly know, it is also a religion that has endured and survived many waves of persecution.

1. A Brief History of Judaism (pages 30–44)

Biblical Period and *Rabbinic Period* and *Medieval Period* and *Modern Period*

Objective

In this section the students will:

- be introduced to the history of Judaism and its impact on western civilization;
- become familiar with the major events of the Rabbinic Period, a stretch of almost 1,000 years that precedes and follows the birth and death of Jesus;
- learn the meaning of key vocabulary terms—**Hellenization, Dead Sea Scrolls, Diaspora, rabbis, the Torah,** and **Talmud;**
- be able to describe the Emperor Constantine and the impact of his Christian reign;
- identify cultural adaptations and compromises that the Jews had to make to survive in difficult or even hostile settings;
- familiarize themselves with vocabulary terms such as **monotheistic, Holy of Holies,** and **Hassidim.**

Preview

The history of Judaism begins in the desert, moves to a land "flowing with milk and honey" and continues with a "destroy, disperse, return, and rebuild" cycle. The land is sacred to the Jews, for God gave it to them. From the holy city, the radiant city of Jerusalem, God's goodness has been reflected to all the nations. Yahweh, Jews believe, has remained faithful—even permitting the unlikely establishment of the State of Israel in 1948. Helping students to get a broad-brush picture of Jewish history is important. In the Rabbinic Period, the Jews were overrun by foreign powers and dispersed throughout the world. Once the Temple was destroyed in Jerusalem in 70 CE, synagogues—Jewish centers of learning and prayer—were established around the world. The Talmud, a collection of commentaries on the Hebrew code of laws, emerged in the second century CE.

Using the Text

- Display a wall map of the biblical world. Call on a variety of students to locate and point out key cities, regions and travel routes on the map, including:
  - the route that Abraham and Sarah would have traveled from Ur to Canaan during he time of the patriarchs
  - the likely route to Egypt from Canaan during the days of famine for the family of Joseph
  - the way traveled by Moses and the Hebrews as they escaped from Egypt and traveled to Mount Sinai
  - the likely path taken by the Hebrews re-entering Canaan
  - the area of King David's United Kingdom and its capital, Jerusalem
  - the borders of the kingdom of Israel and the kingdom of Judah
  - the northern Kingdom of Israel under the Assyrians in 722 BCE
  - the southern Kingdom of Judah, including Jerusalem, which was destroyed as the Hebrews were taken in slavery to Babylon in 586 BCE

- the devastated Holy City of Jerusalem and its Temple, to which the exiled Jews returned in 537 BCE
- To better understand the implications of repeated displacement of the Jews, have students share their views on the following:
  1. What is "holy ground" to you?
  2. Where are the places for you alone or for family or friends that are "very special" or "sacred"? Why are these places "sacred?"
  3. How would you feel if "foreigners" destroyed your "sacred place"? What would motivate you to continually return and rebuild it?
- Assign for journal writing the Reflection Question about a family's defining moment (on page 32).
- After giving students fifteen minutes or so to read "Rabbinic Period," orally quiz them to highlight some of these events that are pivotal in Judaic history—and Christian history.
- Return to the map of this region and trace the route of nations or empires who conquered Israel and Judah and then left. Point out the locations where Jews fled to colonize Jewish Diaspora communities.
- Show a brief segment of the film *Judaism: The Religion of a People* to recap much of this material, and give students a chance to view Jewish traditions mentioned early in this chapter.
- Ask three students to volunteer to present a short skit based on the famous story of the heathen and Rabbi Shammai and Rabbi Hillel. If students want to spend a bit more time developing the skit and researching these two first century rabbis, offer additional extra credit for their efforts.
- Note the Reflection Question about Hillel's teaching on page 36. Ask the students to quietly reflect on this question and then share their responses with the whole class.

Extending the Text

- Hand out index cards to students with terms featured throughout these four subsections. Include such terms as: idolatry, Hellenization, monotheistic, pogroms, Spanish Inquisition, King Ferdinand and Queen Isabella, the Black Plague, Martin Luther, Ba'al Shem Tov, Hassidim, and Moses Maimonides. Challenge students, one by one, to recall and share one fact about their subjects. If they can't, they must hand the card to another student who has no card. Set a time limit on the exercise.
- Invite students to review the section and locate any statements made about treatment (positive or negative) of Jews. Have students reread the statement and discuss the historical and cultural context briefly.
- Distribute copies of the handout, "Excerpts from the Talmud" on p. 56 of the Teacher's Manual. Divide students up into small groups (2 to 4) and give them fifteen minutes to read and discuss the excerpts. Follow up and ask the groups:
  1. What are these rabbis saying about proper speech?
  2. What message is given about respect for parents?
  3. What does the Talmud predict about the Messiah's coming?

- Outside of class, assign students to create 8.5" x 11" inch posters featuring a Talmud saying that would be useful for all people to read and heed. Refer students to the Internet where there are many sites where they can locate Talmudic sayings. Students should also try to illustrate their posters with Judaic symbols and styles.

- Point to the Reflection Question about the jurisdiction of Jerusalem on page 43. Ask students to carefully consider how the jurisdiction of Jerusalem might be handled. Explain that trying to appease or please the Jews, Muslims, Christians, and Armenians would be as complicated as pleasing Hispanics, Blacks, Chinese, and White Americans who would lay claim to the same areas of San Francisco, Chicago, or New York City. Ask for volunteers to participate in a fishbowl exercise in which a group of about six students discuss the issue while the rest of the class looks on. Every few minutes change one or two people within the group with one or two of the spectators. Emphasize that this is an opinion question, so there are no wrong answers. On the other hand, there is such a thing as informed opinion.

- Follow discussion about Jerusalem by showing all or segments of one of the suggested films on Jerusalem.

- Give each student a copy of the handout, "Four Branches of Judaism" (page 55). With the students, review the differences between Orthodox, Conservative, Reform, and Reconstructionist Jews. Have each group discuss how they would answer their respective questions. The handout can also be used to facilitate research.

- As an extra credit project, have students select one of the four branches of Judaism and locate information on the Internet to write a two-page report on "Life as an Orthodox (or Conservative, Reform, or Reconstructionist) Jew."

- Have students read the Mark Twain feature, "Concerning the Jews" on page 44. Students are undoubtedly familiar with Twain as a great American novelist. Challenge students to interpret Twain's comments about the Jews in light of his novels about heroic individuals like *Huckleberry Finn*, *Tom Sawyer*, *The Prince and the Pauper*, and so forth. What qualities and virtues does he see in the Jews?

Section Review Questions and Answers

1. What did the Hebrews become in the forty years it took to return to Canaan from Egypt?

   In the forty years it took to return to Canaan from Egypt, the Hebrews became a covenantal community, owing their allegiance to one God only.

2. After the death of Solomon, why did the kingdom become more vulnerable to outside attacks?

   The kingdom was divided into two kingdoms after the death of Solomon. The kingdom of Israel to the north was comprised of ten tribes while the kingdom of Judah in the south included two tribes. Both kingdoms weakened when they fell prey to idolatry. Israel fell to Assyrians in 722 BCE, and Judah was conquered by the Babylonians two centuries later.

3. What is the Diaspora?

   The Diaspora originally referred to the large community of Jews who lived outside of Palestine. Driven out by many foreign conquerors, the Jews were dispersed and set up Jewish communities throughout the world. Today, the term refers to Jews living outside of Israel.

4. According to the rabbi Hillel, what is the summation of the Torah?

   According to Hillel, the summation of the Torah is that whatever is hateful to you, you are not to do to your neighbor.

5. Who was Moses Maimonides, and what did he argue for?

   Moses Maimonides was a medieval Jewish philosopher who argued that there was no contradiction between the philosophy of Aristotle and the Jewish religion.

6. Define Hasidism.

   Hasidism was a spiritual movement founded by Rabbi Israel ben Eliezer in the eighteenth century. In this era of darkness and persecution, Eliezer's teachings stressed the presence of God—light—in all aspects of Jewish life. It was a comforting teaching that helped Jews endure their trials.

7. Name and briefly differentiate the four types of Judaism that are present in the Modern Period.

   The four types of Judaism present in the Modern Period are Orthodox, Conservative, Reform, and Reconstructionist. Orthodox Jews interpret Torah in the most literal manner. Conservative Jews modify Jewish traditions in a limited manner. Reform Jews advocate full integration into the culture where one lives. Reconstructionist Jews advocate Judaism as a culture rather than a religion.

2. Sacred Stories and Sacred Scriptures (pages 45–47)

Tanakh and *Talmud* and *Midrash*

Objective

In this section the students will:

- get an overview of Judaic Sacred Stories and Sacred Scriptures, especially the Torah, the first five books of the Bible;
- become familiar with the origins and use of the Talmud, commentaries, and discussions about the Torah and how it should be lived;
- gain a working familiarity with the terms **Torah** or **The Five Books of Moses, Tanakh, Nevi'im, Ketuvim, Written Torah, Oral Torah, Mishnah, Talmud,** and **Midrash**

Preview

Several sources of sacred Jewish writing or Scriptures center on the **Torah**, the first five books of the Hebrew Bible. Jews also often call this pivotal resource "The Books of Moses." Even in modern times, this holy book is produced as a hand-sewn scroll of handwritten Hebrew on parchment. A part of the Torah is read aloud each Sabbath. The whole Bible, called the **Tanakh**, is divided into three sections: the **Torah**, the **Nevi'im** or the books of the prophets, and the **Ketuvim** or writings. In the Torah, traditional Jews find the roots of the 613 laws they must follow. Interpretations of Jewish laws were written down by Yehudah HaNasi in 200 CE. This written interpretation is called **Mishnah** or teaching. The **Talmud** is a collection of rabbinic discussions pertaining to Jewish law, ethics, customs, and history. **Midrash** is another kind of interpretation of biblical texts through the use of stories.

Using the Text

- Have students read these short sections on their own—*Tanakh, Talmud, Midrash*. Review the material, posing questions about how Jews use and see these sacred writings.
- If possible, read a cross section of the 613 laws observed by Jews. These laws together constitute the Torah.

Extending the Text

- Give students fifteen minutes or so to answer the Section Review Questions on page 47 on paper. Call on several students for each answer, and discuss any discrepancies in the way students have answered these questions.
- Distribute copies of the *Judaism Word Search* from p. 57 of the Teacher's Manual, and have students do the search.
- Share, if possible, some stories from the contemporary book, *Does God Have a Big Toe? . . . Stories About Stories in the Bible* by Marc Gellman and Oscar de Mejo.

Judaism Word Search Answers

```
L O U H S R R L R T K I W K A
G B C F A B T A H A R O T D X
O Q N A R B B M X L L B J B L
Q B A B W B I M T M X K W V F
F S V Z I F E R S U F S A V K
H Y C L C K H Y U D A F W G T
B A X O U J N G D O R T Z L G
I Y Z Z W A Z I S H O F A R R
D E B U G V W W X Y P C R B B
E K D O Z H A V U H S I T H R
I N G B P Z H F O U A G E E N
S U C Z D W E W Z Q I G H K W
E X B I Z V J M I U D S J F M
H K V Z C D F F O U O S U Z G
I D N G R C W T V K Y M J R Q
```

Section Review Questions and Answers

1. What are the three divisions of the Tanakh?

   Tanakh is an acronym for the three divisions of the Hebrew Bible. The first is the Torah, or the first five books of the Bible. The second is the Nevi'im, the books of the major and minor prophets. The third is Ketuvim, or the writings which includes the Book of Job, Psalms, and Proverbs.

2. What is the Talmud?

   The Talmud is two long collections of Jewish literature that are commentaries on the Mishnah, the Hebrew code of laws that emerged about 200 CE.

3. What is the difference between the Oral Torah and the Written Torah?

   The Oral Torah is an explanation and interpretation of the Written Torah. It explains how the Torah is to be lived and applied.

4. What is Midrash?

   Midrash is a type of literature that explains the meaning of a religious text in an imaginative way. Often, Midrash is expressed in stories which elaborate on the holy texts in memorable and appealing ways.

3. Beliefs and Practices (pages 48–52)

God and *Torah* and *Israel*

Objective

In this section the students will:

- learn that the essence of Judaism is God, Torah, and Israel;
- understand that when Jews follow and respect the commandments within Torah, the Torah becomes alive in the world;
- explore the *Sh'ma*, a prayer recited daily by devout Jews that addresses the central Judaic belief that there is one God who created all things and who is good.

Preview

In Judaism, an expression of their fundamental monotheistic belief is the *Sh'ma*, a prayer recited daily by devout Jews. The central source of knowledge guiding Jews, the Torah is kept in a place of honor in the Jewish synagogue and reverenced by the congregation. Studying and living the Torah and the 613 commandments it contains is the essence of Jewish practice. The Ten Commandments and the other laws given in the Torah are called **mitzvot.** Israel is not only a political entity but a term for "God's Chosen People." Jews trace their chosen (and holy) status to Abraham. A covenant or mutual agreement between God and his people (Israel) commits Jews to living a holy, righteous life, a commitment termed **halakhic** obligations. It is commitment of the individual Jew to the covenant.

Using the Text

- If possible, arrange a tour of a local Jewish synagogue. Or, show pictures of a typical Jewish synagogue, particularly the **Ark** where the scrolls of the Torah are held. Show students what Hebrew writing looks like.
- Locate the phonetic Hebrew pronunciation of the short Jewish prayer, the *Sh'ma*, which is recited daily by Jews. Recite the prayer in Hebrew and challenge students to learn it in both English and Hebrew.
- Emphasize to students that Israel is both a land and a people. In addition, the Jews were God's Chosen People because of God's initiative, not their own.
- Ask students to describe the terms of the ancient covenant (contract) between God and Israel (aka the Jews). Draw students more deeply into the topic, asking: "What effect did knowledge of this covenant with God likely have on Jews over many centuries? How might it have molded and motivated them?"

Extending the Text

- Assign the Section Review Questions on pages 51–52 as a written assignment to recap this section's material and to prepare students for the next section on Sacred Times.
- Present the Reflection Question about Jewish law and the refrigerator light on p. 50 as a debating topic. Allow students to choose a "Yes" or "No" position on the topic but remind them to consider the question more broadly as well. Say: "Are there customs within your own religious tradition that you have learned that seem strange to 'outsiders' but not strange

to you?" (Examples might be Catholics eating no meat on Friday during Lent or kneeling in prayer before statues.) Recruit four students on each side of the issue to open the debate with sixty-second presentations. Allow other students to replace the eight team members after five minutes of debate. Plan fifteen to twenty minutes for this debate, after giving students time for some rereading and preparation.

- Play "Blessing Before the Torah Reading" from the audiocassette *Teaching Christian Children About Judaism*. This will give the students another opportunity to hear a traditional blessing in Hebrew.

- Direct students to respond through a journal entry or a written theme to the Reflection Question on p. 48 about a personal experience of God as good, as Creator, and as one.

Section Review Questions and Answers

1. What do Jews believe about God?

   Jews believe God exists, God is one, God is creator, and God is good.

2. What do Christians understand the Torah to be?

   Christians understand the Torah to be the first five books of the Bible—Genesis, Exodus, Leviticus, Numbers, and Deuteronomy.

3. How are both reverence and familiarity operational with the Torah?

   When not in use, the Torah scrolls are reverently kept in a specially made Ark in the synagogue. But, Jews are delighted when the Torah is carried by the rabbi on special occasions. It is common for Jews to touch, kiss, or dance near the Torah. They believe that God's word—represented by the Torah—is among them in an ordinary, but also an extraordinary way.

4. When did the call to be a Chosen People originate with the Jews?

   Jews see themselves as the children of Abraham. They believe that Abraham was called to holiness and to a different path when God called him to leave Ur and to leave pagan idolatry behind. The "children of Abraham" believe that they have inherited this "chosen" status.

5. What does it mean to say that Jews are God's Chosen People?

   To say Jews are God's Chosen People means that they are holy or separate.

4. Sacred Times (pages 52–61)

Festivals and Holy Days and *Rosh Hashanah and Yom Kippur* and *Sukkot* and *Pesach* and *Shavuot* and *Hanukkah* and *Purim* and *Shabbat* and *Birth* and *Coming of Age* and *Marriage* and *Death*

Objective

In this section the students will:

- learn the difference between a Jewish and a civil calendar;
- become familiar with the major festivals, holy days, and occasions celebrated by Jews—Rosh Hashanah, Yom Kippur, Sukkot, Pesach, Shavuot, Hanukkah, and Purim;
- examine the observance of Shabbat or the Sabbath.

Preview

In Jewish belief, every moment of life is holy. Time is a gift from the Creator. Jews believed that God is a God of history, and they created a calendar that "estimated" the creation of the world. The Jewish calendar begins there. The Jewish year has 354 days, and the eleven-day discrepancy with the civil calendar is reconciled in different ways. Rich with many religious feasts and festivals, Jewish celebrations are divided into two main cycles—the Tishri cycle in the autumn and the Nisan cycle in the spring. Shabbat, the Jewish Sabbath, is the weekly celebration of God's goodness. It begins at sunset on Friday and ends at sunset on Saturday.

Using the Text

- Divide the class up into three groups and give each group markers and large sheets of newsprint or poster board. Have one group create a civil or non-religious calendar that could be used by anyone that year. Give the second group a list of major religious feasts and liturgical seasons and have these students create a Christian liturgical calendar. Provide school-related information for the third group and have them create an academic calendar. Each calendar should note key days (e.g., holidays and seasons) and particular starting and ending points. These do not have to be elaborate calendars, but students should be encouraged to be creative.
- If you do not have time for the group work described above, locate the three types of calendars and hang them in front of the classroom. Take a few moments and have students to locate the following in each calendar:
  - the first day of the year
  - the last day of the year
  - how many months each calendar contains
  - what events are celebrated in the civil calendar that are not celebrated in the other two calendars
  - what events are celebrated in the Christian calendar that are not celebrated in the other two calendars
  - what events are celebrated in the academic calendar that are not celebrated in the other two calendars

- Assign two to three students to each of the Jewish festivals (Rosh Hashanah, Yom Kippur, Sukkot, Pesach, Shavuot, Hanukkah, Purim) throughout this section. Have all groups each read the introductory paragraphs of this section and then the subsection Festivals and Holy Days. Groups should then research their festival through the Internet and prepare a three to five minute presentation. If they can find them, students should bring photos, recordings of festival music, etc. to illustrate the festival they are reporting on.

Extending the Text

- Play all or part of the video *The Jewish Holidays Video Guide* (especially the sections on Shabbat or Passover Seder). Or, play the audiocassette *Teaching Christian Children About Judaism* that has a number of traditional Jewish holiday songs.
- Invite a Jewish adult or a rabbi to talk briefly about the weekly celebration of Shabbat or Sabbath, as well as the life cycle celebrations—birth, coming of age, marriage, and death.
- Bake or purchase challah bread and bring in some of the foods used in the feast of Pesach or Passover. Encourage students to sample all of these foods used during Jewish sacred times.
- Use the reflection questions in this section on pages 54, 56, and 59 as you move through and focus on the material. Consider assigning the third one as a written reflection. This will prompt students to consider what it means to keep a day "holy." Call on students to read their reflections to the whole group.

Section Review Questions and Answers

1. What are the two main cycles on the Jewish calendar?

   The two main cycles are the Tishri cycle in the fall and the Nisan cycle in the spring. Tishri is named for the first month of the cycle. Nisan is the first month of the spring cycle and the word "Nisan" comes from the Sumerian word for "first fruits."

2. How is the Jewish calendar different from the Roman or civil calendar?

   The Jewish calendar is different from a civil calendar in that a Jewish calendar runs on a lunar cycle while a civil calendar runs on a solar cycle.

3. What happens on Yom Kippur?

   Yom Kippur is generally accepted as the holiest day of the year for Jews. It is a day of prayer, fasting, and repentance. Jews ask forgiveness for both communal and personal sins. In cases involving personal forgiveness, Jews try to go directly to the person they have offended.

4. Cite the similarities between Rosh Hashanah and Pesach.

   Rosh Hashanah and Pesach are similar in that they are both memorials of creation. Rosh Hashanah memorializes the creation of the world while Pesach memorializes the creation of the Jews as a people.

5. What are the "days of awe" and what is their significance?

   The "days of awe" are Rosh Hashanah and Yom Kippur. Rosh Hashanah is the first day of the Jewish New Year while Yom Kippur is the "Day of Atonement." Rosh Hashanah is the first day of a ten-day penitential period while Yom Kippur is the last day of that period. During these "days of awe" Jews turn back to the proper way of living.

6. Why did a relatively minor feast, Hanukkah, take on more significance, especially in America?

   Hanukkah gained more significance as Jewish parents saw that it was important to counteract the strong influence of Christmas on all non-Christians in America. Since Hanukkah is also a winter celebration and has light as one of its symbols, Jewish celebration of it "answered" the Christian celebration of Christmas.

7. Explain what takes place on Shabbat.

   On Shabbat (known to Christians as Sabbath) Jews attend synagogue service, study Torah, and engage in a ritual dinner. The Sabbath dinner table includes a white tablecloth, two candles, wine, and a braided loaf of bread called challah. Sabbath begins eighteen minutes before sunset Friday evening with the lighting of the Sabbath candles. A prayer of blessing over the candles is generally recited by the woman of the house. There is a blessing over the wine and bread. After these blessings, the meal begins. The Sabbath candles are not extinguished, but are allowed to burn themselves out. Sabbath ends at sunset Saturday. A brief ceremony called Havdalah concludes this sacred time. A braided candle is lit and held in the hand so one can see its reflection of light on the fingertips. Again, wine accompanies this closing ceremony as a symbol of thanksgiving and joy. A box of aromatic spices is lit, carrying the aroma of the Sabbath into the week.

5. Sacred Places and Sacred Spaces (pages 61–65)

Synagogue and *Home* and *Land of Israel* and *Jerusalem*

Objective

In this section students will:

- learn that the synagogue and home are sacred places to Jews;
- examine the design and use of the Jewish synagogue;
- study the rituals that make a Jewish home holy;
- grow in appreciation for the central importance of the land of Israel and the city of Jerusalem.

Preview

We have already discussed the sacredness of the land of Israel for Jews. This section focuses on the other sacred places for Jews—the synagogue and the home. While some observances are primarily in the home or in the synagogue, others are in both. A traditional Jewish home has a mezuzah on at least one doorpost of the house. A kosher home has one set of dishes for eating and cooking meat, and one set for eating and cooking milk products. Keeping milk and meat dishes separate, and avoiding "unclean" foods, such as pork and shellfish, maintains the proper or "kosher" nature of the home. Israel as a political state and the city of Jerusalem are tremendously significant for Jews around the world. This is holy ground—the land given to their fathers in faith 3,000 years ago, the land they view as "promised" to them by God. Jerusalem is David's capital, a city that held the Temple and still holds its remnants.

Using the Text

- Play several Catholic liturgical music selections that feature Jerusalem as a holy city, as the destination of those journeying to God. Many hymnals now include some of the excellent, spirited music from the charismatic renewal that often focused on Jerusalem.
- Remind students of a synagogue's three main functions. It is a place for prayer, for studying Torah, and for socializing. Recall that the reason synagogues came into existence was because Jews were denied the freedom to worship in the Temple in Jerusalem. The Temple was destroyed twice, first by the Babylonians and then by the Romans. Some Orthodox Jews are praying for the establishment of a third Temple, but the site of the destroyed Temple presently is home to the Muslim mosque known as the Dome of the Rock.
- Point out the photo of the synagogue on page 62. Note the standard synagogue features that are visible or have students identify them.
- Refer to the traditions used to make a Jewish home sacred and then sample student responses to the Reflection Question on page 63. What ways do Catholic families use to designate their houses as holy?

Extending the Text

- Show the class a more detailed map of Israel, pointing out the major cities and the Arab neighbors surrounding Israel.
- Draw this section to a close by posing the Reflection Question about the survival of religious traditions if places of worship closed. The question appears on page 63. Challenge students

to imagine that their parish church—in fact all parish churches in their community—were closed. How could the practice of their Catholic faith continue? How would it be very different?

- Read the extract from Psalm 137 about Jerusalem on page 65. Invite comments about the intensity of feeling in this brief and ancient statement.

Section Review Questions and Answers

1. What does the word "synagogue" mean?

   The word "synagogue" means "place of assembly" outside one's homeland.

2. What takes place in a synagogue?

   The synagogue is a place for prayer, for studying Torah, and for socializing.

3. What makes a home kosher?

   A kosher or "proper" home has one set of dishes for eating and cooking meat and one set for eating and cooking milk products. Keeping milk and meat dishes separate and avoiding "unclean" foods such as pork and shellfish maintains the proper or "kosher" nature of the home.

4. What is the significance of Israel and the city of Jerusalem for Jews?

   The state of Israel and the city of Jerusalem are tremendously significant for Jews around the world. This is holy ground—the land given to their fathers in faith 3,000 years ago, the land they see as "promised" to them by God. Historically, Jerusalem is David's capital, a city which held the Temple and now the Temple's remnants.

6. Judaism through a Catholic Lens (pages 66–73)

Messiah and *Incarnation* and *Scripture* and *Liturgy* and *Holy Thursday and Passover* and *Pentecost and Shavuot* and *Challenges of Dialogue*

Objective

In this section the students will:

- look more closely at the history, Scripture, liturgy, and theology shared with the Jews;
- compare the Jewish vision of Messiah with the Catholic vision of Jesus as Messiah;
- examine Jewish teaching about Scripture, liturgy, Passover, and Pentecost in the light of Catholic teaching and practice.

Preview

Like cousins with the same grandparents, Catholicism and Judaism have much in common. Catholicism finds its roots in Jewish history, Scripture, liturgy, and theology. Above all, Catholics share with Jews a belief in one God and a common Scriptural heritage. Both Catholics and Jews see the Ten Commandments as the platform for moral teaching. The principle difference between Judaism and Catholicism is in their perceptions of the Messiah. For Catholics, Jesus is the Messiah, the divine Son of God. Catholics and Jews also differ in the Old Testament books they accept as revealed by God. Major feasts celebrated by Jews and Catholics also have common roots. They are Holy Thursday, or Passover, and Pentecost. Catholics must also grow in their understanding of the Shoah, the devastating massacre of millions of European Jews by the Nazis during the Holocaust.

Using the Text

- Share some researched background information about the primary symbol of Judaism—the Star of David—and the primary symbol of Christianity—the cross. Show students examples of these symbols and describe their respective histories and symbolic content.
- Have students review the "Messiah" and "Incarnation" sections. Pause and ask students to help you make a list of things that would be different if they did not believe that Jesus was the Messiah, the promised savior and Son of God. *(They wouldn't wear crosses as jewelry, no crosses on walls in their homes, would never make the "Sign of the Cross," might worry or wonder when the Messiah would come, wouldn't celebrate Mass, wouldn't read the Gospel or Gospel passages, etc.)*
- Show students a list of the forty-six Old Testament books that Catholics recognize. Then show them the thirty-nine books that Jews recognize in their "Hebrew Bible." Share with students any information you have discovered that explains the differences.
- Ask students if any of them have attended a "Seder," a Jewish ritual meal that is celebrated on the first day of Passover. *(Many students may have attended a Christian variation of this ritual since Jesus also celebrated this meal in Jerusalem on the night before his death. Some Catholic parishes or communities offer a "Christian Seder" meal and celebration during Holy Week.)* Solicit student reactions or memories of the Seder they attended.
- On the blackboard, overhead projector, or with a PowerPoint program, review the links between Jewish and Catholic feasts, especially Holy Thursday/Passover and Pentecost/Shavuot.

Extending the Text

- Direct students to the Research and Activities section on page 77. Have students choose one project and allow a week to ten days for its completion. Permit students to work in teams of two if they wish.

- Randomly ask what students know about the **Shoah.** When did it occur? Where did it take place? Who promoted and then carried out this persecution and extermination of millions of Jews?

- Show a twenty to thirty minute portion of *Schindler's List*, a true account of one man's attempt to save Polish Jews from prison and death in concentration camps because the **Shoah** was wrong in his eyes.

- Devote at least twenty to thirty minutes on a class period to help students review for the Chapter 2 Test. Ask a student volunteer to read aloud the two paragraphs of the Conclusion on page 74. Repeat the central point—that the faithful adherence by Jews to God has given them heroic strength and cohesion as a people. Have students independently review the section and chapter Summary statements as well as vocabulary terms, etc. Ask students if they have any other questions about the major beliefs and practices of Judaism.

- Make sure that students know the date of this chapter's test. Use the remainder of the review session for prayer. Recite together the Aleinu, a traditional Jewish prayer said at the end of synagogue services.

Section Review Questions and Answers

1. List four areas in which Jews and Catholics are in agreement.

   Jews and Catholics share a great deal of common ground historically, scripturally, liturgically, and theologically. Each religion is monotheistic. They share Abraham as their Father in faith and the moral heritage of the Ten Commandments. They share most of the books of the Old Testament except that Catholics also include 1 and 2 Maccabees, Judith, Tobit, Baruch, Sirach, and Wisdom in their list of Old Testament books inspired by God.

2. What is the difference between what Catholics believe about Jesus and what Jews believe about Jesus?

   Catholics believe that Jesus is the only Son of God who was sent into the world as the Messiah. He is, Catholics believe, the savior and redeemer promised by God to our fathers in faith. The Jews acknowledge that Jesus was a historical figure, a charismatic figure, and a prophet. They do not agree that Jesus was divine and do not acknowledge him as the Messiah. Many Jews are still waiting for the arrival of the Messiah.

3. What are some similarities between the Mass and Passover, and Shavuot and Pentecost?

   In both the Mass and the Passover celebration, there is reading of Scripture, an offering, the blessing and breaking of unleavened bread, and the offering and drinking of blessed wine. Both liturgies are also opened with very similar prayers. The Jewish Passover begins this blessing ritual with the prayer: "Blessed are you, King of the universe." In the Mass, we pray, "Blessed are you, God of all creation."

4. What are some other topics that can further Jewish-Catholic dialogue in a positive way? Explain why.

    Jews and Catholics can explore their shared histories. Christians must remember and continue to discuss the Shoah, the horrendous murder of millions of Jews that took place in the 1930s and 1940s in Christian Europe. Because of their rich common heritage of faith, these two groups should also talk about ways to deal with materialism and contemporary issues of justice, ecology, and peace.

Chapter 2 Review Questions and Answers

1. What is the significance of Mount Sinai?

   On Mount Sinai, in the thirteenth century BCE, God gave Moses the Ten Commandments. This event, described in Exodus 19–20, gave to both Judaism and Christianity the foundation for moral teaching and practice.

2. Compare and contrast the experience of Jews in Babylon during the sixth century BCE with the Jews of Babylon during the sixth century CE.

   In the sixth century BCE, the Babylonians conquered Judea, destroyed their land and the Temple and led the Jews off to Babylon in bondage. More than one thousand years later, during the sixth century CE, Jews flourished in Babylon, building great schools and synagogues. Jews later helped to translate Greek works into Arabic for Muslims and into Latin for Christians.

3. Why would Jews say that the year 70 CE was one of the worst in Jewish history?

   Roman soldiers destroyed the Temple in Jerusalem.

4. Why did the synagogue gain importance during the Rabbinic Period?

   With the Diaspora of the Jews and the destruction of the Temple, Jews around the world constructed synagogues. A synagogue functioned as a house of prayer, a house of study where Jews studied the Torah, and as a house of assembly where the local Jewish community met socially.

5. Define *Diaspora*.

   The Diaspora refers to those Jews exiled or "dispersed" from the Jewish homeland of Israel.

6. What was the general experience of Jews in Spain under Muslim rule?

   For about four hundred years—from the eighth to the twelfth centuries—Jews flourished in the areas of Spain where Muslims were in power. In Cordoba, which became the capital of the Muslims, Jews helped to create a cultural revival and excelled in science, math, medicine, philosophy, metal crafts, and trade.

7. Who was Moses Maimonides?

   Moses ben Maimon was a Jewish rabbi, scholar, and physician, who worked in the court of the Muslim sultan Saladin in Cairo. Most famous for his theological and philosophical writings, Maimonides maintained that there was no contradiction between Greek philosophy and the teachings of Judaism.

8. Define *conversos*.

   Jews who converted to Christianity were known as "conversos." In the Medieval period of Judaism, some Jews converted because they felt forced to. In private, they continued to practice Judaism.

9. Define *Hassidism*.

   Hassidism was a movement within Judaism that began in the seventeenth century. Rabbi Israel ben Eliezer taught that Jews should look for the presence of God in all aspects of life—especially the difficult and dark times of persecution.

10. Why can it be said that the Age of Enlightenment in Europe was an age of emancipation for Jews?

    In eighteenth-century Europe, the Age of Enlightenment urged the use of reason and rational thought to assess doctrines and social traditions and to create new systems of government. A parallel movement in Jewish thought advocated the freeing of Jews from social and legal constraints. Like other people, Jews were finally freed from the yoke of feudal control that had denied their fundamental human rights and treated them as chattel.

11. Why do Jews call the Hebrew Bible "Tanakh"? Why do they not call the Hebrew Bible "the Old Testament"?

    The Hebrew word Tanakh is an acronym for the three divisions of the Hebrew Bible—the Torah, or the first five books of the Bible, the Nevi'im, or the prophets, and the Ketuvim, the writings. They do not call the Hebrew Bible the Old Testament because they do not acknowledge the authenticity of the Christian New Testament.

12. What is the Mishnah?

    The Mishnah is extended teaching about the Torah that tells Jews how to apply the Ten Commandments and other laws. The oral teaching about the Torah was first codified and arranged by Yehudah HaNasi around 200 CE.

13. What is the Talmud? What is considered the most authentic version of the Talmud?

    The Talmud is the rabbinic commentary on the Hebrew Scriptures. Two very different Talmuds or "learnings" developed as rabbinic scholars studied the Mishnah. One was called the Palestinian Talmud, and the other was called the Babylonian Talmud. The Babylonian Talmud is seen as the more authoritative.

14. Define *Sh'ma*.

    The Sh'ma is a daily prayer recited by Jews. Its message is recognized as the central tenet of Judaism— belief in one God. The prayer is taken from Deuteronomy 6:4.

15. How is the Torah reverenced? What does it represent?

    The scrolls of the Torah—God's revelation to the Jews through the Ten Commandments and 613 other laws—are kept in a special place in each synagogue. Usually constructed as a highly decorated box, the Ark holds the Torah when it is not in use. A portion of the Torah is read on every Sabbath.

16. What are the two meanings of the term "Israel" to Jews?

    To Jews the term "Israel" refers to not only a land or political state, but also to a people.

17. Define *halakah*. Give an example.

   The process of interpreting the total body of Jewish law or the Torah is called halakah. This work has been done by rabbis who have categorized the laws in order to help Jews apply them.

18. What are major characteristics of Orthodox, Conservative, Reform, and Reconstructionist Judaism?

   Orthodox Jews interpret Torah in the most literal manner. Conservative Jews modify Jewish traditions in a limited manner. Reform Jews advocate full integration into the culture where one lives. Reconstructionist Jews advocate Judaism as a culture rather than a religion.

19. Define *Ashkenazim* and *Sephardim*.

   The Ashkenazim were Jews living in Poland and in other parts of Eastern Europe who developed their own culture and language which was called Yiddish. The Sephardim were Jews living in Spain or in the Iberian Peninsula who developed their own distinctive culture and approach to Judaism.

20. Briefly describe the significance of the time between Rosh Hashanah and Yom Kippur, including each of those holy days.

   Rosh Hashanah is the first day of the Jewish New Year while Yom Kippur is the "Day of Atonement." Rosh Hashanah is the first day of a ten-day penitential period while Yom Kippur is the last day of that period. During these "days of awe" Jews turn back to the proper way of living.

21. What festivals are in the Tishri cycle? In the Nisan cycle?

   Tishri contains Rosh Hashanah as well as Yom Kippur and Sukkot. Nisan contains two festivals—Pesach and Shavuot.

22. How is Passover related to both the Mass and to Holy Thursday?

   There are striking similarities between the Passover meal and the Mass, a celebration rooted in the Holy Thursday Last Supper of Jesus with his apostles. In each, there are readings from Scripture, offerings, and the blessing and breaking of unleavened bread, as well as the blessing and consuming of wine. Additionally, in the Passover meal, an unblemished lamb is sacrificed. In the Mass, Jesus is the Lamb of God who was slain and who released us from the bondage of sin.

23. What is the significance of Hanukkah?

   Hanukkah celebrates the victory of Judas the Maccabean over the Syrian Greeks and Antiochus IV in 165 BCE. The Maccabean revolt regained the Temple for the Jews. Triumphantly, the victors lit the temple menorah, but had only enough oil for one night. Miraculously, the oil replenished itself and the menorah stayed lit for eight days. Though not a major feast, Jews now celebrate Hanukkah by lighting the menorah—one candle the first night, two the second, etc. The celebration continues for eight days and now includes the sharing of gifts. This custom was added in modern times to answer the Christian Christmas traditions that take place around the time that Hanukkah is celebrated.

24. How do Jews mark major times in the life cycle: birth, coming of age, marriage, and death?

Eight days after birth, boys are circumcised, and girls have a naming ceremony. For coming of age, there is the bar mitzvah for boys and the bat mitzvah for girls. The three major elements of the marriage ritual include the hupah, the blessings, and the breaking of the glass. For Jews, funerals take place as soon as possible, often within twenty-four hours of death. At the burial, blessings are made, prayers are said, and psalms are read aloud.

25. How is a Jewish home made sacred?

A traditional Jewish home attaches a mezuzah to at least one door post of a house. In some Jewish homes one wall is designated the mizrakh, or eastern wall. This wall is sometimes marked with a special picture or embroidery, showing the direction one must face for prayer. A kosher home is one that has special dishes for eating and cooking that separate meat from dairy products. Since a traditional Jewish table is not only a place for building familial relationships but also a place for ritual, food must be kosher or "proper." Pork and shellfish are forbidden. Other meats must be slaughtered in a kosher manner. The combination of meat and dairy products is forbidden. On Shabbat, a "Sabbath-like" atmosphere prevails in the home. The house must be especially clean, and a Shabbat cloth must be on the table along with the Shabbat candlesticks.

26. Why are some Jews wary to engage in meaningful dialogue with Catholics?

The history of relations between Jews and Christians was troubled and painful for centuries. Jews were often persecuted by Christians and told that they were responsible for the death of Christ. Jews were also often told that they would not see salvation unless they accepted Jesus as the divine Son of God.

27. Who is Jesus according to the Jewish faith?

Jews acknowledge the historical existence of Jesus and his traditional Jewish background and education. According to the Jewish community, Jesus was an itinerant preacher and wonder worker who was crucified by the Romans around 30 CE.

28. What is Shoah?

Shoah is the modern Hebrew word for the Holocaust, the extermination of six million European Jews by the Nazis in the 1930s and 1940s. Literally, "Shoah" means catastrophe or devastation.

29. What are some of the Jewish roots of Catholicism? Give examples.

Catholicism and Judaism have more in common than any other two religions. Catholics and Jews both believe in one God and share Abraham as their father in faith. These two religious traditions also acknowledge God's many covenants with the Jews as his chosen people. They both also see the Ten Commandments as the foundation of moral teaching. The Catholic "Old Testament" is also almost the same as the Hebrew Scriptures. The Catholic canon adds seven books not included in the Hebrew Bible: 1 and 2 Maccabees, Judith, Tobit, Baruch, Sirach, and Wisdom.

30. How do Jews see the New Testament?

The Jews accept that the New Testament consists of documents written primarily by first-century Jews. They do not accept that the New Testament was divinely inspired.

31. How did the Second Vatican Council begin to right wrongs done to Jews?

In a council document titled Nostra Aetate, the Church addressed wrongs done to the Jews and erroneous thinking towards our elder brothers in faith. Insulting terms used in Good Friday prayers were changed. The Church also disavowed a long-standing opinion among Christians that all Jews were somehow responsible for the death of Jesus. The Church also made it clear that Jews do not need to become Catholics or Christians to be saved.

Chapter 2 Test Answers

Multiple Choice (3 points each)

1. d, 2. c, 3. a, 4. d, 5. b, 6. b, 7. a, 8. d, 9. c, 10. a, 11. d, 12. b, 13. b, 14. d, 15. c, 16. d, 17. d, 18. d, 19. d, 20. c

Short Answer (8 points each)

1. The essence of Judaism is God, Torah, and Israel.

2. The lunar calendar used by Jews has a 24-hour day that begins and ends at sunset. The year begins in the fall on Rosh Hashanah, the Jewish New Year. In addition, the Jewish calendar is 354 days, eleven days shorter than the civil calendar. The Jews found it necessary to adjust this eleven-day discrepancy so that a holiday that is celebrated in the fall as commanded in the Bible will not eventually end up in the spring. The eleven-day discrepancy is reconciled in two ways. First, a month is added seven times in nineteen years. Second, one day is added or subtracted each year to two different months.

3. A typical synagogue is built to replicate Zion in the shape of a square with the bimah in the center representing Mount Zion. There is a gathering space for men, women, and children and a central chamber for the reading of the Torah and for prayer. The Torah is kept in an Ark on the eastern wall. The people face the east, not only facing the Ark, but also facing Jerusalem.

4. The role of the Jewish prophets was to be God's mouthpiece and to pass along to the Jewish people what God wanted of them.

5. The most notable difference between Catholics and Jews is their view of who Jesus is. Both groups agree that Jesus was a historical figure but Catholics—and other Christians—believe that Jesus of Nazareth was the promised Messiah. Jews still expect a Messiah to come. For them, Jesus was a teacher who was a political figure executed by the Romans.

Name _____

The Four Branches of Judaism

	Orthodox	Conservative	Reform	Reconstructionist
Torah	Literal interpretation Accepts Jewish law and teachings as binding	Subscribes to the divine authority of Torah but respects biblical scholarship	Repository of ethical teachings rather than divinely revealed Commandments lacking in moral purpose ignored.	Torah not given by God Emphasis on Jewish culture and history
Observances	Strict observance of dietary and kosher laws Separation of men and women in worship services Strict attention to details of customs found in traditional texts Wear traditional scull cap, prayer shawl, and phylacteries Prayers exclusively in Hebrew recited at fixed times	Permits modification and modernization of observances Preserves the uniqueness of that which is Jewish Traditional dress just at services Uses more Hebrew than vernacular No separation of men and women	Removed traditional garb Eliminated repetition of prayers and references to the Temple sacrificial system Introduced musical instrument and choirs in place of cantor Modified the liturgy, use of Hebrew limited, most in vernacular, sermon by rabbi as focal point of services Less strict observance of dietary laws Call house of worship a "temple"	Reflects the needs of the community rather than prescribed observances
Jewish law and teaching	Accepts as binding	Accepts most as binding	Does not see Jewish law and tradition as divinely in origin Men and women equal	Jewish law created by people

Excerpts from The Talmud

On the power of the spoken word

63. R. Eleazar said, "Whence do we learn that speech is equivalent to action? Scripture states: (Ps. 3:6) 'By the word of the Lord were the heavens made.'"[See Gen. 1:6f] Sabbath, 119b

On the evil potential of speech

64. R. Johanan said in the name of R. Simeon b. Johai, "Verbal wrongdoing is more evil than cheating in matters of money; for concerning the former, Scripture states: (Lev. 19:14) 'but thou shalt fear thy God, while this is not said of the latter.'"

R. Eleazar said, "Harmful speech is more wicked because it affects the person [of the injured] while the latter affects only his money." And R. Samuel b. Nahmani declared, "Harmful speech is worse because money can be returned, but words once uttered cannot easily be recalled." Baha Metzia, 58h

On honoring one's parents

48. R. Judah said, quoting Samuel, that R. Eliezer was once asked, "How far should one go in honoring his father and mother?" He replied, "Just see what a Gentile of Ashkelon, Dama ben Nathina, did. The Sages wanted to buy a jewel from him for the epbod [a sacred ritual object], but the key [to the safe where it was kept] was under the pillow of his father [who was asleep]. Dama refused to disturb him [and lost the sale].

"The following year the Holy One rewarded him with the birth of a red heifer. When the Sages offered to buy it, he said to them, 'I know that I could ask of you any amount of money, and you would pay the price. However, I only want you to make good the loss I sustained in honoring my father.'"

R. Hanina declared that if one who is not commanded to honor his parents does so, and is so richly rewarded, how much more certain is the reward of one who is commanded to do so!

On the Messiah's role in creation

792. Our rabbis taught that seven things were created before the world itself—the Torah, repentance, the Garden of Eden [Paradise], Gehinnom, the Throne of Glory, the Temple, and the name of the Messiah. Nedarim, 39b

On the terrible conditions that will precede the Messiah's coming

793. R. Isaac said in the name of R. Johanan, "In the generation in which the son of David will come, scholarly men will be few in number, and the eyes of the people will protrude from sighing and sorrow. Many afflictions and many evil government decrees will be imposed upon them; one will not have passed when another will come." Sanhedrin, 97a

794. R. Nehorai said, "The Messiah, son of David, will appear when the young will expose the old to shame in public, and the old will rise up in respect before the young; a daughter will rebel against her mother, a daughter-in-law against her mother-in-law. The leaders of that generation will be like dogs, and a son will feel no shame when reproached by his father." Sanhedrin, 97a

This material is quoted from *The Talmud for Today* by Rabbi Alexander Feinsilver, ed., trans. (New York: St. Martin's Press, 1980).

Judaism Word Search

Test your skills on Jewish terms by completing this word search. Words can be found horizontally, vertically, or diagonally. Words may be spelled from left to right or right to left, from top to bottom or from bottom to top. Letters may overlap between two words.

```
L  O  U  H  S  R  R  L  R  T  K  I  W  K  A
G  B  C  F  A  B  T  A  H  A  R  O  T  D  X
O  Q  N  A  R  B  B  M  X  L  L  B  J  B  L
Q  B  A  B  W  B  I  M  T  M  X  K  W  V  F
F  S  V  Z  I  R  E  R  S  U  F  S  A  V  K
H  Y  C  L  C  K  H  Y  U  D  A  F  W  G  T
B  A  X  O  U  J  N  G  D  O  R  T  Z  L  G
I  Y  Z  Z  W  A  Z  I  S  H  O  F  A  R  R
D  E  B  U  G  V  W  Q  X  Y  P  C  R  B  B
E  K  D  O  Z  H  A  V  U  H  S  I  T  H  R
I  N  G  B  P  Z  H  F  O  U  A  G  E  E  N
S  U  C  Z  D  W  E  W  Z  Q  I  G  H  K  W
E  X  B  I  Z  V  J  M  I  U  D  S  J  F  M
H  K  V  Z  C  D  F  F  O  U  O  S  U  Z  G
I  D  N  G  R  C  W  T  V  K  Y  M  J  R  Q
```

1. Jews forced to live outside Israel

2. An ancient term for "Hebrew"

3. That which is "proper" or "clean"

4. Hangs on the door post of many Jewish homes

5. The title for a religious leader in Judaism

6. A ram's horn

7. Where Jews hold their community religious services

8. Contains commentaries on the Torah

9. A Hebrew term for returning to proper behavior

10. Traditional Jews believe Moses wrote this

Chapter 2 Test

Name _____

Multiple Choice. *Write the letter of the best choice in the space provided.* (3 points each)

_____ 1. Israel is
   a. a country belonging to the international community.
   b. a people.
   c. another name for David.
   d. both a and b

_____ 2. The word Torah means
   a. Jewish Law.
   b. Mosaic Law.
   c. instruction.
   d. institution.

_____ 3. The foundation of Judaism is
   a. in the Sinai desert.
   b. near the Jordan River.
   c. in Egyptian captivity.
   d. in the Talmud.

_____ 4. Judaism is
   a. a historical religion.
   b. a monotheistic religion.
   c. an Abrahamic religion.
   d. all of the above

_____ 5. The United Kingdom of Israel was under
   a. King Saul.
   b. King David.
   c. Herod the Great.
   d. Herod Antipas.

_____ 6. The first Temple of the Jews was destroyed by the
   a. Assyrians.
   b. Babylonians.
   c. Persians.
   d. Romans.

_____ 7. In the Exile, many Jews were deported to
   a. Babylon.
   b. Ur.
   c. Jerusalem.
   d. Qumran.

_____ 8. The _____ led a revolt against the Greeks in 168 BCE.
   a. Pharisees
   b. Sadducees
   c. Essenes
   d. Maccabees

_____ 9. The existence of the Essene community was revealed in modern times through the discovery of
   a. the Jerusalem Temple.
   b. the Dome of the Rock.
   c. the Dead Sea Scrolls.
   d. Mount Sinai.

_____ 10. The _____ began a process of systematically transforming the Temple rituals for practice outside the Temple.
   a. rabbis
   b. habiru
   c. Sadducees
   d. Pharisees

_____ 11. During the _____ period the Jews began to gain equality before the law.
   a. Rabbinic
   b. Classical
   c. Medieval
   d. Modern

_____ 12. Though the State of Israel was established in 1948, it was not until _____ that Jews gained full control over Jerusalem.
   a. the Gulf War
   b. the Six-Day War
   c. the Maccabean Revolt
   d. the Granada Conflict

_____ 13. How many Torahs are there?
   a. 1
   b. 2
   c. 3
   d. 4

_____ 14. Being a "Chosen People" means
   a. God gives the Jewish people many privileges.
   b. God gives the Jewish People many responsibilities.
   c. Jews are the only ones who are the People of God.
   d. both a and b

_____ 15. Which of the following does not take place in a synagogue?
     a. socializing
     b. studying Torah
     c. ritual sacrifice
     d. prayer

_____ 16. Both Tishri and Nisan are
     a. harvest cycles.
     b. planting cycles.
     c. solar cycles.
     d. creation cycles.

_____ 17. _____ is generally considered the holiest day of the Jewish year.
     a. Pesach
     b. Shavuot
     c. Shabbat
     d. Yom Kippur

_____ 18. During a Jewish wedding, the "breaking of the glass" symbolizes
     a. the heartaches the couple will endure during their marriage.
     b. _Kristlnacht_ (literally, "crystal night") when Nazis went on a rampage breaking windows of Jewish establishments.
     c. the time for no more wine drinking.
     d. the destruction of the Temple in 70 CE.

_____ 19. What is not used in a Sabbath ritual?
     a. spice box
     b. candles
     c. braided bread
     d. shofar

_____ 20. The Sh'ma is
     a. "Keep holy the Sabbath."
     b. "I will make a covenant with you and you shall be my people and I will be your God."
     c. "Hear O Israel, the Lord our God, the Lord alone."
     d. "Create in me a clean heart, O God."

Short Answer. *Briefly answer the following questions.* (8 points each)

1. What is the essence of Judaism?

2. Describe the lunar calendar used by the Jews.

3. Describe a typical synagogue.

4. What was the role of the Jewish prophets?

5. What is the difference between the way Catholics and Jews view Jesus?

Chapter 3: Christianity

Introduction

In the study of the world's religions, it is natural to have Christianity follow Judaism, for Christianity has its roots in Judaism. Ancient Jews awaited a promised Messiah that would bring peace to Jerusalem and salvation to the Jewish people. Jesus himself was a Jew. Some Jews accepted Jesus of Nazareth as the Messiah while others rejected him. Those Jews who accepted Jesus as the Messiah ultimately found it necessary to break off from Judaism.

What became known as Christianity is now the largest religion in the world. However large, Christianity has fractured into hundreds of denominations over the past five hundred years. These denominations can be categorized into four main branches—Catholic, Orthodox, Anglican, and Protestant. Though Christianity has many faces, there is a set of beliefs that is core to all Christians. These beliefs are summarized in the Apostles' Creed, a second century creedal statement of beliefs.

The scripture of the Christians, the Bible, is a source of God's self-revelation. For all Christians the Bible is the source for beliefs and moral decision-making. For some Christians it is the only source of authority. For others, both scripture and tradition are the source of moral and religious authority. The foundation for moral living is the Great Commandment that demands love of God and love of neighbor.

Christians live the mystery of Jesus' life through the liturgical year. The Christian calendar begins each year on the First Sunday of Advent. All Christians celebrate the great feasts of Easter and Christmas, while many others celebrate the liturgical seasons of Advent, Christmas, Lent, Easter, and Ordinary Time. In addition, there is a sanctoral calendar superimposed on the liturgical calendar that commemorates the feasts of Mary, the Mother of God, and of many of the saints.

To be a Christian, one must be baptized in the name of the Trinity and live out that baptism. Catholics, Orthodox, and Anglicans all have a sacramental life in which Jesus can be encountered through the ordinary that is made extraordinary. Bread, wine, oil, and water all become signs of God's grace.

In preparation for this chapter, make sure to secure the necessary audio-visual resources and speakers. In addition, schedule a visit to one or more local churches.

Resources for Chapter 3

Books

Anderson, Bernhard W., Bruce Manning Metzger, and Roland Edmund Murphy. *The New Oxford Annotated Bible with the Apocryphal/Deuterocanonical Books.* New York: Oxford University Press, 1991.

Bainton, Roland Herbert, and Jaroslav Pelikan. *The Reformation of the Sixteenth Century.* Boston: Beacon Press, 1985.

Benedict of Nyssa. *The Rule of Saint Benedict.* Trans. Leonard J. Doyle. 6th ed. Collegeville: Liturgical Press, 2001.

Binns, John. *An Introduction to the Christian Orthodox Churches.* New York: Cambridge University Press, 2002.

Borelli, John, and John H. Erickson, eds. *The Quest for Unity: Orthodox and Catholics in Dialogue.* Crestwood, NY and Washington, D.C.: St. Vladimir's Seminary Press and the United States Conference of Catholic Bishops Publishing, 1996.

Brother Roger. *Brother Roger of Taize: Essential Writings.* Marcello Fidanzio, ed. Maryknoll, NY: Orbis Books, 2006.

Brown, Raymond E. *Responses to 101 Questions on the Bible.* New York: Paulist Press, 1990.

Chapman, David M. *In Search of the Catholic Spirit: Methodists and Roman Catholics in Dialogue.* Norwich, UK: Epworth Press, 2005.

Cross, F. L., and Elizabeth A. Livingstone. *The Oxford Dictionary of the Christian Church.* 3rd ed. New York: Oxford University Press, 2005.

Deepening Communion: International Ecumenical Dialogue with Roman Catholic Participation. Washington, D.C.: United States Conference of Catholic Bishops Publishing, 1998.

Dillenberger, John, and Claude Welch. *Protestant Christianity Interpreted Through Its Development.* 2nd ed. London: Collier MacMillan, 1988.

Fitzgerald, Michael L., and John Borelli. *Interfaith Dialogue: A Catholic View.* Maryknoll, NY: Orbis Books, 2006.

Frend, W. H. C. *Martyrdom and Persecution in the Early Church.* Garden City, NY: Anchor Books, 1967.

Haddad, Yvonne Yazbeck, and John L. Esposito. *Daughters of Abraham: Feminist Thought in Judaism, Christianity, and Islam.* Gainesville: University Press of Florida, 2001.

Kelly, J. N. D. *Early Christian Creeds.* 3rd ed. New York: Continuum, 2006.

———. *Early Christian Doctrines.* 5th ed. London: A. C. Black, 1977.

Leith, John H. *Creeds of the Churches: A Reader in Christian Doctrine, From the Bible to the Present.* 3rd ed. Atlanta: John Knox Press, 1982.

Marty, Martin E. *Protestantism.* London: Weidenfeld and Nicolson, 1972.

———. *A Short History of Christianity.* 2nd ed. Philadelphia: Fortress Press, 1987.

Marty, Martin E., and R. Scott Appleby. *The Glory and the Power: The Fundamentalist Challenge to the Modern World.* Boston: Beacon Press, 1992.

McBrien, Richard P. *Catholicism.* New Edition. San Francisco: HarperSanFrancisco, 1994.

Moorman, J. R. H. *A History of the Church in England.* 3rd ed. New York: Morehouse Publishing, 1986.

Neill, Stephen. *Anglicanism.* 4th ed. New York: Oxford University Press, 1978.

Pope John Paul II. *Ut Unum Sint (That They May Be One).* Washington, D.C.: United States Conference of Catholic Bishops Publishing, 1995.

Ratzinger, Joseph Cardinal. *Introduction to Christianity.* San Francisco: Ignatius Press, 2004.

Robertson, Ronald. *The Eastern Christian Churches: A Brief Survey.* 6th ed. Washington, D.C.: United States Conference of Catholic Bishops Publishing, 1999.

Rusch, William G., and Jeffrey Gros, eds. *Deepening Communion: International Ecumenical Documents with Roman Catholic Participation.* Washington, D.C.: United States Conference of Catholic Bishops Publishing, 1998.

Slattery, Edward J. *Catholic Evangelization in an Ecumenical and Interreligious Society.* Washington, D.C.: United States Conference of Catholic Bishops Publishing, 2004.

Ware, Timothy. *The Orthodox Church.* 2nd ed. New York: Penguin Books, 1993.

Witmer, Joseph W., and J. Robert Wright. *Called to Full Unity: Documents on Anglican-Catholic Relations, 1966–1983.* Washington, D.C.: United States Conference of Catholic Bishops Publishing, 1986.

Audio-visual Resources

Byzantium: The Lost Empire. DVD/VHS. (BMG Video, 1997, 200 minutes)

Catholicism: Rome, Leeds and the Desert. The Long Search Video Series. DVD/VHS. (Ambrose Video Publishing, 2001, 60 minutes) Study Guide available for separate purchase.

Christianity. Essentials of Faith Series. DVD/VHS. (Films Media Group, 2006, 24 minutes)

Civilizations in Conflict: Byzantium, Islam, and the Crusades. VHS. (United Learning, 1998, 18 minutes) Includes teacher's guide and blackline masters.

History of Orthodox Christianity. DVD/VHS. (Vision Video, 1992, 90 minutes) Includes study guide.

Inside the Vatican. DVD/VHS. (National Geographic Video, 2001, 90 minutes)

Luther. DVD (Eikon Film, 2003, 123 minutes) Starring Joseph Fiennes as Martin Luther.

Mine Eyes Have Seen the Glory. DVD/VHS. (Vision Video, 1992, 2006, 165 minutes)

Orthodox and Roman Catholic Christianity. Religions of the World Video Series. DVD/VHS. (Schlessinger Media, 1996, 50 minutes)

Orthodox Christianity: The Romanian Solution. The Long Search Video Series. DVD/VHS. (Ambrose Video Publishing, 2001, 60 minutes)

The Protestant Reformation (1517–1550 AD). DVD/VHS. (United Learning, 1997, 20 minutes) Includes teacher's guide and blackline masters.

Protestant Spirit USA. The Long Search Video Series. DVD/VHS. (Ambrose Video Publishing, 2001, 60 minutes)

Religions of the World: Christianity. VHS. (United Learning, 2001, 27 minutes) Teacher's guide included.

Taize: That Little Springtime. VHS. (Journey Films, 1985, 26 minutes)

Internet Resources

Catholic Association of Diocesan Ecumenical and Interreligious Officers (CADEIO)— www.cadeio.org

Official website of the Vatican— www.vatican.va

Official website of the United States Conference of Catholic Bishops— www.usccb.org

Pontifical Council for Promoting Christian Unity— www.vatican.va/roman_curia/pontifical_councils/chrstuni/index.htm

Followers of the Nazarene (pages 81–83)

Using the Text

- Have students cluster in small groups of three or four. Give them a few minutes to read the material that introduces this chapter on Christianity.

- The beginning of the running text sets the context for evoking what students already know, and how they have personally observed the various forms of Christianity, especially on television. This is an opportunity for you, as the teacher, to get an idea about where students are with regard to Christianity as a whole.

- Assign the Reflection Question about a unique Christian television program as a small group discussion topic. Allow fifteen minutes before you call on the small groups to share about the television programs that impressed them.

1. A Brief History of Christianity (pages 83–99)

Jesus of Nazareth and *The Early Church* and *Legalized Christianity* and *Growing Divisions* and *Seeds of Reformation* and *The Catholic Reformation* and *The Modern Period*

Objective

In this section the students will:

- survey the long history of Christianity as a worldwide religion;
- review the timeline of important Christian dates and developments;
- recognize the Jewish roots and identity of Jesus Christ and of Christianity;
- become familiar with the external and internal challenges to early Christianity.

Preview

The history of Christianity details a movement from a small Jewish sect begun in Palestine to the world's largest religion today. Christianity spread throughout the Roman Empire and later into the Byzantine Empire. Though Christianity eventually established strong ties between church and state, divisions within Christianity often damaged its unity. Frequently, Christian groups split off over doctrinal differences. Sometimes, however, cultural differences and corruption in some areas of the church contributed to Christians splitting off to go in their own direction.

Using the Text

- Ask students what they think it must have been like for Christians in the first three centuries when practicing the faith was "illegal?" (Fill in with some general information about the persecution of Christians throughout the Roman Empire.) Challenge students to describe what practicing an illegal faith would be like today in the United States.
- Ask: "What are the many names or titles Christians gave to Jesus over the centuries?" List all the names the students come up with on the board. Call on volunteers to share what each name says about the kind of person Jesus is.
- Backtrack and have students look again at the BC and AD timeline of Christian dates on page 83. How many years are covered by the timeline? Can students think of any Church events they would add to the timeline?
- Read aloud the Reflection Question about the Christian belief in the resurrection of Jesus on page 85. Then read 1 Corinthians 15:12–19 to help students consider their answers to the question.
- Call on several students to locate the cities of the five patriarchates on a large map of Europe and Eastern Europe. Enlarge upon information presented in "Growing Divisions," the development of the papacy, the spread of Muslim control through Africa and southern Europe, the "Great Schism of 1054" that separated Eastern Christianity from Western Christianity, etc.
- Randomly distribute 3"x 5" index cards to students with one key word or term from this section. As they consult the text, give these students ten minutes to write a good question that only this word or phrase will answer. In the meantime, have the rest of the class write their

own responses to the Reflection Question on page 91 about the leading division between East and West.

- Ask several students to read their reflection question responses. Then ask the group to suggest possible solutions to one or more of these ancient causes of division.

- Display some images of Martin Luther and the church at Wittenberg. Describe Luther's disillusionment with the Roman Catholic Church and the divisions between Lutherans and Catholics that soon developed. The Protestant Reformation hastened the Catholic Reformation. The ensuing Council of Trent defended and expounded on traditional doctrine. While the English Reformation was more political in nature, the Protestant Reformation led to a deeper split due to its theological and doctrinal disputations with the Catholic Church.

- Have students share what they may know about the English Reformation and King Henry VIII's creation of the Church of England. (Students may have heard about the six wives of Henry the VIII or perhaps the fictionalized account of Prince Edward, Henry's only son in the Mark Twain novel, *The Prince and the Pauper*, which was also presented in film.)

- Elaborate on the teachings of the Council of Trent and the impact of many of its reforms, such as the requirement that bishops and pastors preach on Sundays and holy days and that diocesan seminaries be established to assure the proper education of priests. After the Council of Trent, all branches of Christianity accelerated their missionary efforts to include the new lands discovered by the explorers of the sixteenth and seventeenth centuries. By the twentieth century, Christians found less reason to exploit differences and more reasons to embrace things that are similar among the various branches of Christianity. The ecumenical movement is that movement which moves towards a growing understanding among the various Christian denominations.

- Have students read the special sidebar feature, "Movements within Protestantism" about Fundamentalism, Evangelicalism, and Pentecostalism on pages 96–97. These three words are often interchanged in the mass media, but they are distinctively different. Explain that examples of fundamentalists are Jimmy Swaggart and Bob Jones. Billy Graham has been the preeminent evangelical spokesman of modern times. Many of the television preachers are evangelicals rather than fundamentalists. Ministers that exhibit the "gifts of the Holy Spirit" such as speaking in tongues are Pentecostals, but may also be evangelicals.

Extending the Text

- As persecutions ceased and Christianity became more complacent, some men and women found it necessary to take up an austere life in the desert. This lifestyle, which also included celibacy, became a substitute for martyrdom. Read several short selections from the Desert Fathers or Mothers, such as St. Anthony the Hermit, Athanasius of Alexandria, etc.

- Bring to class a copy of St. Benedict's Rule. Read part of the Rule to the students. Then say, "Imagine that you are about to establish a Christian community dedicated to the Gospel of Jesus Christ. Write your own rule calling it The Rule of (Your Name). Have an opening paragraph stating the overall mission of your community and then list ten rules by which community members should live. Limit your rule to approximately two pages in length.

- Show a twenty to thirty minute segment from Franco Zeffirelli's 1977 movie *Jesus of Nazareth*. After the viewing ask the students what they found attractive about Jesus and his message and what they found disturbing.
- Refer to the Pentecost experience for the disciples of Jesus and the missionary work of the early Christians, especially Paul. After students have read this text, have them share any first-hand experiences they have had of contemporary missionaries—parish visitors, door-to-door missionaries from other denominations, foreign missionaries.
- Focus in briefly on the major accomplishments of some early Church councils. Using the following information, highlight the significant outcome of these councils as follows:
  1. Nicaea and Constantinople—doctrine of the Trinity; Nicene Creed
  2. Ephesus—Mary is the mother of Jesus and Mother of God
  3. Chalcedon—declared Jesus fully human and fully divine and established five major centers of Christianity: Alexandria, Antioch, Constantinople, Jerusalem, and Rome
- As an extra credit project, have students compare and contrast the Apostles' Creed with the Nicene Creed. Then, have them write their own brief creeds or belief summaries.
- Remind students that Jesus was a Jew, not a Christian. Christianity became a religion separate from Judaism at the beginning of the second century of the Common Era when differences between those who accepted Jesus as the Jewish Messiah and those who did not became irreconcilable. Jesus did not set out to found a new religion. On the contrary, the presence of Jesus was a fulfillment of a promise made by God to the Jews. God promised to send a Jewish Messiah, not a Christian one. Use this background information to underscore the Reflection Question on page 86 about Jesus not being a Christian and the one on page 87 about anti-Semitism. Have students answer these questions as a graded, written assignment.
- Have students who composed questions from the words and terms of this section take turns quizzing the class orally with their questions.
- Show twenty to thirty minutes of a video or DVD that highlights themes from this section, such as *Civilizations in Conflict: Byzantium, Islam and the Crusades* or *Orthodox Christianity: The Romanian Solution*.
- For extra credit, have students research and then create posters about the Christian Crusades. Topics to focus on could include the life of a crusader, the battle for Jerusalem, why Christians joined the Crusades, St. Francis of Assisi and the Fifth Crusade, Thirteenth-century Moslems, or why Christians wanted to reclaim the Holy Land.
- Distribute copies of the worksheet, "Theses of Martin Luther" from p. 86 of the Teacher's Manual. Allow fifteen minutes for students to read the worksheet and answer the questions at the end. Call on a sampling of students to share their questions.
- Show a portion of the film *Luther*, that portrays Luther's protest of Catholic practices. A 2003 release, this film stars Joseph Fiennes as Martin Luther. Directed by Eric Till, this 123-minute film won a number of film awards at German film festivals.
- Refer to the Reflection Question on page 96 about whether or not Christian divisions are a sort of scandal to Christianity. Solicit student input and share your own views.

- Show a pre-selected segment of the film *Catholicism: Rome, Leeds and the Desert* to launch a bit more discussion of the Modern Period.
- To further enrich this section you may want to bring in (or have students bring in) religious paintings or music of various eras of Christian history. Intersperse the lessons with these audio-visual masterpieces which portray Christian mysteries.
- Consider having the students view a commercially released "classic" film. Or assign different videos to small groups of students to watch at home. Some suggestions:

  The Robe

  The Mission

  The Silver Chalice

  Becket

  A Man for All Seasons

  Song of Bernadette

  Joan of Arc

  The Day the Sun Stood Still

  Going My Way

  The Bells of St. Mary's

  Brother Sun, Sister Moon

  Romero

  Roses in December

  Entertaining Angels

- Have students report back with oral "film reviews" to the class. Each student viewing a film should keep the following questions in mind: Was the film based on a true story or purely fictional? What was my reaction to the film? What feelings did the film evoke? How was Christianity portrayed? Did the characters or the plot make Christianity appealing?
- To review this large section, go over the Summary points and have students answer the Review Questions.

Section Review Questions and Answers

1. What do Christians believe about Jesus of Nazareth?

   Christians believe that Jesus is the only begotten Son of God, conceived by the Holy Spirit. They also believe that Jesus was born of the Virgin Mary, was a storyteller and healer, was crucified and raised from the dead on the third day, and lives today.

2. Why is Pentecost significant to Christians?

   Pentecost is significant to Christians because it recalls that God made a new covenant with the Christians and sent His Holy Spirit. Pentecost is known as the birthday of the Church.

3. What was the role of Paul in the spread of Christianity?

   Paul founded Christian communities in Asia Minor and Greece. He wrote letters called epistles to the fledgling communities to encourage their new life in Christ.

4. Explain the significance of the Emperor Constantine in the history of Christianity.

    Constantine legalized Christianity and made it the official religion of the Roman Empire in the fourth century.

5. Name two important Christian doctrines that were defined at the Church councils between the fourth and fifth centuries.

    Two important Christian doctrines that were defined at the Church councils between the fourth and fifth centuries were the doctrine of the Trinity and the doctrine of the two natures of Jesus.

6. Who was Benedict?

    Benedict was the founder of Monte Cassino, a monastery in Italy. He wrote a "rule" for his monks that became a foundation for monasticism throughout the centuries. Benedict's rule emphasized a balanced life of prayer, work, and study.

7. Briefly trace the events that led to the division between the Church in the east and the Church in the west.

    Several things led to the division between the Church in the east and the Church in the west. Among them were the claim of primacy by the bishop of Rome, the crowning of Charlemagne as the Holy Roman Emperor in the west, and the missionary efforts of the east into Slavic lands. In addition, at the Council of Toledo, western bishops added a line ("the Holy Spirit . . . who proceeded from the Father and the Son") to the Nicene Creed without consulting eastern patriarchs. Unhappy with the addition and excluded from the discussion, eastern patriarchs found the statement heretical. Known as the filioque ("and the son") controversy, this was the final straw. In 1054, a mutual excommunication between Rome and Constantinople took place. Even if that event had not occurred, the destruction of Constantinople by western Christian Crusaders in 1204 would have completed the split.

8. What major doctrines and beliefs do most Protestants share?

    Most Protestants believe that the Bible is their sole religious and moral authority, in the justification by faith, and in the priesthood of all.

9. How did Anglicanism begin?

    Anglicanism began with the English King Henry VIII claiming to be supreme head of the Catholic Church in England. Since Catholicism could not accept this arrangement, the Church of England initiated the Anglican Communion.

10. How did rationalism and empiricism affect Christianity during the modern period?

    Rationalism and empiricism affected Christianity in that there was an increasing emphasis in the belief that people could determine their own destiny and had little need for God.

11. What is the ecumenical movement?

    The ecumenical movement attempts to bring about understanding among the various religious groups, including the different Christian denominations.

12. Define fundamentalism, evangelicalism, and Pentecostalism.

Fundamentalism is a movement that believes the world has become too secularized, especially in the area of science, and advocates the infallibility of the Bible on historical and scientific matters. Evangelicalism emphasizes a personal faith in Jesus Christ and the Bible as an individual's sole religious authority. In addition, "witnessing" or sharing faith with others is important. Pentecostalism is a movement that emphasizes the "gifts of the Holy Spirit" as recorded in the Acts of the Apostles. These gifts may include speaking in tongues, healing, holy joy, and holy tears.

2. Sacred Stories and Sacred Scriptures (pages 99–103)

The Bible and *Apologetics*

Objective

In this section the students will:

- learn about the Old and New Testaments and variations in the books that different denominations include in the Old Testament;
- recognize the Gospels as the preeminent New Testament sacred Scriptures;
- discuss the different ways that Christian denominations interpret sacred truths;
- become familiar with the origins and style of Christian apologetics.

Preview

In this short but important section, students will have an overview of the Bible, the sacred Scripture shared with Judaism. They will note that while all Christians have the same twenty-seven New Testament books, not all denominations recognize or accept the same books in their Old Testaments. The Catholic Old Testament canon includes forty-six books, including seven books that most Protestant bibles omit or label as "apocryphal" or of dubious authority. Apologetics is also introduced and explored as a unique style of Christian writing that emerged to help Christians defend or explain their faith.

Using the Text

- Distribute Bibles to the students and have them explore them, noting the difference in length of the Old Testament compared to the New, locating the Gospels, etc.
- Once students have read "The Bible" and "Apologetics," have them look through the Bible again locating the individual books or types of writings described.
- Survey students to see if they already have any favorite books of the Bible or favorite passages, such as a Psalm.
- Amplify the short explanation of Christian apologetics as a style of writing that emerged in the early Christian centuries to defend and explain Christian teachings. Add that, in a way, each Christian generation must defend and explain its beliefs. Can students think of any new ways to "defend" their Catholic Christian beliefs?

Extending the Text

- Show twenty to thirty minutes of the film *Where Jesus Walked*, a Reader's Digest film that was filmed in Israel and is widely available.
- As an extra-credit project, invite students to research, copy and display—in poster style—persuasive or encouraging quotations from one of the early Christian apologists, such as Irenaeus of Lyon or Justin Martyr.
- Use a little tape recorder with an exterior mike—or enlist a student—to use it playing the role of a reporter on the street randomly asking the Reflection Question on page 102 from St. Jerome: "Ignorance of Scripture is ignorance of Christ." Is that valid? Why or why not?"
- Consider having students write answers to the Review Questions on page 103.

Section Review Questions and Answers

1. Name the four literary genres represented in the New Testament.

   The four literary genres in the New Testament are: the four Gospels; one narrative history of the early Church, the Acts of the Apostles; twenty-one letters; and one apocalyptic book, Revelation.

2. What is the difference among the various Christian branches with regard to the understanding of the Word of God?

   Some Christian groups believe that God dictated the Word of God literally word for word. For them, the Bible is without error both in spiritual matters and in secular concerns as well. Other Christians see the Bible as the inspired Word of God which should guide us in spiritual matters, but not necessarily in areas like science and history.

3. List two ways in which Christians use the Bible in their lives.

   All Christian groups use the Bible in their worship services. Many Christians also make the reading and study of the Bible part of their individual prayer lives.

4. What were the intentions of apologetic writings?

   Apologetic writers wrote to defend and explain the Christian faith. Their audience was primarily Christians who did not always understand the tenets of their own faith.

3. Beliefs and Practices (pages 103–109)

Trinity and *Jesus* and *Sin* and *Salvation* and *Christian Living* and *The Church*

Objective

In this section the students will:
- explore fundamental Christian beliefs as expressed in creeds;
- review basic teachings about the Trinity, Jesus, sin, salvation, Christian living and the Church;
- be able to define crucial vocabulary terms such as creed, Incarnation, Original Sin, the Great Commandment, church or assembly.

Preview

As students explore Beliefs and Practices, the second element of a religious tradition, they will obviously encounter much that is familiar. Nonetheless, looking more carefully at the creeds and fundamental Christian beliefs about God, the Trinity, Jesus, sin, and salvation can still help them see Christianity in a fresh way. Emphasize the importance of key concepts and terms such as Incarnation, Original Sin, the Great Commandment and their connection with interlocking teachings and principles of Christianity.

Using the Text
- Have students read the introductory paragraphs of this section and then display two posters—one with the Apostles' Creed and the other with the Nicene Creed printed in large type. Ask students to compare and contrast the two summaries of fundamental beliefs. Does one creed tell them more? Why do they think the Nicene Creed was developed and is used now at Mass?
- Recap what the text presents about the Trinity, Jesus, Sin, etc. Invite students to voice any confusion or questions about these teachings.
- Distribute three 3"x 5" index cards to each student. Have students write three simple "Trivial Pursuit" or "Jeopardy" style questions from their reading and then write the answer in parentheses under the question.
- Have students break down into small groups of four or five. Tell students to put their questions in a box or basket—question-side down. Have students take turns drawing and asking questions of the group until they have emptied the box or basket.
- The students learned in Chapter 2 that Jews believe Israel is both a people and a nation. In similar fashion, as the New Israel, Christians believe the church is both a people and a building. It is important to emphasize to students that even if there were no longer church buildings, the church would survive through its most precious resource—its community of faithful people.

Extending the Text
- Reinforce one of the messages given in "Christian Living" that the Great Commandment of loving God and loving neighbor is *the* foundation for Christian moral living.
- Read or have one of the students read the parable of the Good Samaritan in the Gospel of Luke (Luke 10:25–37). Briefly discuss the parable and its message. Then, have students gather in small groups to rewrite and act out a contemporary "take" on the parable. For instance, the

injured person could be a member of the cross-town basketball rival. The Samaritan might be a student from their own school who looks beyond the rivalry to give compassion and help. If possible, videotape the Good Samaritan skits.

- Offer some brief biographical background on Søren Kierkegaard, the nineteenth-century Danish philosopher and theologian whose statement about the difficulties of living a Christian life appears with a Reflection Question on page 108. Challenge students to react and answer Kierkegaard's statement in a one- to two-page essay to be done outside of class.

Section Review Questions

1. According to the Apostles' Creed, what do Christians believe about God?

   Christians believe that there is only one God, but that there are three Persons in One God—Father, Son, and Holy Spirit. God is the Creator and Sustainer of all life and all things. Christians also believe that Jesus was the Son of God who was conceived in time by the Holy Spirit and born of the Virgin Mary.

2. Define the major Christian beliefs in the Trinity, Jesus, sin, and salvation.

   Christians believe that there are three persons in one God—Father, Son, and Holy Spirit. Jesus is the second person of the Trinity. Jesus is fully human and fully divine. Sin is an offense against God, and Adam and Eve committed the first sin by disobeying God's command not to eat from the tree of the knowledge of good and evil. Salvation is the redemption of humankind through Jesus Christ.

3. Give examples of two different ways Christians have interpreted the Great Commandment.

   Some Christians have interpreted the Commandment's mandate to love God above all as a mandate to destroy what they see as the enemies of God. Others have simply viewed the commandment as a statement that love—love of God and love of neighbor—is the foundation of all religion.

4. Define *Church*.

   Church means the assembly or the gathering of all those who believe, under the guidance of the Holy Spirit, that Jesus is God.

5. What does it mean to say that the Catholic Church possesses the "fullness of the means of salvation"?

   The Catholic Church possesses the fullness of the means of salvation because it has the complete confession of faith, full sacramental life, and an ordained ministry in apostolic succession.

4. Sacred Times (pages 109–116)

The Christmas Cycle: Advent, Christmas, Epiphany and *The Easter Cycle: Lent, Easter, Pentecost* and *Sacraments* and *Prayer*

Objective

In this section the students will:

- become more familiar with the Christian liturgical cycle;
- learn that Baptism and Eucharist (the Lord's Supper) are the two sacraments common to most Christians;
- review and discuss sacraments as sacred times not tied to a particular season; discuss prayer and different prayer forms as "sacred times" for Christians.

Preview

Try to introduce the liturgical year by showing a calendar or chart with the major seasons and feasts to the class. Remind students that just as human beings draw comfort and inspiration from the changing seasons of the year, so too do people of every faith, including Christians, find special meaning in liturgical seasons. The Christian liturgical season follows the birth, life, and death of Jesus so that Christians can more closely follow in Christ's footsteps. Celebrating the birth of Jesus at Christmas each year helps Christians to "relive" the dramatic miracle of the Incarnation. Marking the forty days season of Lent reminds the followers of Jesus and his forty days of fasting and prayer in the desert, a preparation for his public ministry. Discussing their own experiences with sacraments and prayer will complete this look at Christian "sacred times."

Using the Text

- Divide the class into six groups, giving each group one of the following topics for further study: Advent, Christmas, Epiphany, Lent, Easter, or Pentecost. The groups should read the text about "their" season or sacred time. Then, provide prepared materials about each feast to the groups. Allow several days for the groups to gather additional background information from the library or internet. Have each group give a presentation to the entire class to teach what the season or feast day commemorates, how it is celebrated, what symbols, liturgical colors, and customs are used, and what the symbols represent.
- Invite students to individually tell about their family customs and practices that enrich the celebration of Advent, Christmas, Lent or Easter.
- Refer to the Reflection Question about "Good" Friday on page 112 and sample the group for their responses.
- Review the Catholic sacraments and how they function as "signs from Christ to give grace," but emphasize that Baptism is the only sacrament recognized by all Christian denominations.

Extending the Text

- Assign students to research how one non-Catholic denomination prepares its people for and ritualizes baptism. Reserve time for the students to share their research with the rest of the class.
- Show all or parts of *Taize: A Little Springtime*, a film about an ecumenical community in the province of Burgundy, France. Tie the film to common sources for ecumenical or interdenominational Christian prayer. How can all Christians join in prayer?

- Back up to the Reflection Question on page 113 that asks students to tell about any times they might have been afraid (or embarrassed) to admit to their faith. Before students offer responses, remind them that after the crucifixion and resurrection of Jesus, the Apostles hid in Jerusalem for fear of the Jews and the Romans until they were filled with gifts and new courage at Pentecost.

- Complete this section by having the students reflect on the "Our Father" or "The Lord's Prayer." Though there are various translations, it is the one prayer common to all Christians.

- Point students to the Reflection Question about "The Lord's Prayer" on page 115. Have students write their answers to the question.

- Have one student read aloud the section summary statements before having the class do the Review Questions as a written assignment.

Section Review Questions and Answers

1. Why did the early Christians change their Sabbath from Saturday to Sunday?

   The early Christians changed their Sabbath from Saturday to Sunday because Sunday was the day Jesus rose from the dead.

2. How is the Christian calendar different from the civil calendar?

   The Christian calendar is different from the civil calendar in that it begins on the first Sunday of Advent and throughout the year celebrates the life, ministry, death, and resurrection of Jesus.

3. What are the special events in the Christmas cycle?

   The special events in the Christmas cycle are Advent, Christmas, and Epiphany.

4. What are the special events in the Easter cycle?

   The special events in the Easter cycle are Lent, Easter, and Pentecost.

5. What are two sacraments that most Christians celebrate?

   The two sacraments that most Christians celebrate are Baptism and Eucharist.

6. Name some of the characteristics of prayer.

   Some characteristics of prayer are that it is a two-way conversation between God and an individual or group; it can be formal or informal, long or short, verbal or silent. Prayer can involve different postures and different gestures and can be done at any time.

5. Sacred Places and Sacred Spaces (pages 116–118)

Church and *Holy Land*

Objective

In this section the students will:

- learn that churches are the sacred places of worship for Christians;
- appreciate that the Holy Land where Jesus was born, lived, and died is especially sacred;
- understand that how God is worshipped is more important than where God is worshipped.

Preview

Like people of other faiths, Christians hold certain places as sacred. The land where Jesus was born, lived, preached, and died—present day Israel—is called "the Holy Land." Individual churches, no matter what their architectural style or decoration, are also seen as holy or sacred. In these houses of worship, Christians gather to pray, to initiate new members, and to reverently observe major rites of passage for members such as baptisms, marriages, and funerals.

Using the Text

- Plan a class visit or, if possible, a walking tour to various nearby Christian churches.
- Assign students to bring photos of any church—both interior and exterior views. Have them share their photos with the rest of the class and explain how the design and style of their churches are specifically Catholic, Protestant, Orthodox, or Anglican. Conclude the presentations with a brief discussion of the photo on page 116 which opens this section.

Extending the Text

- Distribute copies of the "Christianity Crossword Puzzle" as a worksheet and review for this chapter. Copy the puzzle from page 88 of the Teacher's Manual.
- Direct students to read the Summary statements, and note the Section Review Questions.

Section Review Questions and Answers

1. Describe the various church architectures depicted in the photos on pages 116–117.

    Answers will vary.

2. Why are Protestant churches often less formal interiorly than Catholic, Orthodox, or Anglican churches?

    Since some Protestant churches often put more emphasis on the scriptures, there is need for only a pulpit.

3. Name and explain the significance of several sacred places in the Holy Land.

    Bethlehem, where Jesus was born, Nazareth, where Jesus grew up, and the region of Galilee, where Jesus did much of his preaching and healing, are especially sacred. In addition, Jerusalem and areas surrounding it are holy spaces. Jesus preached and healed the sick in that locale. Inside the walls of Jerusalem, Jesus was tried as a criminal. Outside the walls of Jerusalem, Jesus was crucified, died, buried, resurrected, and ascended to heaven.

Other Christian Denominations through a Catholic Lens
(pages 118–125)

The Book of the Church and *Understanding Inerrancy* and *Interpreting the Bible*

Objective

In this section the students will:

- learn that "catholic" means "for everyone," though not everyone belongs to the Church in the same way;
- become familiar with ecumenism, the ongoing effort to seek unity within the Christian faith;
- recognize that Catholicism sees the Bible as "the book of the Church" while many Christian denominations see themselves as the "church of the Book" since they believe that the Scriptures contain the fullness of God's revelation;
- examine and discuss the topic of "inerrancy," the belief of some Christian churches that the Bible is completely free from error.

Preview

When guiding students to examine how other Christian denominations differ from Catholicism, it's good to first revisit the meaning of the term "catholic." "Catholic" means "universal," or "for everyone." Although not all people belong to the Church in the same way, the Church takes the message of salvation to everyone. Many Christians do not profess the Catholic faith for a variety of reasons. Ecumenism is the movement to promote Christian unity, and the Catholic Church works hard to dialogue with many other Christian churches. Some of those churches are "churches of the Book," which means that they see the Bible as God's final revelation that is free from all error. Catholics, on the other hand, believe that the ongoing teaching or Tradition of the Church also shares God's word, and that the Bible is not meant to guide us in many areas of science, geography, and history. The Catholic Church, through its teaching authority, helps to interpret scripture for Catholics.

Using the Text

- Recap the introductory paragraphs about the ways that other Christian denominations belong to the Church but not in the fullest way. An analogy might be the variety of ways that teens really call their peers "friends." Some friends are for shopping or for a certain period of time. They may also be teammates on the court or field. Other friends, however, are more fully our friends. They share deepest values and experiences with us. But all see each other as friends who have some fundamental interests in common.
- Ask students how they would organize—and then promote—a large ecumenical prayer service for Christian youth. In what ways would they need to be sensitive about making sure all teens felt invited and welcomed—despite their different faiths? What kind of prayer or prayer experiences could include different religious traditions?
- Discuss the view of Biblical inerrancy held by some Protestant groups. Bring greater clarity to this issue for students by discussing the teaching of the Catholic Church and the views that

some Protestant churches have on a specific Bible passage such as the seven days of creation described in Genesis 1.

Extending the Text

- Show the film *Taize: A Little Springtime* (Journey Films, 26 minutes). Invite students to comment on the different ways that Christian unity is found and celebrated in this ecumenical community.

- Make use of the Reflection Question about different Christian denominations on page 124 and engage students in a discussion about religious divisions they see or sense.

- Have the group review the list of Section Summary statements on pages 124–125 and Chapter Summary statements on pages 126–127. Then, have students number off and write short answers to the twenty-two Chapter Review Questions on pages 128–129. (If needed, have some students do more than one question.) Call on students to share their answers. Correct or expand on student answers if it's needed.

- Lead the students in a review of this chapter. Draw on the work the students did in reviewing the summary statements and answering the review questions. Announce the date for the chapter test. Then read aloud the "Conclusion" about the symbol of the cross and then light a "unity candle" where all students can see and gather around it. Together, recite the "Prayer" from the Pontifical Council on page 130 as this chapter is completed.

Section Review Questions and Answers

1. Define *ecumenism*.

   Ecumenism is the attempt and mission to establish a visible unity of the Christian faith. It is the application of the prayer of Christ at the Last Supper that "all may be one."

2. What are the two understandings of inerrancy described in this section?

   Some Protestant groups interpret "inerrancy" to mean that the Bible is free of errors of all kinds—even in statements made about history, geography, and science. Other Christian groups see "inerrancy" as related only to truths necessary for salvation.

3. What is *sola scriptura*?

   The term means "scripture alone" and was originally connected with the attempt to limit the authority of the Catholic Church to what the Bible says. Catholic teachings on papal authority and the veneration of images, for instance, could not be verified in the Bible.

4. Why does the Catholic Church say that both Scripture and Tradition are sources of authority for Catholics?

   The Catholic Church believes that, in addition to the teaching authority of Scripture, God continues to guide the successors of the Apostles—the Pope and the bishops—in every generation. This ongoing teaching is known as Tradition.

5. What is the difference between describing the relationship between the Church and the Bible as "the book of the Church" versus "the Church of the book?"

   Christians who see the Bible as "inerrant," or without error, look to the Bible as the only legitimate moral guide. This group could be described as the "church of the Book." Catholics and other Christians who do not rely only on the Bible for moral guidance see the Scriptures as the "Book of the Church."

Chapter Review Questions and Answers

1. Who was Jesus?

   For Christians, Jesus was the long-awaited Jewish Messiah as prophesied in the Hebrew Scriptures, and he was the Son of God. He was a storyteller and healer who did most of his ministry in the region of Galilee. He was brought before trial and crucified on a Roman cross. He rose from the dead on the third day and was seen by many of his followers before his ascension to heaven.

2. What are epistles?

   Epistles are letters from some of the apostles or first disciples of Jesus to Christian communities that are found in the New Testament.

3. How was the Christian life different after the Edict of Milan?

   After the Edict of Milan Christians were no longer persecuted. Rather, Christianity was legalized and became the official religion of the Roman Empire.

4. What did the monastic rule of Benedict emphasize?

   The monastic rule of Benedict emphasized prayer, study, and work.

5. What doctrines were defined at the Council of Nicaea and Council of Ephesus?

   At the Council of Nicaea, the doctrine of the Trinity was defined. At the Council of Ephesus, the doctrine that Mary was the Mother of God and the mother of the human Jesus was defined.

6. How did the eastern patriarchs regard the bishop of Rome?

   The eastern patriarchs regarded the bishop of Rome as one to be respected because Rome is the place where Peter is buried.

7. Explain how Christian conversion of Germanic tribes often occurred.

   Often when the head of the tribe converted, the whole tribe converted as well.

8. What was the stated purpose of the Crusades?

   The stated purpose of the Crusades was to get back the Holy Land from the Muslims.

9. What were some of the beliefs stated by Martin Luther in his Ninety-five Theses?

   Martin Luther believed that church authority should come from the Bible, not Church tradition or leaders. He believed salvation was by a person's faith. He also believed in the priesthood of all believers, not just a few.

10. What is the derivation of the word *lent*?

    The word lent comes from an Old English word meaning "springtime."

11. How did the Council of Trent respond to the reformers?

    The Council of Trent responded to the reformers by reiterating Catholic doctrine and countering Protestant doctrine. The Council reiterated papal as well as biblical authority, the need for works as well as faith, and said there were seven true sacraments, not just two.

12. Why was religion in the modern period diminished?

    Religion in the modern period was diminished because of the increased emphasis in the belief that people could determine their own destiny and had little need for God.

13. What is the ecumenical movement? How is it manifested today?

    The ecumenical movement attempts to bring about understanding among the various Christian groups. Today it is manifested through the World Council of Churches that presently has over 300 members from Orthodox, Anglican, and Protestant denominations. Also, the Second Vatican Council (1962–65) made major strides in recognizing the validity of the existence of the various religions in the world.

14. What are some of the ways Christians use the Bible?

    Christians use the Bible in both public and private settings. Individuals may read the Bible as part of their prayer life. The Bible is often used as part of family devotions or study groups. All Christians use the Bible in their worship services.

15. Name the Great Commandment that is the foundation of Christian living.

    The Great Commandment is, "You shall love the Lord your God with all your heart and all your soul and with all your mind. This is the greatest and the first commandment. The second is like it: You shall love your neighbor as yourself."

16. Define church.

    The word church means "the assembled."

17. How can the interior design of a church indicate which denomination worships there?

    The interior design of a church is more telling than the exterior. A church with an altar in the middle and a pulpit on the side would tend to be Catholic, Anglican, Orthodox, or perhaps Lutheran. If, in addition, there are statues of Jesus, Mary, and the saints, then the church is likely to be Catholic. If, instead of statues, there are icons, it is most likely Orthodox. Protestant churches tend to be simpler in ornamentation, some with just a pulpit in the center of the sanctuary.

18. What two sacraments are accepted by most Christians?

    The two sacraments accepted by most Christians are Baptism and Eucharist.

19. What are some of the ways that Christians pray?

    Prayer can be formal or informal, long or short, verbal or silent. Prayer can involve singing. Different postures and different gestures can be used at different times for prayer. A person can pray anytime and anywhere.

20. What do all Christians agree about the Bible?

    All Christians agree that the Bible is the inspired Word of God and the fundamental sacred text to guide their spiritual lives.

21. Why does the Catholic Church say that both Scripture and Tradition are sources of authority for Catholics?

    The Catholic Church believes that, in addition to the teaching authority of Scripture, God continues to guide the successors of the Apostles—the Pope and the bishops—in every generation. This ongoing teaching is known as Tradition.

22. What is the role of the Magisterium in the Catholic Church?

    The Magisterium is the official teaching authority of the Church made up of the Pope and the college of bishops. The Magisterium interprets matters of faith and morals in the light of the long apostolic tradition of the Church, the teachings of the Church Fathers and ecumenical councils. The Magisterium does not base its teaching on the Bible alone.

Christianity Crossword Puzzle Answers

Across

2. filioque
5. evangelization
6. mendicant
9. Anglican
10. Pentecostalism

Down

1. fundamentalism
3. icon
4. ecumenical
7. Sect
8. anti-Semitism

Chapter 3 Test Answers

Multiple Choice (3 points each)

1. b, 2. d, 3. d, 4. d, 5. d, 6. a, 7. d, 8. d, 9. a, 10. a, 11. b, 12. c, 13. b, 14. a, 15. d, 16. d, 17. b, 18. a, 19. a, 20. d

Short Answer (8 points each)

1. The Catholic Reformation was an attempt to both reform the Catholic Church and restate long-held doctrine and tradition. The outcomes of the reforms were stated at the Council of Trent.

2. Protestants accept only two sacraments—Baptism and the Eucharist. According to Protestants, they are the only two sacraments mentioned in the Bible.

3. The special events in the Christmas cycle are Advent, Christmas, and Epiphany. Advent is a preparation for the coming of Jesus. Christmas celebrates the birth of Jesus. Epiphany is a celebration of the manifestation of Jesus to the Gentiles.

4. The special events in the Easter cycle are Lent, Easter, and Pentecost. Lent is a forty day penitential period in preparation for Easter. Easter celebrates the resurrection of Jesus. Pentecost celebrates the coming of the Holy Spirit.

5. The major difference between the Catholic and Protestant Bible is the number of books in Old Testament. The Catholic Bible has seven more books in the Old Testament than the Protestant Bible.

Theses of Martin Luther

On October 31, 1517, the German Augustinian monk Martin Luther is said to have nailed his 95 *Theses* to the castle church door at Wittenberg, Germany. Though this incident may be legendary, he definitely gave his *Theses* to some friends and students. And this event, true or not, has been portrayed in numerous manners and is the great symbol of what came to be known as the Protestant Reformation. Listed below are some selected entries from Luther's *Theses*:

Therefore, those preachers of indulgences err who say that, by the Pope's indulgence, a man may be exempt from all punishments, and be saved.

Yea, the Pope remits the souls in Purgatory no penalty which they, according to the canons, would have had to pay in this life.

All penalties may be granted, it is certain that it is granted only to those most approaching perfection, that is to very few.

Therefore the multitude is misled by the boastful promise of the paid penalty, whereby no manner of distinction is made.

Christians should be taught that it is not the Pope's opinion that the buying of indulgence is in any way comparable to works of charity.

Christians should be taught that he who gives to the poor, or lends to a needy man, does better than buying indulgence. For, by the exercise of charity, charity increases and man grows better, while by means of indulgence, he does not become better, but only freer from punishment.

Christians should be taught that he who sees his neighbor in distress, and nevertheless buys indulgence, is not partaking in the Pope's pardons, but in the anger of God.

Christians should be taught that unless they are rich enough, it is their duty to keep what is necessary for the use of their households, and by no means to throw it away on indulgences.

Christians should be taught that the buying of indulgences is optional and not commanded.

Christians should be taught that the Pope in selling pardons, has more want and more desire of a devout prayer for himself than of the money.

Christians should be taught that the Pope's pardons are useful as far as one does not put confidence in them, but on the contrary most dangerous if through them one loses the fear of God.

Questions:

1. How does Luther portray God?

2. How does Luther portray the Church?

3. With what is Luther most concerned?

4. What feelings does Luther emit from this document?

God's Grandeur

by Gerard Manley Hopkins

The world is charged with the grandeur of God.

It will flame out, like shining from shook foil;

It gathers to a greatness, like the ooze of oil

Crushed. Why do men then now not wreck his rod?

Generations have trod, have trod, have trod;

And all is seared with trade; bleared, smeared with toil;

And wears man's smudge and shares man's smell: the soil

Is bare now, nor can foot feel, being shod.

And for all this, nature is never spent;

There lives the dearest freshness deep down things;

And though the last lights off the black West went

Oh, morning, at the brown brink eastward, springs—

Because the Holy Ghost over the bent

World broods with warm breast and with ah! bright wings.

Quoted from Norman H. MacKenzie, ed. *The Later Poetic Manuscripts of Gerard Manley Hopkins in Facsimile.* New York and London: Garland Publishing, 1991.

Christianity Crossword Puzzle

Across

2. "and the Son."

5. witness the good news

6. beggar

9. outgrowth of the Church of England

10. manifests gifts of the Holy Spirit

Down

1. back to the Bible basics

3. window to heaven

4. movement encouraging understanding among various Christian groups

7. splinter group from main religious body

8. discrimination against Jews

Chapter 3 Test

Name _____

Multiple Choice. *Write the letter of the best choice in the space provided.* (3 points each)

_____ 1. Regarding the historical Jesus, we know
  a. very much.
  b. very little.
  c. only what historians tell us.
  d. only what the church tells us.

_____ 2. The epistles of Paul were written
  a. before the Gospels in all cases.
  b. predominantly to churches in Asia Minor and Greece.
  c. both a and b
  d. neither a nor b

_____ 3. The state-sponsored persecutions of early Christians
  a. ceased with the Edict of Milan.
  b. ceased during the reign of Constantine.
  c. was strongest in the areas around Rome.
  d. all of the above

_____ 4. The Rule of St. Benedict
  a. emphasized an austere lifestyle.
  b. emphasized prayer, teaching, and work.
  c. became the model for monastic rule over the centuries.
  d. all of the above

_____ 5. The first seven councils of the Christian Church
  a. are the only ones recognized by the Eastern Orthodox churches.
  b. were convened by the emperor of Constantinople.
  c. were convened to address doctrinal disputes.
  d. all of the above

_____ 6. The eastern patriarchs regarded the Pope
  a. as one to be respected.
  b. as the successor of Jesus on earth.
  c. as one with primacy above all patriarchs.
  d. all of the above

_____ 7. Generally, Constantine's decision to move the capital of the Roman empire to Constantinople
  a. resulted in two political centers.
  b. exasperated differences between Greek-speaking east and Latin-speaking west.
  c. further divided Christianity.
  d. all of the above

_____ 8. Which one of the following was not held by Martin Luther:

    a. the common priesthood of all

    b. the supreme authority of the Bible

    c. justification by faith alone

    d. believers' baptism

_____ 9. The results of the Crusades were

    a. that Muslims maintained jurisdiction over the Holy Land.

    b. that Catholic Christians regained jurisdiction over the Holy Land.

    c. that Orthodox Christians regained jurisdiction over the Holy Land.

    d. none of the above

_____ 10. The World Council of Churches

    a. is a product of the ecumenical movement.

    b. is a European response to the ecumenical movement.

    c. has both Protestants and Catholics as members.

    d. is a response to the growing Christian fundamentalist movements.

_____ 11. The two sacraments accepted by most Christians are

    a. Baptism and Matrimony.

    b. Baptism and Eucharist.

    c. Baptism and Holy Orders.

    d. Baptism and Confirmation.

_____ 12. The Christian liturgical year

    a. begins on January 1.

    b. begins on Ash Wednesday.

    c. begins on the first Sunday of Advent.

    d. begins on Christmas Day.

_____ 13. The Anglican Communion

    a. emerged during the Anglo-Saxon era.

    b. is a loose confederation of national churches.

    c. emphasizes Communion under both species.

    d. all of the above

_____ 14. Which of the following movements places a strong emphasis on witnessing the Good News of Jesus Christ?

    a. evangelicalism

    b. fundamentalism

    c. anti-Semitism

    d. pentecostalism

_____ 15. Christians commemorate Jesus' Last Supper on

    a. Good Friday.

    b. Epiphany.

    c. Pentecost.

    d. Maundy Thursday.

_____ 16. Which of the following saints was a mendicant?
   a. St. Paul
   b. St. Leo
   c. St. Benedict
   d. St. Francis

_____ 17. Which of the following did *not* contribute to the Great Schism between the Eastern and Western Church?
   a. the *filioque* controversy
   b. the belief in saints
   c. Crusaders devastating Constantinople
   d. the cultural gap between Latin west and Greek east

_____ 18. Which of the following did *not* contribute to the Protestant Reformation?
   a. the difference between the Apostles' Creed and the Nicene Creed
   b. corruption in the selling of indulgences
   c. doctrinal differences
   d. corruption in papal leadership

_____ 19. That which is *most* prominent in Eastern Orthodox churches is
   a. icons
   b. statues
   c. the reading of the Bible
   d. priests

_____ 20. The foundation for Christian moral living is
   a. the Apostles' Creed.
   b. the Nicene Creed.
   c. the Lord's Prayer.
   d. the Great Commandment.

Short Answer. *Briefly answer the following questions.* (8 points each)

1. What is the Catholic Reformation?

2. Why do most Protestants accept only two sacraments?

3. What are the special events in the Christmas cycle, and what does each commemorate?

4. What are the special events in the Easter cycle, and what does each commemorate?

5. Describe the major difference between the Catholic and Protestant Bible?

Chapter 4: Islam

Introduction

In spite of much negative publicity accompanying some of its more militant elements, Islam is one of the fastest growing religions in the United States.

Islam is a worldwide religion. After the death of Muhammad, Islam spread rapidly throughout the Middle East and North Africa and into India and southern Europe, especially the Iberian Peninsula. During the Middle Ages, Islam was very influential in the creation of Western civilization, especially in the areas of science, philosophy, and medicine. At the dawn of the Modern Period Islam was pushed out of the Iberian Peninsula and Britain began to colonize places once ruled by Muslims. Now in the twenty-first century, Islam is striving to return to the greatness it once possessed.

Islamic beliefs are centered squarely on the absoluteness of one God. Islam's seven articles of faith and Five Pillars are simply stated beliefs and practices for Muslims throughout the world. Like Judaism and Christianity, Islam is a historical, monotheistic religion of the book (the Qur'an). In addition, sacred time is clearly marked and Muslims are required to pray five times daily, facing the sacred city of Mecca in present day Saudi Arabia.

Islam does not separate the secular from the sacred. Muslims hold that all of life—physical, social, economic, and political—is to submit to the will of Allah. That is the nature of all creation. While plants and animals submit to Allah's will, many human beings make the choice to go against the natural tendency to submit to Allah. Yet, Muslims believe, Allah remains compassionate and merciful.

Resources for Chapter 4

Books

Armstrong, Karen. *Islam: A Short History*. New York: Modern Library, 2002.

———. *Muhammad: A Biography of the Prophet*. San Francisco: HarperSanFrancisco, 1992.

Donohue, John J., and John L. Esposito. *Islam in Transition: Muslim Perspectives*. 2nd ed. New York: Oxford University Press, 2006.

Esposito, John L. *Asian Islam in the 21st Century*. New York: Oxford University Press, 2007.

———. *Islam: The Straight Path*. 3rd ed., New York: Oxford University Press, 2005.

———. *The Oxford Dictionary of Islam*. New York: Oxford University Press, 2003.

———. *The Oxford Encyclopedia of the Modern Islamic World*. New York: Oxford University Press, 1995.

———. *What Everyone Needs to Know About Islam*. New York: Oxford University Press, 2002.

Esposito, John L., Darrell J. Fasching, and Todd Thornton Lewis. *World Religions Today*. 2nd ed. New York: Oxford University Press, 2005.

Feiler, Bruce. *Abraham: A Journey to the Heart of Three Faiths*. New York: William Morrow, 2002.

Haddad, Yvonne Yazbeck, and John L. Esposito. *Daughters of Abraham: Feminist Thought in Judaism, Christianity, and Islam.* Gainesville, FL: University Press of Florida, 2001.

————. *Islam, Gender, and Social Change.* New York: Oxford University Press, 1998.

Haddad, Yvonne Yazbeck, and Barbara Freyer Stowasser. *Islamic Law and the Challenges of Modernity.* Walnut Creek, CA: AltaMira Press, 2004.

————. *Muslims in the West: From Sojourners to Citizens.* New York: Oxford University Press, 2002.

Haddad, Yvonne Yazbeck, and Jane I. Smith, eds. *Muslim Minorities in the West: Visible and Invisible.* Walnut Creek, CA: AltaMira Press, 2002.

Hunter, Shireen. *Islam, Europe's Second Religion: The New Social, Cultural, and Political Landscape.* Westport, CT: Praeger, 2002.

Keeler, William Cardinal. "How Mary Holds Muslims and Christians in Conversation." *Origins. CNS Documentary Service*, 25, 36 (February 29, 1996): pp. 610–612.

Lings, Martin. *What is Sufism?* Cambridge, UK: Islamic Texts Society, 1999.

Nasr, Seyyed Hossein. *Islamic Art and Spirituality.* Albany: State University of New York Press, 1987.

————. *Islamic Spirituality: Foundations.* New York: Crossroad, 1987.

————. *Muhammad: Man of God.* Chicago: KAZI Publications, Inc., 1995.

————. *The Heart of Islam: Enduring Values for Humanity.* San Francisco: HarperSanFrancisco, 2002.

Nomachi, Kazuyoshi, and Seyyed Hossein Nasr. *Mecca the Blessed, Medina the Radiant: The Holiest Cities of Islam.* 2nd ed. New York: Aperture, 1997.

The Qur'an Translation. Sayer A. A. Razwi, ed. and Abdullah Yusef Ali, trans. New York: Tahrike Tarsile Qur'an, Inc., 1999.

Renard, John. *101 Questions and Answers on Islam.* 2nd ed. New York: Paulist Press, 2004.

Revelation: Catholic and Muslim Perspectives. Washington, D.C.: United States Conference of Catholic Bishops Publishing, 2005.

Smith, Jane I., and Yvonne Yazbeck Haddad. *The Islamic Understanding of Death and Resurrection.* New York: Oxford University Press, 2002.

Williams, John Alden. *The Word of Islam.* Austin: University of Texas Press, 1994.

Audio-visual Resources

Civilizations in Conflict: Byzantium, Islam and the Crusades. VHS. (United Learning, 1998, 18 minutes) Includes teacher's guide and blackline masters.

Inside Mecca. DVD/VHS. (National Geographic Video, 2003, 60 minutes)

Islam. Essentials of Faith Series. DVD/VHS. (Films Media Group, 2006, 24 minutes)

Islam. Religions of the World Video Series. DVD/VHS. (Schlessinger Media, 1996, 50 minutes)

Islam: Empire of Faith. DVD/VHS. (Gardner Films, Inc., 2000, 180 minutes) Includes web resources at www.pbs.org/empires/islam/index.html.

Islam: The Faith and the People. VHS. (United Learning, 1991, 22 minutes) Includes teacher's guide and blackline masters.

Malcolm X. DVD/VHS. (Warner Home Video, 1994, 201 minutes) A commercially released film starring Denzel Washington.

Muhammad: Legacy of a Prophet. DVD/VHS. (Kikim Media and Unity Productions Foundation, 2002, 120 minutes) Lesson Plans available at www.cie.org/ItemDetail.aspx?id=N&m_id=28&item_id=124 &cat_id=26.

Muslims. DVD/VHS. (The Independent Production Fund, Inc., 2002, 120 minutes) Lesson Plans available at www.cie.org/ItemDetail.aspx?id=N&m_id=28&item_id=111&cat_id=26.

There Is No God But God. The Long Search Video Series. DVD/VHS. (Ambrose Video Publishing, 2001, 60 minutes) Study Guide for series available for separate purchase.

Three Faiths, One God: Judaism, Christianity and Islam. DVD/VHS. (Auteur Productions, Ltd., 2005, 115 minutes) Study Guide available for purchase.

Internet Resources

Center for Muslim-Christian Understanding— www.cmcu.georgetown.edu

Council on Islamic Education— www.cie.org

Pontifical Council for Interreligious Dialogue— www.vatican.va/roman_curia/pontifical_councils/ interelg/documents/rc_pc_interelg_pro_20051996_en.html

www.islam-online.net

Submission Brings Inner Freedom (pages 133–135)

Using the Text

- Have students quietly read the introductory pages of this chapter, taking note of crucial names and terms such as the prophet Muhammad, Islam, Muslims, Allah, etc.

- Ask students if they are surprised that Islam is the second largest religion and the fastest growing religion in the world. Sample a variety of students to see what their 9/11 memories or impressions are with regard to Muslims.

- Discuss the meaning of the term "stereotype." As one dictionary defines it, a stereotype is "a conventional, formulaic, and over-simplified conception, opinion, or image." Randomly call on students to describe "Muslim stereotypes." If any students personally know Muslims, they may want to add to the discussion, sharing their real-life experiences and interactions. Be ready to let them show that real-life experiences and stereotypes don't match.

- Display a large map of the Middle East and point out—or have students locate—places cited in the listing of important Muslim dates—Mecca and Medina (Saudi Arabia), Damascus (Syria), Karbala and Baghdad (Iraq), Egypt, Jerusalem, Constantinople (now Istanbul in Turkey), Iran, Pakistan. Show students the sweep and range of the Muslims spread through southern Europe and northern Africa.

1. A Brief History of Islam (pages 136–151)

Muhammad, Messenger of God and *The Rightly-Guided Caliphs* and *Classical Period* and *Medieval Period* and *Modern Period*

Objective

In this section, the students will:

- become more familiar with the foundation of Islam and its early history;
- learn that Muslims believe that Islam began with Adam and that Muhammad is seen as the last prophet who was given messages for humanity by God;
- learn about the life, struggles, and teachings of Muhammad and the successors or caliphs who followed him;
- identify the Qur'an (Koran) as the sacred scriptures of Islam and Mecca and Medina as its principle holy cities;
- get a broad look at Muslim history from the Classical Period through modern times;
- become acquainted with Muslim cultural and intellectual accomplishments that profoundly influenced Western philosophy, engineering, medicine, science, and literature;
- survey European, Middle Eastern, and Asian maps to track the ebb and flow of Muslim expansion and control;
- learn about the history of Islam in the United States and identify its principle proponents—Elijah Muhammad, Malcolm X, Warith Din Muhammad, and Louis Farrakhan.

Preview

Muslims maintain that God created all humans to be Muslims, that is, people who will submit to the will of God. They believe that Muhammad, born in Mecca in 570 CE, was God's final prophet or messenger. By Muhammad's death in 632, many Arabs had become Muslims. Caliphs, the first successors to Muhammad, collected Muhammad's revelations into the Qur'an and began the territorial expansion of Islam. Two major factions—the Shi'i and the Sunni Muslims—developed within Islam over competing claims to leadership. During the Classical Period, Islamic influence spread throughout the world. Muslim culture emerged and flowered as the "Golden Age of Islam." Muslim scholarship profoundly contributed to many fields. In modern times, Muslim influence declined with the rise of European power and colonial domination in the Middle East. In America, Elijah Muhammad developed the Nation of Islam, combining the practice of Islam with an appeal for Black pride and separatism.

Using the Text

- Repeat the crucial Muslim belief that according to Muhammad, Adam, Moses, Abraham, and Jesus were prophets who submitted to the will of God. Through Muhammad, God's will was once again being revealed to humanity. He destroyed the many idols found at the Ka'bah. The one God (Allah) was to be worshipped.
- Sort through any questions or comments students may have about who Muhammad was and how his revelations were eventually written down in the Qur'an.

- Show the film *Islam: The Faith and the People,* a twenty-two minute overview of Islam or a pre-viewed twenty- to twenty-five-minute portion of the longer film, *Islam: There is No God But God.* Solicit comments or questions and discuss with the students.

- Obtain several copies of the Qur'an and encourage students to look through them and hand them on.

- Emphasize key terms used in these first two sections—Ka'bah, Hijrah, caliph, Qur'an, caliph-ate, and imam. Then call on individual students to explain them and their origins.

- Remind students that during the Classical Period of Islam, great expansion of Islam occurred. The most holy of Islamic books, the Qur'an, was codified and distributed. Muslims were able to erect the great mosque in Jerusalem known today as the Dome of the Rock, just forty years after the death of Muhammad.

- Show pictures of the famous Dome of the Rock and detail some of its recent history as a controversial Islamic monument. Ask students if they recall seeing pictures or news about the Dome.

- Also show examples of Arabic writing. Recap points made in the book about the way the language unified Islamic culture since the use of Arabic was required.

- Share some examples of Islamic literature, poetry, philosophy, or pictures of Islamic architecture from around the world.

- Divide students into small groups of two or three and give them blank outline maps that show the Middle East, northern Africa, and the Mediterranean basin. Have students look back through the text from "Classical Period" through "The Nation of Islam" (pages 140–149), identifying cites or regions that were of significance in Islamic history. (Baghdad, Istanbul, Cairo, Mecca, Cordoba, Turkey, etc.) Give each group a historical atlas and a contemporary political atlas. Each group should collaborate to locate and label as many locations as possible.

- Talk about Islam in America, bolstering information offered in the text with material from recent attention in national news magazines and in other media. What is it really like to be Muslim in America? Encourage student discussion and follow-up research.

Extending the Text

- Direct students to the Reflection Question about similarities between Christianity and Islam on p. 138. On the board, call on students to help create a list of five to six similarities and then a list of differences.

- Have students find the area of the text that explains the split between the Shi'i and the Sunni Muslims. What do students know about that split as it's expressed today in Iraq and other Middle Eastern nations?

- Offer extra-credit to students willing to prepare a three- to five-minute oral report or a poster on contemporary Shi'i-Sunni conflicts in one or more Middle Eastern nations.

- Refer all students to the Research and Activities list on pages 179–180. Have students work in pairs to do one project from any of the project topics listed. Allow a week to ten days for completion of the projects.

- Show the segment in the video *Living Islam: What It Means To Be a Muslim in Today's World* on the festival that commemorates the martyrdom of Hussein.
- The feature "The Nation of Islam" on pages 148–149 describes a sect of Islam indigenous to the United States. The Nation of Islam has raised important questions about racism in the United States. Describe these in a bit more detail and encourage student comment.
- At this point, you may want to show a previewed portion of the film *Malcolm X* starring Denzel Washington and directed by Spike Lee. (Violence gives it an R rating.)
- Refer students to the Reflection Questions on page 147 about being ruled by a government that was totally Catholic or one with a religion different than their own. Invite students to offer their perspectives, reminding them to honor a variety of opinions.
- Have students read through the Section Summary statements on page 150 and then answer the Section Review Questions on pages 150–151

Section Review Questions and Answers

1. Explain how Muhammad received his first revelation.

   Muhammad received his first revelation in 610 CE when the angel Gabriel appeared to him in a cave. The angel began to give Muhammad teachings from Allah, the one true God. He commanded him to recite to the people what he heard.

2. As a messenger of God, what was Muhammad's chief message to mankind?

   Muhammad's message was that there is only one God, and that God wanted his people to worship him alone. Care for the poor and disadvantaged was also said to be a priority.

3. What was the major cause of the rise of the two major groupings of Muslims—the Sunni and the Shi'i?

   Although there are no fundamental differences in beliefs and practices between the Sunni and the Shi'i Muslims, there is a long-standing dispute over who is to lead the Muslim community. In the seventh century, the Shi'it could not accept the successor of Ali as caliph because Shi'ites believe the successors of Muhammad should be his direct descendants.

4. On a map, locate the capitals of the following: the first capital of Islam, the capital extablished by Ali, Umayyads, Abbasids, Fatimids, Mughals, Safavids, Umayyads, and Ottomans.

   Provide a large map of the Middle East, North Africa, and the Mediterranean Basin for students to use.

5. Summarize some of the major contributions of Islamic civilizations during its Golden Age.

   During its Golden Age, in the Medieval Period, the Muslim capital was moved to Baghdad, and it became an intellectual center for many disciplines. Scientific, literary, and philosophical works from Greek, Persian, and Indian sources were translated into Arabic. Scientific research also flourished in Muslim lands. Many books were written on engineering, geography, astronomy, mathematics, and chemistry. The rich and abundant analysis of Muslim scholars in the sciences and in the humanities contributed greatly to Western scholarship for centuries.

6. What were some of the major causes of the decline of Islamic political power in the early Modern Period?

    One of the major causes was the growth of European industrial, economic, and political power at a time when the influence of Muslim political influence was declining. The English and French, in particular, took political control and colonized many areas of Africa and the Middle East that had once been under Muslim control. A fall-off in economic power accompanied the political decline. Enduring political conflicts developed when European Christians attempted to evangelize some regions in the Holy Land. Political realignments without respect for cultural, ethnic, and religious differences also sabotaged long-term peace and security in some areas of the Middle East, where historic Muslim rights and influence were ignored.

7. Summarize the history of the Nation of Islam in the United States.

    (Answers may vary.) An African-American named Fard, who wished to separate his followers from the dominant American culture, began the Nation of Islam in Detroit. Elijah Muhammad succeeded Fard and greatly expanded the Nation of Islam, advocating a strong work ethic and a high standard of moral living. Malcolm X was a strong leader in the movement in the 1960s until he began to move toward the more orthodox Sunni branch of Islam. Malcolm X was assassinated in 1965, but Elijah Muhammad's son Wallace moved the Nation of Islam toward mainline Islam. Louis Farrakhan did not like the "integrationist" movement that Wallace Muhammad was leading, so he splintered off and moved back toward the ideals of Elijah Muhammad.

2. Sacred Stories and Sacred Scriptures (pages 151–154)

Qur'an and *Sunnah*

Objective

In this section the students will:

- recognize that Muslims see the Qur'an as precious since it was dictated by God;
- learn how the Qur'an, the most sacred Muslim text, was written and structured;
- become familiar with the Sunnah and the Hadith, books that guide Muslims to holy living;
- recognize that Muslims believe the Torah, Psalms, and Gospels to be human words, not the direct words of God;
- practice memorizing Sacred text as do Muslims.

Preview

The Qur'an (also spelled Koran) is the most sacred of books to Muslims. They believe that it contains direct revelations from God to his prophet Muhammad over a twenty-two year period. Since Muhammad was unschooled, he memorized these words from God and shared them with his followers over the years. They too memorized these sacred words but 'Uthman, one of the early successors of Muhammad, wanted to assure that these words would be passed on in uncorrupted form to later generations. 'Uthman had these holy words written down to create the "Qur'an," an Arabic word that means "to read." Another source for spiritual guidance is the Haddith, a collection of stories about Muhammad. Together, these sacred writings are the main sources for Islamic belief, known as the *al-imanul-mufassal*, the Islamic creed.

Using the Text

- Revisit the Muslim belief that the Qur'an is infallible or uncorrupted by human interpretation or alteration. Muslims maintain that God's revelation to Muhammad came in exquisite Arabic without any human deflection by Muhammad nor by the followers of Muhammad who wrote down the revelations recited by Muhammad.
- Leaf through a copy of the Qur'an, pointing out where the one hundred and forty-four surahs or chapters separate the material. If possible, add to the information provided in the text about how Muslims show reverence for the book itself—washing one's hands before opening it, etc.
- Have a half-dozen short verses from an English translation of the Qur'an that deal with a variety of topics written on a half-sheets of paper. Distribute them among the students. Call on students to read them aloud, giving them the dramatic emphasis or reverential tone that a Muslim teenager might give.

Extending the Text

- Adapt the Reflection Question about memorizing verses from Sacred Scripture on page 153. Ask students if any of them can quote a Scripture verse by heart.
- Refer to the Reflection Question about memorized sacred writings on page 153. Then call on students to share a passage they have memorized. *Option:* Divide the class into two sides.

Play a game of "Can you top this?" where the winning side is the one that can recite the most Scripture passages from memory.

- Discuss the Muslim practice of memorizing Scripture verses. Point out that imams (Muslim prayer leaders) must memorize the entire Qur'an. Sample the class for opinions about the value of this kind of "faith knowledge."

- Direct students to the Research and Activities lists on pages 179–180. Have students choose a short research topic from among the first three larger categories. Allow a week for completion of the written or oral reports.

- Delve more directly into Hadith, sharing, explaining, and even demonstrating specific teachings about Islamic lifestyle that many Muslims feel they must follow and respect.

- Assign the Section Review Questions on page 154 to be answered in writing as an open book activity.

Section Review Questions and Answers

1. What does the word Qur'an mean?

   The word Qur'an means "to read" and refers to the instruction that Muhammad received when the angel Gabriel appeared and told him that he was to be God's messenger. God wanted Muhammad to read or learn this message and then share it with the world.

2. Why is the Qur'an the most sacred writing for Muslims? What are the other sacred writings that Muslims revere?

   The Qur'an is the most sacred Muslim text because it was dictated by God through his angel Gabriel. Muhammad memorized every word given to him and orally passed on these scriptures. The Hadith is another revered resource for Muslims. It is a collection of transmitted oral and written accounts of Muhammad's teachings and actions.

3. Why can it be said that the Qur'an and the Sunnah go hand in hand?

   The Qur'an and the Sunnah go hand in hand because the Qur'an presents God's word and the Sunnah presents Muhammad's way of life. Muslims believe both are needed to fully live and act as a Muslim.

4. Compare the Hadith to the Jewish Talmud. How are they alike?

   In many ways, the Hadith is similar to the Jewish Talmud since it is a sort of handbook, describing how adherents are to put teachings into practice.

3. Beliefs and Practices (pages 154–165)

The Five Pillars of Islam and *Islamic Living*

Objective

In this section the students will:

- learn about the seven articles of the Islamic creed;
- become familiar with the Five Pillars of Islam;
- learn more about the way scriptures are used by Muslims;
- know the meaning of Islamic terms—ummah, wudu, Jum'ah, Zakah, Sawm, Hajj, Shahadah, muezzin, Salah, and Shar'iah;
- become familiar with the foundations and actions of Islamic moral law.

Preview

The Qur'an (also spelled Koran) is the sacred scripture of Islam. The Haddith is a collection of stories of Muhammad and forms the core of Islamic law. These are the main sources for Islamic belief, known as the *al-imanul-mufassal*, the Islamic creed.

Monotheism is at the core of Islamic belief and Muslims proclaim this daily with the statement, "There is no god but Allah; Muhammad is the Messenger of Allah." Muslims hold that Allah is an all-knowing judge of human history. Human beings are free to make choices, but will be judged for the choices they make, the lives they lead. Muslims also revere and claim that prophets have received messages about God's will. Among these prophets are Adam, Noah, Moses, and Job. Muslims also see Jesus as a prophet. Muslim practice is guided by the Five Pillars of Islam—religious duties that every Muslim must perform. These pillars are: Shahadah (witnessing); Salah (prayer); Zakah (almsgiving); Sawm (fasting); and Hajj (pilgrimage).

Using the Text

- List the Five Pillars of Islam on the board, (or overhead overlay, flipchart, PowerPoint, etc.) and call on different students to pronounce the Arabic words for these pillars and explain what they mean to Muslims.
- Recite the Arabic Shahadah in English and then in Arabic. (Check pronunciation guides to pronounce it accurately.) Have students repeat the prayer. As the text states, this prayer is said several times each day by every Muslim. Ask students to share their opinions about what effect saying this prayer so often would have on a Muslim's faith, behavior, view of life, etc.
- Present the last three pillars—Zakah, Sawm, and Hajj—with additional background information drawn from other sources. Invite students to react or offer personal reactions to these Muslim practices. Ask students to imagine themselves as Muslims living in America. What would it be like to pray throughout the day, to give alms generously, to fast each day during Ramadan?
- Show previewed segments of the video series *Living Islam: What It Means To Be a Muslim in Today's World* that focus on Muslim practice of the Five Pillars.
- Switch gears and divide the class into small groups of three or four students. Have the groups discuss and respond to the Reflection Question on page 161 that asks them to compose

"pillars" for their own faith. Give students fifteen to twenty minutes. Then, have groups share their pillars.

- Recap and elaborate on the crucial section, "Islamic Living." This section makes it clear that for Muslims there is nothing distinguishable between the secular and the religious. (This is very different from the historical American view that some separation between church and state is desirable.) Add to what the text presents about the Muslim nations of Iran and Pakistan.

Extending the Text

- Invite four or five students to work together to create a word scramble of six to eight key Islamic terms. Photocopy it so that the rest of the class may unscramble the words at a later date.
- Offer extra credit to students interested in art who will present a five-minute oral report from one of the Research and Activities topics from section 3 on page 179. The topics include Islamic architecture, Islamic geometric art, Islamic calligraphy. Remind students that for Muslims, God is so sacred that there can be no artistic representation of God. For example, Michelangelo's masterpiece depicting the creation of Adam by God in the Sistine Chapel would never be acceptable Islamic art.
- If possible, have a small group of students identify and interview a Muslim teen using a video camera or cassette tape to record the interview. (This is Research and Activities project four on pages 179–180.)
- Alternatively, invite discussion of the show *Aliens in America*, a TV sitcom launched in 2007 about a Wisconsin family with teenage children. Unknowingly, the family agrees to host a guileless Pakistani exchange student named Raja Musharaff. *Little Mosque on the Prairie* is a Canadian sitcom on CBC Television created by Zarqa Nawaz. The series focuses on the Muslim population in the fictional rural prairie town of Mercy, Saskatchewan. Poll the class to see how many students have seen or heard about these series. What do they think about the cultural issues raised in these plots? Do they think it is helpful to have television sitcoms about Muslim culture? Discuss.
- As a homework assignment, ask the students to research more about Muslim beliefs about Jesus.
- The special feature on Muslim women seeks to expand students' image of Muslim women. Some Muslim women can be easily identified by their clothing. Everyone has heard the cliché, "The clothes make the man." Ask students whether they think clothes can make a statement about what one believes, especially in the area of religious beliefs.
- Take up the term "submit," a word commonly used in Islam. Poll students to find what thoughts and feelings come to mind when they hear the word "submit?" Muslims claim that submission to God's will is liberating, not oppressive. How can this be true? Have they experienced any "submissions" that were liberating?
- Review this section with students by going over the summary points in the text, and having students answer the review questions at the end of the section. Distribute as well the Islamic word scrambles done by students.
- Share the story of Mahmoud Abdul-Raulf, a Muslim professional basketball player with the NBA who had changed his name from Chris Jackson after converting to Islam in 1991. Soon

after becoming Muslim, Abdul-Raulf refused to stand for the American national anthem when it was played before games. On one occasion when he remained seated on the bench and was noticed, public reaction was decidedly negative. Abdul-Rauf said that his Muslim faith prevented him from worshipping at any nationalistic ceremonies. He said: "It's a belief, and I won't compromise my beliefs." Another Islamic player, Hakeem Olajuwon held a different view, saying that Islamic belief requires every Muslim to obey and respect the law of the countries they live in. Later, Abdul-Rauf compromised by standing during the national anthem, but refusing to sing. Ask the students to share their reactions to this story.

Section 3 Review Questions and Answers

1. Explain what Muslims believe about the two main sections of the Islamic Profession of Faith.

   The Islamic Profession of faith, the Shahadah states, first of all, a belief in one God. The second statement declares that Muhammad is the messenger or prophet of God. This second part is also said to imply that Muhammad was the final prophet sent by God to give direction to his people.

2. Name and explain each of the Five Pillars of Islam.

   1) Profession of Faith—there is no god but God and Muhammad is God's messenger.
   2) Prayer—Muslims pray daily at five specified times, always facing Mecca.
   3) Almsgiving—Muslims give a percentage of their income to the needy.
   4) Fasting—A one-month fast during the Islamic month of Ramadan where no food or drink passes the lips of a Muslim between sun-up and sundown.
   5) Pilgrimage—An obliged pilgrimage to Mecca at least once in one's lifetime, if at all possible.

3. How does one become a Muslim?

   One becomes a Muslim by submitting to the will of Allah. One demonstrates this submission through practicing the duties of a Muslim, that is, the Five Pillars of Islam. A ritual cleansing and a proclamation of the Shahadah before two witnesses is the extent of the initiation ceremony.

4. What are the sources of shar'iah and what is its role in Islam?

   The primary sources for shar'iah are to be found in the Qur'an and the Sunnah. Shar'iah is the centerpiece of Muslim life. It provides the guidance from God about how individuals and society should live.

5. Discuss the role of women in Islam.

   Although many in the Western world view Muslim women as oppressed because of the way some dress and view their roles as wives and mothers, it is really a much more complex issue. In fact, women who dress in a traditional Islamic style today may be professionals or even government officials. The rise of Islam brought higher status to women. They were able to inherit, buy, and sell property. They had independent legal status before the law and could also make choices with regard to marriage, divorce, education, and careers. Many of the traditions that have isolated and discriminated against Muslim women entered Muslim cultures from non-Islamic sources. Today, families are still the backbone of Muslim life, and women play key roles there.

4. Sacred Time (pages 166–168)

Eid al-Fitr (Festival of Breaking the Fast) and *Eid al-Adha (Festival of Sacrifice)* and *Ashura*

Objective

In this section the students will:

- read that Muslims would say that the five times reserved for prayer each day are very sacred;
- learn the significance of the observance of Ramadan and Eid al-Fitr;
- become familiar with the commemoration of historical events that are significant for Muslims, such as the birth of Muhammad, the renewal of the year, and the birth of the world;
- study the Islamic life cycles of birth, marriage, and death.

Preview

Like Jews and Christians, Muslims mark sacred times. The most obvious is the five times marked for daily prayer—between dawn and sunrise; after mid-day; between late afternoon and sunset; between sunset and the end of daylight; at night until dawn. Like the Jewish calendar, the Muslim calendar is lunar and has only 354 days. Celebrations are set to move through the seasons of the solar year over the course of two decades. In addition, there are sacred times that commemorate historical Muslim events, while others celebrate the goodness of Allah. Two of the most important Islamic feasts are Eid al-Fitr, the Festival of Breaking the Fast at the end of Ramadan, and Eid al-Adha, the Festival of Sacrifice which is celebrated at the conclusion of the hajj rituals each year. Ashura, a third festival, has an atonement theme. Mawlid al-Nabi celebrates the birthday of Muhammad.

Using the Text

- Once students understand how the lunar system is different, display a Muslim calendar if you can locate one. Indicate where Islamic holy days and seasons will appear on the calendar. Then, using a Roman calendar, point out when some of the upcoming Muslim sacred times take place.
- Eid al-Fitr marks the end of Ramadan and a month of daily fasting—reason to celebrate. Ask students to participate in an exercise in which they imagine that they are Muslim teenagers observing Ramadan:

    You are a practicing Muslim. You do your chores, go to summer school, have a summer job, and spend time with friends. The month is July, the month of Ramadan. From the time the sun comes up at six in the morning until the sun sets at nine in the evening, you fast from food and drink. That is, not one thing passes your lips until 9:01 p.m.

- Ask: "How is this fast affecting your activities? How difficult is it?" Call on students to share their honest responses.
- Now connect this imagination exercise with the Reflection Question about the spiritual benefits of fasting on page 167. Have students write their responses in their journals. Then ask them to share what they wrote.

- Recap information presented in the book about other Islamic festivals such as *Eid al-Adah*, which commemorates Abraham's planned obedience when God told him to sacrifice his son, Ishmael. (Muslims believe Abraham was preparing to sacrifice Ishmael, not his son Isaac as Christians and Jews believe.) It is celebrated at the end of the hajj, whether one is a pilgrim that year or not. Ask students why they think this ultimate submission to God's will is so important in Islamic thinking and theology.
- Call on students to tell about the feasts of *Mawlid al-Nabi* and *Ashura*.

Extending the Text

- If possible, invite a Muslim adult or high school student (or students) from the area to talk about their personal experiences with Islamic celebrations, especially if this person has made a pilgrimage to Mecca.
- Assign students to select a topic for a written two-page report from the activities listed for Research and Activities four and five, or other research topics that explore Islamic life, culture, or history. Allow a week for the completion of these research reports.
- To complete this subsection, direct students to the summary points in their textbook. In addition, have students answer the section Review Questions.

Section Review Questions and Answers

1. Explain the difference between the Jewish calendar, the Christian calendar, and the Islamic calendar.

   (Answers may vary.) The Jewish calendar is a lunar calendar of 354 days. The Christian calendar is a solar calendar of 365 days. Jews make adjustments for the missing eleven days so that their festivals land in the same season each year. The Islamic calendar is a lunar calendar, but does not make adjustments for the missing eleven days. Thus, Islamic festivals gradually move from season to season.

2. What are the two great Islamic festivals and what do they celebrate?

   Two of the most important Islamic festivals are Eid al-Fitr, the Festival of Breaking the Fast celebrated at the end of the month-long fast during Ramadan, and Eid al-Adha, the Festival of Sacrifice that commemorates the willingness of Abraham to obey God and sacrifice his son Ishmael. This feast is celebrated at the end of the hajj, the pilgrimage to Mecca.

3. What are the two main reasons for the celebration of the feast of Ashura?

   Muslims believe that on Ashura, Allah created the heavens and earth and Adam, the first man. Also on this date, according to Muslims, Noah left the ark after the flood and Allah saved Moses from the Pharaoh. Muslims also believe that this is the date that Allah will judge the people.

5. Sacred Places and Sacred Spaces (pages 168–171)

Mosque and *Mecca* and *Medina* and *Jerusalem* and *Karbala*

Objective

In this section the students will:

- learn that the mosque is the primary place for Islamic public worship;
- recognize the importance of Mecca, Medina, Jerusalem, and Karbala to Muslims;
- appreciate that mosques are also the social, educational, and business centers of Muslim communities.

Preview

For Muslims, the mosque is the primary place for public worship. Muslims pray five times daily, and if a person lives near a mosque, it is likely he or she would pray at least some of the daily prayers there. Though Friday is not a Sabbath in the sense that the Jews see Saturday or the Christians see Sunday as Sabbaths, the midday prayer on Friday at a mosque is a little more elaborate and includes a sermon. Besides the mosque, Muslims can be found praying in their homes, in their offices, in the fields, in the marketplace, or wherever they happen to be at prayer time. Besides the mosque, four places in the Middle East are most sacred to Muslims. They are Mecca and Medina in present day Saudi Arabia, Jerusalem in Israel, and Karbala in Iraq. Mecca is the most sacred for it is where the Ka'bah resides. It is toward Mecca that all Muslims face during prayer.

Using the Text

- Divide students into three groups—one for Mecca, one for Medina, and one for Jerusalem. Have students research the city and give one presentation on it to the rest of the class. The presentation should include the following information:
  - a map that locates the city
  - the significance of the city during the time of Muhammad
  - the significance of the city for Muslims today
  - photographs highlighting special sites for Muslims in the city
  - what distinctive activities, in relation to Islam, take place in the city
- If possible, take the students on a field trip to a local mosque that would include a Muslim as a "tour guide" after they have read the material in this section.
- Give students the "Islamic Word Search" from page 118 of the Teacher's Manual to initiate a review of this chapter.

Extending the Text

- Offer extra credit to students who will make a short presentation on Muslim music or the foods prepared for Islamic feasts.
- Referring to the Reflection Question on page 169, sample students for opinions on how a person can best prepare before entering a place of worship. Is clothing important? Is it best to be quiet before entering—getting into a prayerful mindset?
- Remind students to look through the Section 5 Summary and Review Questions on page 171, but don't require them to write their answers.

Section Review Questions and Answers

1. Define mosque.

    The word "mosque" means "a place of prostration."

2. How did Mecca become a holy place for Muslims?

    Mecca is a holy place for Muslims because that is where the Ka'bah, the first Islamic shrine, is located. According to Islamic teaching, the Ka'bah was built by Abraham, destroyed by pagans, and reclaimed by Muhammad in the seventh century.

3. Why are Medina and Jerusalem also holy cities for Muslims?

    Medina is holy because Muhammad migrated there when he and his followers were initially persecuted in Mecca. Jerusalem is holy because it is the place where Muhammad had his "night visit." The angel Gabriel transported Muhammad from Mecca to the temple mount in Jerusalem. There, on what is presently the site of the Dome of the Rock, Muhammad visited with Abraham, Moses, and Jesus and ascended to heaven to be greeted by Allah.

4. What is the significance of Karbala, Iraq for Shi'i Muslims?

    Karbala is the site of the massacre of the grandson of Muhammad and the son of Ali, Husayn, and his companions and family. Shi'ites consider that this heir of Muhammad had legitimate claim to leadership of the Muslim community.

Islamic Word Search Answers

6. Islam through a Catholic Lens (pages 172–175)

Objective

In this section the students will:

- recognize that the fundamental shared belief of Muslims and Catholics is belief in one God;
- learn that the major difference between Islamic and Catholic belief is the belief among Muslims that Jesus was a prophet, but *not* divine;
- identify topics where Catholics can fruitfully dialogue with Muslims—especially with regard to secularism, materialism, prejudice, poverty, and the environment.

Overview

Since Vatican Council II, the Catholic Church has consistently promoted dialogue with Muslims as logical and desirable. Catholicism shares a monotheistic theology with Islam. Catholics and Muslims also see the Old Testament as sacred texts. Clearly, however, there is an essential difference in the way Catholicism and Islam see Jesus. Muslims see Jesus as a prophet, second only to Muhammad. They do not acknowledge the divinity of Jesus, and therefore, do not see the New Testament as sacred text. In today's world, there are many ways that Muslims and Catholics can fruitfully dialogue and collaborate to address mutual concerns about the world. Topics such as growing global poverty, systemic prejudice, materialism, and needed care for the environment would be among the topics that these two world religious could and should address in the light of faith.

Using the Text

- Read several statements made by Pope John Paul II about Islam and Catholicism and their shared heritage. In his long papacy, the pope often visited Muslim leaders and prayed in Muslim mosques, giving Catholics—and all Christians—a model for ecumenical outreach.
- Revisit the discussion about Muslim stereotypes held as students began this chapter. Call on students to share specific facts they've learned about Islam. Have a student record a dozen or more facts on the board. Remind students that negative images of Muslims are widely prevalent, and have often been the root of discrimination against them.

Extending the Text

- Assign students to read the feature "Faith and Football at Notre Dame" on page 175. It profiles Ryan Harris, an All-American football player at Notre Dame who became a Muslim in the eighth grade. Point out that the close relationship that Harris had with fellow teammates, most of whom were Catholic, constituted a sort of informal, but ongoing ecumenical dialogue between Harris and his teammates.
- Query students about their friendships with those of other faiths. Is it intimidating or uncomfortable to be involved with people who think and pray differently?
- Have students quietly read the Conclusion on page 176. Then have students number off. Assign the twenty-eight Chapter Review Questions, giving a second question to some students if there are less than twenty-eight students in the class. Have one or two students compile the questions and provide a photocopied set for each student for the chapter review.

- Spend part of a class session reviewing for a test over this chapter. Make sure that students are aware of the date for the test. Collect all projects and homework related to this chapter. As a conclusion to the review session, read aloud the Fattiha, the "Lord's Prayer of Islam" on page 180. Save time for silence and perhaps some meditative music. Invite students to offer prayers of petition or praise as well as comments about this study of Islam and its adherents.

Section Review Questions and Answers

1. List some similarities between Catholics and Muslims.

   Both Catholics and Muslims believe in one God, the Creator of all. These two religious groups also revere the prophets of the Old Testament—Abraham, Moses, David, Solomon, and many others. Muslims and Catholics also share a strong and abiding commitment to help the poor and homeless.

2. Explain two major differences between Catholics and Muslims.

   Catholics believe in the Trinity, a unity of Three Persons in One God. Muslims do not share this belief in the Trinity. Catholics believe that Jesus is divine—the Son of God. Muslims see Jesus as a prophet, but not as God.

3. What are two areas of concern when Muslims engage in interreligious dialogue with Catholics?

   Catholics must be aware that most Westerners have a skewed and negative image of Muslims as a whole. Especially since September 11, 2001, this prejudiced view has jeopardized fair and honest dialogue between the groups. Catholics must also understand that many Muslims believe that too much contact with the West has diluted and perverted their own societies and religious communities. Some Muslims want little or no contact with Westerners.

4. List some suggested areas of dialogue between Catholics and Muslims.

   Major areas of dialogue for Catholics and Muslims are shared concerns about modern -isms—secularism, materialism, racism. These groups could also usefully discuss protecting family life and preserving religious values and practices.

Chapter 4 Review Questions and Answers

1. Briefly outline the life of Muhammad.

   Muhammad was born in the area of Mecca and orphaned at a young age. He was raised by an uncle, became a caravan trader, met a businesswoman named Khadija, and married her. In 610, Muhammad received his first revelation from God through the angel Gabriel. He was told to recite, that is, to share these revelations with others. He destroyed the more than three hundred idols at the Ka'bah. He was exiled from Mecca, so he migrated to Medina. There Muhammad became a political and religious leader, gained military strength, and returned to Mecca in triumph. He continuously received revelations until shortly before he died.

2. Why is Muhammad called the "Seal of the Prophet?" How was he chosen as a prophet?

   Muhammad is called the "Seal of the Prophet" because he was said to be the last prophet sent by God to guide people back to the straight path of submission. In 610 CE, an angel appeared to Muhammad and commanded him to read "in the name of your Lord." Muhammad was illiterate, but memorized the angel's words. These revelations continued for a number of years and Muhammad began to share them with his wife and close friends.

3. Name five biblical prophets recognized by Muslims as prophets.

   Five prophets recognized by Muslims are Adam, Noah, Abraham, Moses, and Jesus.

4. What is the difference between Muhammad's Night Journey and the Night of Power?

   Muhammad's Night Journey to the holy city of Jerusalem occurred when the angel Gabriel took him from Mecca to the temple in Jerusalem. There on the site of the present day Dome of the Rock, Muhammad visited with Abraham, Moses and Jesus. The Night of Power or Destiny is an extremely important night for Muslims. It is the night in which the Holy Qur'an was revealed to Muhammad. Traditionally, Muslims celebrate the Night of Power on the twenty-seventh night of Ramadan.

5. Who are the Rightly-Guided caliphs?

   The first successors of Muhammad are called the Rightly-Guided caliphs. The first was Abu Bakr who was one of Muhammad's disciples. The next was Umar, and the third was Uthman, who was instrumental in the publication and distribution of the Qur'an.

6. What was the catalyst for Islam to split into two major factions so early in its history?

   A dispute over the right to lead the Muslim community began with the third caliph, Uthman. When a protracted power struggle developed in the late seventh century, some members of Uthman's clan supported the claim of Mu'awiyah while Ali insisted that he was the rightful successor to Muhammad. When Ali was assassinated, a deep rift developed in the Muslim community that never healed. The separation grew still more serious when Ali's younger son Husayn and his companions and family were murdered near Karbala in Iraq. Shi'i Muslims developed from a faction of Muslims who saw Husayn as a martyr. Sunni Muslims supported the ruling faction.

7. What is the major difference between Sunni and Shi'i Muslims?

    There are no major fundamental differences in the beliefs and practices of Sunni and Shi'i Muslims, but these two groups still disagree about who should lead the Muslim community. Sunnis call their leaders "caliphs" while Shi'i Muslims refer to their leaders as "imams."

8. What is the difference between an imam and a caliph?

    "Imam" is the term for a Muslim leader among the Shi'i Muslims while "caliph" is the title for leaders of the Sunni Muslim community.

9. Name the starting date and center for each of the following Islamic empires: Umayyad, Abbasid, Fatimid, Safavid, Mughal, and Ottoman.

    In 661, the Umayyad empire began at Damascus. In 750, the Abbasid empire was founded at Baghdad and continued until 1258. In 909, the Fatimid empire began in Egypt and lasted there until 1171. The Safavid dynasty was founded in 1502 in Iran and survived until 1736. The Mughal empire was founded in India in 1526, and the Ottoman caliphate was established in 1517 in Constantinople and ended in 1918 at the end of World War I.

10. What was the Golden Age of Islam?

    The Golden Age of Islam occurred during the Medieval period when the Abbasid empire enthusiastically fostered civilization and culture. In the new Muslim capital of Baghdad, scientific, literary, engineering, and philosophical works were translated from Greek, Persian, and Indian sources. In many disciplines, Muslim scholars translated or wrote works that guided Western scholars for centuries.

11. What are some of the struggles some Muslims have with contemporary Western society?

    Many Muslims see Western society as materialistic, weak, and depraved in its orientation to sexual freedom. The word "Islam" means "submission," and many Muslims maintain that many people in Western cultures aren't submitting to God's will for their lives.

12. How does the Nation of Islam as a movement differ from Islam as a world religion?

    W. D. Fard Muhammad founded the Nation of Islam in Detroit for blacks only. Fard taught that Christianity was for white people and that it had been used to suppress blacks. Fard allowed his followers to call him God or Allah. Many, but not all, of the succeeding leaders of the Nation of Islam separated themselves from some of Fard's teachings. Some disagreed with the "Blacks only" policy and aligned themselves more closely with the Five Pillars of Islam and orthodox Islamic teaching.

13. What is the importance of the Qur'an to Muslims?

    The Qur'an is the primary sacred text for all Muslims. They believe that it is the word of God as it was revealed to his prophet Muhammad. It is revered and displayed in a place of honor in Muslim homes, and many Muslims memorize much of the Qur'an in its original Arabic.

14. Explain how the Qur'an is organized.

The Qur'an is organized into 114 surahs, or chapters. The surahs are arranged by length (except for the first surah), beginning with the longest and ending with the shortest. Each surah, except chapter 9, begins with the words, "In the Name of God, the Compassionate, the Merciful."

15. What types of writings can be found in the Qur'an?

The Qur'an has prose that rhymes, with lines unequal in length. There is no narrative as in most other scriptures. The Qur'an does not "tell" stories of Muslims as a people. The tone is more like prophetic utterances, dictates, prescriptions, and instructions.

16. What is the significance of the Sunnah?

The Sunnah is Muhammad's way of life, meaning it describes what was approved and what was prohibited during the prophet's own lifetime. The Sunnah and the Qur'an go hand in hand, Muslims say. The Sunnah often shows Muslims how to live out the message of the Qur'an.

17. What, to Muslims, is God's most important attribute?

For Muslims, the oneness of God is all-important. Muslims declare their faith in the absolute oneness of God several times a day.

18. Name the Five Pillars of Islam and the duties associated with each.

The Five Pillars are:
1) Profession of Faith—the duty to proclaim that there is one and only one God and Muhammad is God's messenger
2) Prayer—the duty to pray five specified times a day
3) Almsgiving—the duty to give two and one half percent of one's income to the needy
4) Fasting—the duty to abstain from food and drink from sunrise to sunset during the Islamic month of Ramadan
5) Pilgrimage—the duty to make a pilgrimage to Mecca at least once in a lifetime, if at all possible

19. What are the characteristics of the universal ummah? What are the rights and responsibilities of the individual Muslim?

All Muslims know that they will find support to live as good and faithful Muslims within the universal ummah, or world-wide Islamic community. Responsibilities include the responsibility to observe the Five Pillars of Islam. The Five Pillars should be understood as the Muslim "way of life."

20. Why are the Qur'an and the Sunnah the primary sources for shari'ah?

According to Islam, the Qur'an is the literal word of God to humanity. It is the most perfect Scripture and is the original source for shari'ah or Islamic law. Sunnah, a repository of Islamic teaching based on the Qur'an provides Muslims with additional guidance for living properly.

21. When did the Islamic calendar begin? Why do Islamic festivals fall on different dates each year?

The Islamic calendar begins with the year of Muhammad's Hijrah to Medina in 622. Islamic festivals fall on different dates from year to year because they use the 354 day lunar calendar and do not make any adjustments for the eleven-day discrepancy. Instead their feasts are set so that they take place during the appropriate season.

22. Compare and contrast the Judeo-Christian and the Islamic story of Abraham and his sons Isaac and Ishmael.

In the Judeo-Christian story about God's testing of Abraham, it was Isaac whom Abraham was commanded to sacrifice. In the Islamic account, Abraham prepares to sacrifice his son Ishmael when he is stopped by God who honored him for his submission in faith and his obedience.

23. What are the prominent features of a mosque?

There is a prayer hall without seats. A decorated plaque called amihrab is placed on the wall or an alcove within the wall that is in the direction of Mecca. A minbar is a short flight of stairs to a platform where the imam or prayer leader preaches. Mosque walls can be decorated with arabesque patterns, mosaics of geometric patterns, and Arabic calligraphy of verses from the Qur'an.

24. Explain why Mecca is the most sacred city for Muslims.

Mecca is the most sacred city for Muslims because that is where the Ka'bah is present. It is also the city where Muhammad was born and received his first revelations from God.

25. Why is the city of Jerusalem significant to Muslims?

Muslims believe that Jerusalem is the city to which Muhammad was miraculously taken by the angel Gabriel. Muhammad was taken to the temple in Jerusalem where he was reportedly taken up to heaven. He was greeted by Allah and visited with Abraham, Moses, and Jesus. This event was called Muhammad's "Night Visit." When he was returned to earth, Muhammad began to preach and share God's message to the world.

26. In engaging in interreligious dialogue with Muslims, what must be considered?

Catholics should be aware of the fact that their image of Muslims is most likely very distorted by western media. Much of what we hear, see, and read about Islam, a religion with more than one billion members, is unfairly skewed. Additionally, some Muslims do not support interreligious dialogue because they believe that previous contact with the West has diluted and even polluted the purity of Islamic life.

27. Name the three categories of topics in which Catholics and Muslims find common ground for dialogue?

There are many topics which Catholic and Muslims could fruitfully discuss. Three of those are: the promotion of peace in the world, safeguarding family life, concern for the poor and disenfranchised.

28. What commonalities did Ryan Harris find between Islam and Catholicism while at Notre Dame?

Ryan Harris was an All-American football player at Notre Dame and a practicing Muslim. He found that the Muslim mandate to serve generously was matched by a willingness and enthusiasm in his teammates to be involved in community service. Ryan and others even coached football at a local Catholic parish and at a boys' and girls' club. Ryan also saw that prayer was very important to his teammates, most of whom were Catholics. Before each game, players attended Mass to thank God for his many gifts and to ask for God's protection and wisdom.

Chapter 4 Test Answers

Multiple Choice (3 points each)

1. d, 2. b, 3. a, 4. c, 5. a, 6. d, 7. c, 8. a, 9. d, 10. a, 11. a, 12. a, 13. c, 14. b, 15. d, 16. c, 17. a, 18. c, 19. d, 20. c

Short Answer (8 points each)

1. The seven articles of Muslim faith are belief in Allah, in Allah's books, in Allah's angels, in Allah's messengers, in the last day, in Allah's providence, and in life after death.

2. One becomes a Muslim by submitting to the will of Allah. One demonstrates this submission through practicing the duties of a Muslim, that is, the Five Pillars of Islam. A ritual cleansing and a proclamation of the Shahadah before two witnesses is the extent of beginning life as a Muslim.

3. While the Qur'an is the infallible revelation of God to Muhammad through the Angel Gabriel, the Hadith are the words and deeds of Muhammad.

4. The Five Pillars of Islam are: Profession of Faith; Prayer; Almsgiving; Fasting; and Pilgrimage. All Muslims recite the Muslim profession of faith ("There is no god but Allah: Muhammad is the Messenger of Allah") often. It is considered the first and most important pillar. Muslims pray at fixed times five times a day. On Fridays, Muslims who can fulfill the second prayer commitment by praying in the mosque. Muslims see it as an obligation to give alms to the poor. Muslims fast from food, drink and sexual intercourse from sunrise to sunset during the month of Ramadan each year. Muslims feel obliged to make a pilgrimage to Mecca in Saudi Arabia at least once during their lifetimes.

5. With Muslims, Catholics share a belief in one God and in our common Old Testament heritage. Major differences in belief, however, are the Catholic belief in the Trinity and the divinity of Jesus Christ. Muslims see Jesus as another prophet but not as the Son of God.

Name _____

Islamic Word Search

Test your skills on Islamic terms by completing this word search. Words can be found horizontally, vertically, or diagonally. Words may be spelled from left to right or right to left, from top to bottom, or from bottom to top. Letters may overlap between two words.

```
H  P  D  U  T  H  T  S  F  R  P  E  Y  E  F
K  I  D  N  T  E  X  U  K  K  Q  T  X  L  K
T  U  J  I  J  V  R  D  C  S  U  W  H  G  Q
W  D  D  R  P  I  Y  A  B  I  R  P  P  M  Q
D  A  S  A  A  M  U  N  N  P  A  A  O  A  O
H  T  A  O  U  H  S  M  M  I  N  J  B  M  L
Q  N  V  F  N  Z  M  I  C  S  M  C  H  I  I
Z  I  Q  B  D  R  P  G  I  U  H  J  C  G  X
N  Z  H  O  R  J  L  D  A  N  T  J  J  E  M
O  Z  U  G  J  U  T  W  R  Z  I  H  A  A  L
X  E  H  A  M  M  U  W  O  T  I  Q  F  I  H
E  U  G  R  C  W  O  X  J  J  O  I  G  Q  B
I  M  G  W  S  I  K  E  A  P  L  E  V  H  T
H  A  I  R  A  H  S  B  C  A  L  I  P  H  F
G  Q  Z  Y  U  B  V  H  E  R  B  U  O  H  D
```

1. Traditional Islamic political ruler
2. Contains words and deeds of Muhammad
3. Pilgrimage to Mecca
4. Traditional dress of Islamic women
5. Meaning "migration"
6. Islamic leader, usually adept at Islamic studies
7. Tower on mosque
8. One who calls Muslims to prayer
9. Sacred scriptures of Muslims
10. Islamic law
11. The Islamic community
12. The Islamic ritual cleansing before prayer

Chapter 4 Test

Name _____

Multiple Choice. *Write the letter of the best choice in the space provided.* (3 points each)

_____ 1. Muhammad's revelations from God
   a. were kept a secret for several years.
   b. were in Arabic.
   c. are believed to be infallible.
   d. both *b* and *c*

_____ 2. The early expansion of Islam
   a. was hampered by the unbelief of many.
   b. rapidly moved throughout the Middle East.
   c. was welcomed by the conquered who were disappointed with their own religion.
   d. was unsuccessful.

_____ 3. About ninety percent of the world's Muslims are
   a. Sunni.
   b. Shi'ite.
   c. Sufi.
   d. Muhammadans.

_____ 4. The main beliefs of Islam are expressed in the
   a. shari'ah.
   b. Hadith.
   c. Shahada.
   d. Hijrah.

_____ 5. The "Seal of the Prophets" refers to
   a. Muhammad as the last of the prophets.
   b. Muhammad as the source of strength.
   c. Muhammad as the "glue" to hold all prophets together.
   d. Muhammad as the author of the Qur'an.

_____ 6. The holiest of cities for Muslims is
   a. Jerusalem.
   b. Medina.
   c. Istanbul.
   d. Mecca.

_____ 7. For Muslims, Allah
   a. is the one and only God.
   b. is the Arabic word for God.
   c. both *a* and *b*
   d. neither *a* nor *b*

_____ 8. The Ka'bah was built by
   a. Allah.
   b. Abraham and Isaac.
   c. Abraham and Ishmael.
   d. Muhammad.

_____ 9. Muslims pray
   a. twice a day.
   b. three times a day.
   c. four times a day.
   d. five times a day.

_____ 10. The type of calendar used by Muslims is
   a. lunar.
   b. solar.
   c. civil.
   d. secular.

_____ 11. Muslims celebrate _____ at the end of Ramadan.
   a. Eid al-Fitr
   b. Eid al-Adah
   c. Ashura
   d. Mawlid al-Nabi

_____ 12. The successors of Muhammad were called
   a. caliphs.
   b. clersy.
   c. hafiz.
   d. all of the above

_____ 13. One of the greatest contributions of Muslims to Western civilization is
   a. the institution of the caliphate.
   b. their many prophets, though Muhammad is the greatest.
   c. their translation of Greek philosophical classics.
   d. none of the above

_____ 14. Some of the decline of Islamic influence in the Modern Period can be attributed to
   a. a decline in religious fervor of Muslims.
   b. colonization by the British.
   c. more interest in philosophy than politics.
   d. its separation of church and state.

_____ 15. Which of the following countries does *not* use Islamic law as the foundation of its government?
   a. Saudi Arabia
   b. Iran
   c. Pakistan
   d. Turkey

_____ 16. The beginning of the Islamic calendar was precipitated by
   a. the birth of Muhammad.
   b. the death of Muhammad.
   c. the hijrah.
   d. Muhammad's first revelation.

_____ 17. The Hadith
   a. contains words and deeds of Muhammad.
   b. is as sacred as the Qur'an for Muslims.
   c. contains Islamic stories.
   d. none of the above

_____ 18. The _____ is called by a _____.
   a. minaret . . . adan
   b. adan . . . minaret
   c. adan . . . muezzin
   d. muezzin . . . adan

_____ 19. All the following can be found at a mosque _except_ a
   a. minaret.
   b. prayer hall.
   c. place for wudu.
   d. cruciform.

_____ 20. The following about the birth of Muhammad is true _except_
   a. it was not celebrated by Muhammad.
   b. it is not celebrated by some Muslims.
   c. it is the holiest feast day of Muslims.
   d. it was in the sixth century of the Common Era.

Short Answer. *Briefly answer the following questions.* (8 points each)

1. List the seven articles of the Muslim faith.

2. How does one become a Muslim?

3. What is the difference between the Qur'an and the Hadith?

4. What are the Five Pillars of Islam and how do Muslims practice them?

5. What are the shared beliefs and the differences in belief among Catholics and Muslims?

Chapter 5: Hinduism

Introduction

In taking up Hinduism, we move with the students to less familiar ground. No longer are we dealing with the monotheistic religions of Judaism, Christianity, and Islam with their Abrahamic heritages and their influences on western civilization. With Hinduism in Chapter 5 and with Buddhism in Chapter 6, we move to religious traditions that have played a major role in Eastern thought and culture.

As a religious tradition, Hinduism has no clear beginnings. It emerged gradually within the Indian subcontinent and didn't originate from a specific event or founder. From its Indo-Aryan roots to its "missionary" outreach to the West, Hinduism has moved in many directions. It also has been shaped by many influences—from monism to polytheism, from activism to philosophy. Hinduism embraces various beliefs and an even wider range of practices. Even in its scriptures, Hindus have an authoritative set of *shruti* texts, but it is the less authoritative *smriti* texts that are more prevalent and popular among the people.

Important concepts of Hinduism are *Brahman* (the Ultimate Reality), *atman* (equal with Brahman as the unification with one's real self), and *karma* (the actions a person does that will have a direct effect on the present life and also on what type of life he or she will have after rebirth). Yet, with all these concepts, the ultimate goal of every Hindu is *moksha*, that is, liberation from the cycle of rebirth.

In Hinduism, there certainly is a fundamental belief in other-worldliness. On the other hand, the four pursuits of Hindus should dispel the misconception that Hinduism is not grounded in real life. The pursuit of wealth, and artistic and sensual pleasure are said to go hand in hand with the ultimate goal of *moksha*, that is, the end of the death and rebirth cycle. For the attainment of moksha, Hindus generally choose one of three paths—the Path of Action, the Path of Knowledge, or the Path of Devotion.

Traditional Hindu society is divided into four castes plus a fifth group, the "untouchables" (that is, those not worthy to be part of the caste system). Though now outlawed, the caste system is difficult to break down after millennia of use. It was used to define who people were and what roles they were to play. Within the top three caste systems, there are four stages of life through which a Hindu male may travel, though few go beyond the second stage.

It was not until the nineteenth century that Hinduism began to move beyond the Indian subcontinent. It was then that Hindu reformers began to move west, influenced by their Western colonizers. They began to preach that all religions are paths to God and also taught such practices as yoga. In the 1960s, Transcendental Meditation and the International Organization of Krishna Consciousness found supporters in the West.

For Hindus, sacred space begins with the home and village shrines. Temple worship also takes place, but the devotees tend to be more the spectator and less the participant there. One universal sacred place is the waters of the Ganges River, the premiere place for spiritual healing, especially from the effects of karma. With its various languages and subcultures, a universal festival among Hindus is rare. Rather, local festivals abound. Despite all of its diversity, Hinduism can claim to be the oldest worldwide religion.

Resources for Chapter 5

Books

Brockington, J. L. *The Sacred Thread: Hinduism in Its Continuity and Diversity*. Edinburgh: Edinburgh University Press, 1981.

Chatterjee, Margaret. *Gandhi's Religious Thought*. Notre Dame, IN: University of Notre Dame Press, 1983.

Cole, W. Owe, and Piara Singh Sambhi. *The Sikhs: Their Religious Beliefs and Practices*. 2nd ed. Portland, OR: Sussex Academic Press, 1998.

Dundas, Paul. *The Jains*. 2nd ed. New York: Routledge, 2002.

Ellsberg, Robert, ed. *Gandhi on Christianity*. Maryknoll, NY: Orbis Books, 1991.

Emka, Kaur. *Peace Lagoon: Sacred Songs of the Sikhs : The Collected Hymns of Guru Nanak, Guru Amar Das, Guru Ram Das, Guru Arjun, and Guru Gobind Singh*. 4th ed. San Bernardino, CA: Borgo Press, 1985.

Holm, Jean, and John Westerdale Bowker, eds. *Women in Religion*. New York: St. Martin Press, 1994.

Hopkins, Thomas J. *The Hindu Religious Tradition*. Encino, CA: Dickenson Company, 1971.

Huyler, Stephen P. *Meeting God: Elements of Hindu Devotion*. New Haven, CT: Yale University Press, 1999.

Klostermaier, Klaus K. *A Survey of Hinduism*. 3rd ed. Albany: State University of New York Press, 2007.

Mahony, William K. *The Artful Universe: An Introduction to the Vedic Religious Imagination*. Albany: State University of New York Press, 1998.

Miller, Barbara Stoler. *The Bhagavad-Gita: Krishna's Counsel in Time of War*. New York: Bantam Books, 1991.

Mitter, Sara S. *Dharma's Daughters: Contemporary Indian Women and Hindu Culture*. New Brunswick: Rutgers University Press, 1991.

Olivelle, Patrick, trans. *Upanishads*. New York: Oxford University Press, 1996.

Panikkar, Raimundo. *The Vedic Experience: Mantramanjari (An Anthology of the Vedas for Modern Man and Contemporary Celebration)*. Berkeley: University of California Press, 1977.

Audio-visual Resources

Gandhi. DVD/VHS. (RCA/Columbia Pictures Home Video, 1982, 190 minutes) Commercially released film on the life of the twentieth century advocate and practitioner of nonviolence, Mohandas K. Gandhi.

Hinduism. Essentials of Faith Series. DVD/VHS. (Films Media Group, 2006, 24 minutes)

Hinduism. Religions of the World Video Series. DVD/VHS. (Schlessinger Media, 1996, 50 minutes)

Hinduism: 300 Million Gods. The Long Search Video Series. DVD/VHS. (Ambrose Video Publishing, 2001, 60 minutes) Study Guide available for separate purchase.

Religions of the World: Hinduism. VHS. (United Learning, 2001, 24 minutes) Includes teacher's guide and blackline masters.

Varanasi: City of Light. VHS. (United Learning, 1997, 25 minutes) Includes Teacher's Guide and blackline masters.

Internet Resources

Pontifical Council for Interreligious Dialogue— www.vatican.va/roman_curia/pontifical_councils/interelg/documents/rc_pc_interelg_pro_20051996_en.html

www.hindunet.org

www.hindubooks.org

www.hinduwomen.org

www.hindumythology.com

Modern Religion with Ancient Origins (pages 183–185)

Preview

Briefly introduce this world religion as one of the oldest. The origins of Hinduism can be traced to 3000 BCE on the subcontinent of India. Unlike many religions, however, Hinduism cannot be linked to any particular founder or founding event. Rather, it emerged slowly, shaped by many factors. Although Hinduism has moved beyond India, over 95 percent of its adherents still live there. In this sense, Hinduism is not a "world religion" in the same way as religions with members spread across the globe. Hinduism is also unique in its fluid theological attitudes. Hindus claim that no religion can possibly claim to have the complete truth. They encourage personal exploration of many faiths so that people can find the god that is "best" for them.

Using the Text

- Display a large contemporary map of India to point out the subcontinent, the Ganges River, the Indus River, the Indian Ocean, Pakistan, Kashmir, etc. Ask students how they think geography—and the tropical climate—may have played a role in containing Hinduism on the subcontinent.
- Play a bit of modern music popularly influenced by Hindu's Krishna Movement to suggest that Hindu's influence has spread beyond India even if its membership is almost completely confined to the subcontinent. For instance, the Beatles were heavily influenced by Maharishi Mahesh Yogi and his promotion of Transcendental Meditation.

1. A Brief History of Hinduism (pages 185–193)

The Indus Valley Period (3000–1500 BCE) and *The Brahmanical Period (1500–300 BCE)* and *Classical Period (300–1200 CE)* and *The Hindu-Muslim Period (1200–1600 CE)* and *The Modern Period (1600–Present)*

Objective

In this section the students will:

- learn how the roots of Hinduism emerged by 3000 BCE;
- understand how a banyan tree, a tree unique to this region of the world, is an apt symbol of Hinduism, a religion with many roots and branches;
- become familiar with the meaning and impact of Hindu wise writings or Veda;
- be able to identify the roots of the caste system in the Aryan division of labor in the Classical Period;
- be able to trace the influences of both Islamic and Western culture and thought on Hinduism from the sixteenth century;
- identify Mohandas Gandhi as the primary Hindu leader of modern times.

Preview

Western scholars hold that Hinduism began as a distinctive religious tradition by 1500 BCE, though earlier influences had been shaping it for centuries. Chief among those influences was India's Indus Valley dwellers. Early practices stressed the use of baths and the importance of ritual purity. When the nomadic Aryans came into India from the north, they contributed their language and oral wisdom stories called Veda. Eventually the Veda was written but for a time, Brahmins or Vedic priests were the only ones who knew and recited the wisdom stories. They also controlled ritual sacrifices that were made primarily by the wealthy. Scripture commentaries and popular literature called smriti (including the Mahabharata and the Ramayana) enabled other Hindus to learn. Most dramatic was the development of the Hindu concepts of karma and reincarnation, and the three ways of responding to the flow of life and death: the Way of Action, the Way of Wisdom, and the Way of Devotion. Muslim incursions in the sixteenth century and the conquest of India by the British in the eighteenth century brought even further changes in the practice of Hinduism. Mohandas Gandhi, a Hindu, was the primary political leader and voice for Hindu thought and passive resistance rather than violence.

Using the Text

- Direct students to the time-line of Hinduism on pages 184–185. Read through the dates and elaborate on them as you can. Point out that the earliest roots of Hinduism even precede the first date given, making Hinduism more than 4,000 years old.
- Show pictures of a banyan tree, a type of fig indigenous to the region of the subcontinent. Banyans grow in a unique way when birds drop banyan seeds in the top branches of a palm or other kind of tree. When the seeds sprout, branches develop and send roots to the ground. A banyan tree can have many trunks and look like a forest. Ask students why the banyan is a fitting symbol for Hinduism.

- Locate a variety of simple Vedic stories and make copies for the class. Divide the class into small groups of three or four. Give one story to each group to read and discuss. Then have a student from each group tell about the story and its likely moral or teaching. Are the teachings likely to be valuable and relevant for modern Hindus? For anyone?
- Create six to eight simple multiple choice questions using Hindu terms such as Brahmins, shruti, gurus, bhakti, Veda, Sanskrit, karma, ahimsa, and satyagraha, and quiz students orally. Have students immediately locate the correct answer in the text if the question is answered incorrectly.
- Emphasize that Mohandas Gandhi was an important figure on the world scene in the first half of the twentieth century. Various anti-war and civil rights groups in the second half of the twentieth century adopted Gandhi's creed of nonviolence.
- Show a previewed portion of the film *Gandhi* that illustrates the religious tensions between Muslims and Hindus in India in the 1940s. The 1982 award-winning film stars Ben Kingsley in the lead role.

Extending the Text

- Point out the feature on Jainism, an offshoot of Hinduism and Buddhism that arose in India between the ninth and sixth centuries BCE. It emerged, in part, as a reaction to Brahminism that had dominated Indian society and religion and featured nonviolence and non-injury even towards plants and animals.
- Referring to Jainism and the Reflection Question about nonviolence on page 191, have students write four to five paragraphs telling whether they would be willing to use nonviolent methods to defend a cause they deeply believed in. Call on several students to read their answers for all to hear.
- Pick eight students to answer the eight Section Review Questions on page 193 while the other students work independently on the "Hinduism Crossword Puzzle" on page 147 of the Teacher's Manual. Have students read their questions and answers to the group.

Section Review Questions and Answers

1. What was the Aryan influence on the origins of Hinduism?

   The Aryan influence on the origins of Hinduism included Vedic hymns, Vedic gods, and Brahmin priests.

2. Who were Brahmins and what was their main function?

   Brahmins were priests whose main function was to offer ritual sacrifices for the people.

3. What makes up the shruti?

   The shruti is made up of many braminical commentaries of rituals, other reflections of the Brahmins, and the Vedas.

4. Describe Jainism.

Jainism is a religious tradition begun in the sixth century BCE as a reaction to the elaborate rituals of the Hindu Brahmins. It also contains Buddhist elements. Ahimsa, or nonviolence, is a major tenet of Jainism.

5. Why are the years 300 to 1200 CE known as the Classical Period of Hinduism?

The years 300 to 1200 CE are known as the Classical Period of Hinduism because it is the period in which Hinduism becomes recognized as a religion. Ritual forms changed dramatically during this period. Hindu temples were established and home-based rituals grew. Sanskrit, the liturgical and scriptural language of Hinduism that only a few understood, gave way to the vernacular during this time.

6. What happened when the Muslims came to India?

Muslims conquered the northwest, northern, and central regions of India between the seventh and thirteenth centuries, administrating the region from Delhi. Some Muslim rulers were tolerant of Hinduism while others took to destroying Hindu temples and statues. Hindus during this period established practices that clearly distinguished them from Muslims.

7. What are some of the beliefs major Hindu figures of the nineteenth and twentieth centuries advocated?

Some major Hindu figures of the nineteenth and twentieth centuries taught that all religions are paths to God and that they were equal. They also promoted ahimsa (nonviolence), and satyagraha (passive resistance) to British rule.

8. What is one movement of Hinduism that contributed to its expansion outside of India?

One movement of Hinduism that contributed to its expansion outside of India was the Ramakrishna movement (or International Society of Krishna Consciousness more popularly known as the Hare Krishnas or Transcendental Meditation.)

2. Sacred Stories and Sacred Scriptures (pages 193–199)

Shruti Scriptures and *Smriti Scriptures*

Objective

In this section the students will:

- learn that some Hindu scriptures, shruti, are considered to be revealed by gods and therefore sacred;
- recognize that other Hindu texts, smriti, are full of Hindu traditions and are more popular, but not said to be revealed by the gods;
- become more familiar with the style and message of various Hindu writings;
- learn about the plot and significance of the *Bhagavad Gita*, one of the best known Hindu scriptures.

Preview

Shruti are the most sacred scriptures of Hinduism. Hindus believe these writings have been directly revealed by the gods. Smriti, on the other hand, are less authoritative and are valuable as texts to be remembered. These, including the *Bhagavad Gita* and the *Ramayana*, present Hindu morals and lessons in stories or epics. The focus is often on rebirth and the importance of a person's actions. The *Puranas*, also included in the category of smriti scripture, tell stories about the three great gods of Hinduism—Brahma, Vishnu, and Shiva.

Using the Text

- Write the names of the two categories of Hindu texts on the board—shruti scriptures and smriti scriptures. Recap the text that explains why shruti scriptures are considered sacred, given directly by the gods.
- Read samples of the *Vedas* as shruti scriptures and invite students to comment or ask questions about their meaning.
- Distribute copies of the complete *Bhagavad Gita* to small groups of three or four. Have each group peruse the stories and locate and record three to four different sentences that seem to represent a moral or teaching. Allow fifteen to twenty minutes for the group research. Then, have each group read their lines of Hindu wisdom from the *Bhagavad Gita*.
- Show the twenty minute film *Hinduism: An Ancient Path in the Modern World*. Call on four or five students to ask, "What surprised you about what you saw or learned?"

Extending the Text

- Display pictures of artistic renditions (statues, drawings, paintings, etc.) of the Hindu gods—Brahma, Vishnu, and Shiva. Give students additional background on devotional practices for these gods. Tell about and show pictures of any major Hindu shrines for these gods.
- Show examples of Sanskrit writing, the language in which Hinduism's sacred texts were once written.
- For extra credit, invite students to create posters using the lines from the *Bhagavad Gita* identified earlier in their small groups. Allow a week for completion of the posters.

- Invite three students interested in drama to dramatically read and act the parts in the "Knowledge of the Heart" feature on pages 197–198. The three parts are: a Narrator, Svetaketu, Svetaketu's father. (Supply an apple to substitute for the nyagrodha fruit and other simple props that might be helpful.)
- Call on students to answer the four short section Review Questions from page 197.

Section Review Questions and Answers

1. What are shruti scriptures?

   The shruti are the more sacred scriptures in the Hindu tradition. Hindus believe that these scriptures, including the Vedas, have been revealed to ancient seers by the gods.

2. What are smriti scriptures?

   The smriti scriptures are less authoritative scriptures and these include stories about traditions that should be remembered. The smriti include Mahabharata, a Hindu epic poem, and the Ramayan, another epic.

3. What is the dilemma of Arjuna in the *Bhagavad Gita*?

   Arjuna is troubled by two competing claims. He is committed to fight as a warrior to defend his family, but is also pulled by his commitment to nonviolence.

4. What are the *Puranas*?

   The Puranas are a collection of stories about the three most popular Hindu gods—Brahma, Vishnu, and Shiva.

3. Beliefs and Practices (pages 199–207)

Deities and *Female Goddesses* and *Atman* and *Cycle of Rebirth* and *The Sacredness of Life* and *Caste System* and *The Stages of Life*

Objective

In this section the students will:

- learn Hindu beliefs about gods and goddesses;
- become more familiar with the Ultimate Reality known as Brahman and how it is interchangeable with a person's innermost self;
- be able to identify the main categories of Hindu scriptures;
- familiarize themselves with the life goals of Hindus;
- learn about the four caste system and a Hindu's cyclical life pattern.

Preview

Almost all Hindus would adhere to many of the common beliefs and practices of their faith. Among these core beliefs and practices are beliefs about gods and goddesses, belief in the cycle of rebirth, and belief in the sacredness of life. Hindu practices include participation and acceptance of a communal life that includes the caste system and an understanding that there are stages of life.

Using the Text

- Recap an initial point made in the text that Hindus would concede that there are an uncountable number of gods but that these gods are images of the one Ultimate Reality, Brahman.
- Elaborate further on Hindu teachings about Brahman as transcendent, beyond reach. Invite students to offer other adjectives to describe Brahman in a way consistent with Hindu "theology." (Have them reread the text describing Brahman's nature on pages 199–200.)
- Remind students that an avatar is the incarnation of a god or goddess. Challenge students to consider and explain why the Hindu belief in avatars would be a predictable development. (People naturally long for divine intervention here on earth so that wrongs can be righted, etc.)
- Have students write a one-sentence description of the Hindu belief about atman. (Refer them to page 201 before they write.) Call on five or six students to read their descriptions. Have students vote for the statement that seems to be the most accurate Hindu interpretation.
- Redirect student attention to the Reflection Question about symbols for the Cycle of Life on page 202. Print the words "Birth," "Death," and "Rebirth" on the board or where they can be easily seen. Break students up into groups of five or six and give them art supplies and poster board. Each group should design a poster representing the Hindu understanding of the Cycle of Life. They should include the name of the gods who symbolize the cycle: Brahma the Creator god, Vishnu the Preserving god, and Shiva the Destroying god. In representing it as a cycle, they will see that Destroyer is not for the sake of annihilation, but for a new creation.
- Differentiate for students the crucial difference between similar Hindu terms: *Brahman* (Ultimate Reality), *Brahma* (Creator god), and *Brahmin* (priest).

- Note the photos of female goddesses depicted on page 200.
- The text looks at the caste system, including the "untouchables." Point out that this is a very brief description, for Hinduism has numerous sub-castes. Even though one's caste and status in society may be high or low, the reasons for living are the same. After reading aloud the four purposes for living on page 205, seek student reaction to this list.

Extending the Text

- Revisit the Hindu teaching that Brahman is identical with the "real self." One's body, mind, and emotions are not the real self but *maya* or illusions of the real self. Maya keeps one from one's real self, and thus, from the true identity of Brahman and atman. Hindus believe that ridding the self of maya brings liberation.
- Distribute the handout "On the Experience" (from page 145 of the Teacher's Manual) as a poetic expression of the Cycle of Life. The poem is from famed Hindu poet, Kabir. Have students quietly read the poem and offer answers to Questions 1, 2, or 3. At this point, also ask students to respond to the Reflection Question about the transmigration of souls on page 202.
- Because Brahman is in all creation, all creation is sacred. The symbol of the sacredness of life is the cow. Destroying the cow is saying that life is nothing or worthless. *Ahimsa* is an example of the influence of Jainism on Hinduism.
- If possible, invite a Hindu speaker to further elaborate on Hindu teaching about the sacredness of life and the concept of Ahimsa. If no speaker is available, commission three or four students to research and prepare a five to ten minute presentation on how this crucial teaching is lived out in everyday Hindu life.
- Use the Reflection Questions about the Hindu caste system on page 205 to review what students have just learned about this system.
- Give extra credit if students write a one to two page essay offering their opinions about the effectiveness of nonviolence as a means for combating violence. Encourage them to give examples and reasons for their claims.
- Expand discussion based on the Reflection Questions about the Hindu caste system on page 205 and the four stages of life on page 206. Ask students if they can find any liberating or positive values to a caste system. What would they find confining about such a caste system?
- Assign the section Review Questions on page 207 to be answered on paper.
- The completion of this subsection would be a good time to show students all or part of the video *Hinduism: 330 Million Gods*. It has a good interview with a *sannyasin*, a Hindu who has renounced the material world.

Section Review Questions and Answers

1. What is meant by Brahman? How is Brahman linked to atman?

   Brahman is a Hindu name for the Supreme Being, Ultimate Being, or God. Brahman is the ground of all nature as well as the entire cosmos. Hindus believe that the Ultimate Reality or Brahman is identical to the innermost soul, the real self of each person, called the atman.

2. What are the three primary forms of Brahman?

    The three primary forms of Brahman are Brahma as the Creator god, Vishnu as the Preserving god, and Shiva as the Destroying god.

3. Describe the Hindu cycle of rebirth related to the three paths of liberation.

    The Path of Action is karma yoga where selfless service to others brings liberation from the endless cycle of rebirth. In this path the devotee resolves that his or her right actions and deeds will be performed not for personal gain, but for the sake of Brahman. The Path of Knowledge is known as the jnana yoga. There are three steps involved in this path: learning, thinking, and viewing oneself in the third person. Learning is the information the person receives from outside oneself. Thinking is the internal reflection on what one learned. Viewing oneself in the third person is like seeing from God's point of view. Meditation is the most common instrument in jnana yoga. Through meditation a person can see the truth of how he or she is attached to this world. The Path of Devotion, known as bhakti yoga, is the Path followed by most Hindus. A pure, long devotion to Brahman can bring liberation.

4. Name and describe each of the four Hindu castes. Also define the "untouchables."

    The four Hindu castes are Brahmins, Kshatriyas, Vaishya, and Shudra. Brahmins are priests who make up the highest caste. They are from families who are considered the purest, wisest, and most learned. Kshatriyas are warriors. They help protect and rule society. Vaishya, the third level, are made up of those families who are farmers and merchants. Shudra are servants, the lowest in the caste system. Shudra serve those in the other levels of castes. Unlike the other three castes, Shudra are not permitted to study scripture. The "untouchables" are considered so impure that they are not deemed worthy to be part of the caste system, but below it. They are the families that are considered defiled because they have the degrading jobs in society, such as cleaning up human waste.

5. Name and describe the four stages of life for a Hindu male.

    The four stages of life for a Hindu male are Brahmancarin, Grihastha, Vanaprastha, and Sannyasin. Brahmancarin is the student stage where one learns about the Hindu tradition, usually at the feet of a guru. Grihastha is the stage of the householder, when he marries, raises a family, and contributes to society. Vanaprastha is the stage when a man begins to move away from ordinary life to life as a hermit in order to pursue more otherworldly desires. Sannyasin is a spiritual pilgrim who renounces absolutely everything in this world for the purpose of pursuing moksha. In this stage the man abandons family and even family name and lives as if having no memory of his previous life.

6. What are the four life goals for a Hindu male in the first three castes?

    The four life goals for a Hindu male in the first three castes are to be dutiful; to pursue material and political wealth; to pursue artistic, recreational, and sensual pleasures; and to obtain liberation from the cycle of rebirth.

4. Sacred Time (pages 207–214)

Festivals and *Life Cycles*

Objective

In this section the students will:

- learn about the Hindu calendar;
- discover how different Hindu festivals are celebrated;
- study the meaning of life cycle rituals called *samskaras*;
- read about and then discuss Sikhism, a religion that blends elements of Hinduism and Islam.

Preview

Like so many other things in Hinduism, sacred time is cyclical. Hindu time is marked by a lunar calendar that is more complicated than the Jewish or Islamic lunar calendar. The twelve Hindu months vary in length to make up the eleven-day difference between the solar calendar and the Hindu lunar calendar. Hindus also celebrate six seasons, rather than four seasons. Festivals celebrated in common by Hindus include Diwali which is celebrated in the fall in India and Holi, a spring festival commemorating the love between Krishna and Radha. Hindus also celebrate sixteen life cycle occasions called samskaras.

Sikhism, a blending of Hinduism and Islam, began with revelations to Guru Nanak in 1459 CE in the Punjab region of Pakistan. Unlike Hindus, Sikhs are monotheistic, but also believe in karma, samsara, and moksha. However, this group rejects the caste system and performs unique ascetic practices.

Using the Text

- Review the Hindu calendar displayed on page 208. Note some similarities with our calendar, such as the twelve-month year.
- If possible, find out when the next Diwali and Holi festivals will be celebrated on the Hindu calendar and translate that to the Western calendar. Would these be similar to any spring and fall festivals that Westerners know? (*Easter is a spring festival; many harvest festivals are celebrated in the fall.*)
- Assign the Reflection Question about the function of festivals and holidays on page 209 as a written assignment. Students should write one hundred to two hundred words on the topic.
- Review the sixteen samskaras as described in the book and add information from other sources. Ask students where they see parallels with Western life cycle ceremonies and rites.

Extending the Text

- Focus on the feature "Sikhism" on pages 212–213, asking students if they have ever met or seen a Sikh. (Because of their turbans, Sikh men are quickly identifiable.) Make sure that students know what makes Sikh beliefs and worship different than Hindu beliefs and worship.
- Show images of Diwali and Holi celebrations. If possible, share some Indian foods connected with these feasts (from a local Indian restaurant or made at home). Some students may even be adventurous enough to try cooking or baking if recipes aren't too complex or expensive to make.

- Sikhs generally dress in white, wear turbans, and make their religious affiliation very visible in other ways. Direct students to the Reflection Question about wearing visible signs of religious tradition on page 212. Poll students about their own attitudes and practices. Call on volunteers to share any religious symbols they are currently wearing.
- To review this section, have students go over the Section Summary points and answer the Section Review Questions that follow.

Section Review Questions and Answers

1. How do Hindus compensate for the different number of days between the solar and lunar calendars?

   Hindus compensate for the different number of days between the solar and lunar calendars by making an adjustment of one month, but do not give the additional month its own name. Rather, the added month bears the name of either the previous month or next month. Cumulatively, about seven months are added approximately every nineteen years.

2. What do the festivals of Divali and Holi celebrate? How are they celebrated?

   Divali is the autumn festival of Hindus that celebrates the return of Rama, the seventh avatar of Vishnu, from a fourteen year exile. Divali is a festival of lights where Hindus decorate their homes with colorful lights and candles. Bonfires are lit and images of the demon Ravana are burnt. Lights are symbolic for piercing the darkness of life's miseries. Holi is a spring festival of a rather riotous nature that commemorates the love between Krishna and Radha. Often division between castes is suspended during this time of celebration. Fun-loving pranks are part of this day as a reminder of the fun Krishna had as a boy. Hindus squirt each other with colored liquid or throw red powder on each other during the Holi festival. Another story associated with Holi is that of the demon Holika attempting to kill the infant Krishna. Appearing as a lovely woman, Holika tried to feed Krishna poisoned milk from her breast, but Krishna sucked the blood out of her, exposing the dead Holika as the hideous demon that she was. Hence, the reason for the red colored power or liquid.

3. Name and explain at least two of the sixteen stages of the Hindu life cycle.

   (Answers may vary. See pages 210–211 in the student text.)

5. Sacred Places and Sacred Spaces (pages 214–219)

Temples and *Home Shrines* and *Ganges River*

Objective

In this section the students will:

- learn that for Hindus, sacred spaces are found in all of nature;
- discover that Hindu temples, found in towns and major cities, have images of many gods and goddesses;
- discover that the Ganges River is considered the most sacred place for Hindus;
- learn that Hindu homes are considered sacred;
- learn about puja, the practice of honoring a god or goddess in a worship service.

Preview

This section looks at Hindu sacred places and spaces. All rivers are sacred to Hindus, especially the Ganges River. This river is said to have special spiritual healing powers. The notion of flowing water is important in a region where drought is common. Hindu temples are also sacred places and although small villages may not have temples, most towns and all major cities have temples. A brahmin, or priest, typically performs puja, or practices, that honor a god or goddess. There is little participation from the community, however. Most Hindu families also have home shrines that contain murtis, or images of a god. In homes, it is usually women who perform puja.

Using the Text

- Introduce this section by reading aloud the opening paragraph about temples and shrines on page 214. Then, have the class quietly read the other materials on temples, home shrines, puja practices, and the Ganges River.
- Direct students to the photos of Hindu temples on page 215. Call on one or two students to tell how different parts of the temple are used. Emphasize that Hindu temples are not—like Christian churches or Jewish temples—built to accommodate large groups for worship.
- Play or replay parts of a recommended film to show how puja is practiced in the temple or in a Hindu home. In either location, a god or goddess is welcomed into the sacred space and invited to dwell in the *murti*, a statue that represents the deity, but is not, in fact, the deity. The deity is honored with food and flowers. At the end of the service the people present eat the food that was offered.
- Show several scenes of the Ganges River, the most sacred of all rivers for Hindus. More than 1,500 miles long, it begins in an ice cave in the Himalayan Mountains in northern India. The Ganges flows southeast through Bangladesh and finally empties into the Bay of Bengal. Hindus visit cities strung along the Ganges to bathe in its waters. Some people even come to die near the river for Hindus believe that they will be taken straight to Paradise if they die in the Ganges. The cremated remains of a loved one are also frequently disbursed in the sacred waters of the river.

Extending the Text

- Let students know that since many villages do not have temples, the home shrine becomes the most sacred place to Hindus. Some villages do have shrines dedicated to the local god or goddess. All the larger towns and cities have temples dedicated to a Hindu deity.
- Have one student read aloud the feature, "Honoring is Called Puja." Ask, "What does Shankar say about the meaning of puja—for those who perform it? What feelings are identified with the puja actions? What analogies does the author give to explain the spirit that should accompany these rituals?
- Now ask students to consider the Reflection Question about the Catholic practice of placing flowers at shrines on page 216. What's behind this Catholic devotion? Is it like Hindu puja? How is it different?

Section Review Questions and Answers

1. Why is everything sacred to Hindus?

   Everything is sacred to Hindus because Brahman is present in all creation.

2. Describe a home puja and its purposes.

   A home shrine may be as large as a room unto itself or as small as a table. The household typically contains a murti of a god that has special meaning for that family. Flowers or fruit may also be part of the shrine surrounding the murti. The actual puja can be performed individually or collectively. Usually women conduct the home puja. The home puja involves the welcoming of the god or goddess into the house by calling upon it to dwell within the murti. The murti is also washed and dressed in fine clothes so that it is ready to receive guests. Fruits, flowers, and incense are offered to the murti. There may be prayers recited, hymns sung, and sacred texts read. In return for the offering, it is held that the individual or family receives a blessing from the deity. At the end of puja, those present eat the food that was offered to the deity.

3. How does a temple puja differ from a home puja?

   A temple puja differs from a home puja in that a temple puja is often offered by a brahmin, and people participate very minimally.

4. Why is the Ganges River the most sacred place for Hindus?

   The Ganges River is the most sacred place for Hindus because it is the symbol for life without end. The Ganges is the premiere place for spiritual healing. Hindus perform ritual bathing in the river, believing the Ganges has the power to wash away the karma that destines one for another rebirth.

6. Hinduism through a Catholic Lens (pages 219–225)

Jesus, the Incarnate God and *Religious Images*

Objective

In this section the students will:

- review the ways that Hinduism is exceptionally tolerant of other faiths;
- look at the continuing Hindu-Catholic dialogue;
- differentiate Catholic from Hindu views about the nature and history of Jesus;
- re-examine differences in the way that Catholics and Hindus interpret religious images.

Preview

Tolerance is built into Hinduism. Hindus are taught that each religious tradition holds some eternal truths, and that Jews should pursue that truth by being good Jews, Christians good Christians, etc. Catholics and Hindus have dialogued about issues related to human dignity. Though the caste system perpetuates inequities, Gandhi and other Hindus spoke out against it. About Jesus, however, there is little common ground for Hindus and Catholics. Hindus disagree with Catholic teaching that presents Jesus as the Son of God, who was actually born, lived, and executed in Jerusalem. Hindus also have a perspective about religious images that is different than the one Catholics have. Hindus venerate images of their many gods and goddesses which collectively represent the Ultimate Reality. Some Hindu images have multiple arms or heads to indicate greater strength or knowledge. Catholic images—paintings or statues—are primarily of historical figures such as Jesus, Mary, or one of the many saints. Images are venerated, but only to remind Catholics to imitate the Christ-like virtues of these holy ones.

Using the Text

- Ask students to rank the importance of tolerance in their friendships. 1 for not important at all; 10 for most important as a friendship trait. Take a straw poll and find out how students ranked this trait.
- Elaborate on the importance of tolerance within Hinduism in the context of interreligious dialogue.
- Call on some students to tell who Jesus is from the Catholic perspective. Call on others to speak as Hindus would about Jesus. Make sure that the fundamental differences are clear.
- Give a fuller historical picture of the ancient Christian icon controversies and the term **icono-clasm**. In the Eastern Church, Emperor Leo III saw that some people were idolizing icons. He ordered religious images destroyed or covered up. But many monks and lay people treasured their holy images. In the ninth century, a compromise was reached. Holy images—but no statues or large pictures—were permitted. The Western Church never banned statues or religious images.

Extending the Text

- Have students form small groups to research and display pictures of a variety of Hindu gods and how they are venerated.

- Pose the Reflection Questions about what students respect in the Hindu tradition and about religious images on page 225. Conclude the discussion by reading together the prayer on page 230.

- Direct students to independently read through the Section Summary Statements and Review Questions on pages 227–228, the Conclusion on page 226, and the Chapter Summary Statements and Review Questions.

- Reserve thirty minutes or more of the last class session focused on Hinduism for review. Tell students the date for the chapter test and discuss concepts and Hindu customs that might be particularly confusing. Collect all projects and any homework focused on the study of Hinduism.

- Finish the review session with a short prayer service. If possible, play some Hindu music and create space for students to sit comfortably in meditation. Ask for a volunteer to read the Gayatri Mantra, the "mother of the vedas" on page 230. Encourage students to share prayers for worldwide growth in ecumenical understanding and peace. They can also offer their own prayer petitions in the Christian tradition.

Section Review Questions and Answers

1. In dialoguing about human dignity, what topic in particular do Hindus have in mind?

   Hindus wish to dialogue about social issues essential to human dignity, especially poverty and the lack of basic human necessities that plague many in India. Although the caste system has contributed to some of the inequalities, much of the difficulty is due to a fragile national economy.

2. Name at least three views of Jesus that can be found among Hindus.

   Some Hindus believe that Jesus spent his "hidden years" in India learning from Hindu sages. Others acknowledge that Jesus was an ideal spokesman for social and moral change, but one among many avatars. Others believe Jesus was mythical. Both Hindus and Catholics see Jesus as "pure of heart," a great example of human compassion, kindness, sympathy, reconciliation, and justice.

3. List three functions of religious imagery.

   Religious images can tell a story within a religious tradition. Religious imagery can also instruct adherents of a faith tradition, especially those who are unable to read. Religious images are also objects for veneration, a practice that assists one in meditating on the Ultimate Reality.

Chapter 5 Review Questions and Answers

1. Briefly summarize the main characteristics of each of the five main Hindu historical periods.

   In the Indus Valley Period, the Indo-Aryans contributed Vedic hymns, Vedic texts, and Vedic gods that were precursors to Hindu deities and scripture. In the Brahmanical period, ritual sacrifice became elaborate and elusive to most but the rich. Elaborate rituals also required commentaries for explanation. Reaction to Brahmanism included such groups as the Buddhists and the Jains distancing themselves from the caste system and the elaborate rituals. In the Classical period, ritual forms changed dramatically. There was the establishment of Hindu temples and the continual growth of home-based rituals. Sanskrit, the liturgical and scriptural language of Hinduism that only a few understood, gave way to the vernacular. In the Hindu-Muslim period, Muslims conquered the northwest, northern, and central regions of India between the seventh and thirteenth centuries, administrating the region from Delhi. Some Muslim rulers were tolerant of Hinduism while others took to destroying Hindu temples and statues. Hindus during this period established practices that clearly distinguished them from Muslims. In the Modern period, Christianity somewhat influenced reform movements within Hinduism. Ideals such as the equality of all religions and "all religions are paths to God" became prominent.

2. What is the difference between shruti and smriti scriptures?

   Shruti consists of the oldest scriptures, the Vedes, and are said to be more authoritative because they came from the gods. Smriti are more popular and rank below shruti because they are human stories and traditions about sacred topics.

3. What was the major dilemma for Arjuna in the *Bhagavad Gita*?

   Arjuna faced the dilemma of defending his family from the wicked one and remaining faithful to nonviolence.

4. What do Hindus mean by the Ultimate Reality?

   By the Ultimate Reality, Hindus mean that which is "real" and not dependent upon anything else.

5. How are Brahman and atman related?

   Brahman is the Ultimate or Absolute Reality, according to Hindu thought. It is said that all Hindu gods and goddesses have attributes, typically human attributes. Together, these gods and goddesses constitute Brahman, but Brahman has no attributes because Brahman is transcendent, beyond the reach of any attributes. That Ultimate Reality is identical to the innermost soul, the real self of each person. That soul is called atman.

6. There is a perfume sold that is called "Samsara." Why would Hindus find that strange?

   Samsara is the Hindu belief in continuing birth, life, and death until one achieves oneness with Brahman. For Christians, it would be like naming a perfume for a sacred belief.

7. What is moksha?

   Moksha is liberation from samsara. It is achieved by removing the karmic residue that accumulates through countless deaths and rebirths.

8. What are the three main paths to liberation for Hindus? Which of the three paths is the most prevalent among Hindus?

    The three main paths of liberation for Hindus are the Path of Knowledge, the Path of Action, and the Path of Devotion. The Path of Devotion is the most prevalent.

9. How are the caste system and the cycle of rebirth related?

    The caste system and the cycle of rebirth are related in that good actions merit migration to a better situation, including caste, in the next life, while bad actions merit migration to a worse situation.

10. Name and explain the four stages of life for Hindu males in the first three castes.

    The four stages of life for Hindu males in the first three castes are Brahmancarin, Grihastha, Vanaprastha, and Sannyasin. Brahmancarin is the student stage where one learns about the Hindu tradition, usually at the feet of a guru. Grihastha is the stage of the householder, when he marries, raises a family, and contributes to society. Vanaprastha is the stage when a man begins to move away from ordinary life to life as a hermit in order to pursue more otherworldly desires. Sannyasin is a spiritual pilgrim who renounces absolutely everything in this world for the purpose of pursuing moksha. In this stage, the man abandons family and even family name and lives as if having no memory of his previous life.

11. Why is the Ganges River so sacred to Hindus?

    The Ganges River is the most sacred place for Hindus because it is the symbol for life without end. The Ganges is the premiere place for spiritual healing. Hindus perform ritual bathing in the river, believing the Ganges has the power to wash away the karma that destines one for another rebirth.

12. What is the significance of the city of Varanasi to Hindus?

    Varanasi, also known as Benares, is a particularly holy city since hundreds of temples line the banks of the Ganges nearby.

13. What are the four pursuits in life for Hindus? Which of the four is the most important?

    For Hindus, the four pursuits in life are Dharma, performing one's duties in life; Artha, the pursuit of both material and political wealth; Kama, the pursuit of artistic, recreational, and sensual pleasure; and Moksha, the pursuit of liberation from the cycle of rebirth through actions, thoughts, and devotions. The most important of these is Moksha.

14. What elements of Hinduism can be found in Sikhism?

    Like Hindus, Sikhs believe in karma, samsara, and moksha.

15. Describe the various views about Jesus that can be found among Hindus.

    Some Hindus believe that Jesus spent his "hidden years" in India learning from Hindu sages. Others believe that he is an avatar like Rama or Krishna. Still other Hindus see Jesus simply as a wonderful role model for righteous and moral living. And there are also some Hindus who question the historical existence of Jesus; they believe that Jesus is a myth.

16. What are the "five Ks" of Sikhism?

    The "five Ks" are ascetic practices that Sikhs commit themselves to. The "Ks" are: "Kesh," unshorn hair; "Kanga," carrying a comb, a symbol of cleanliness; "Kacha," short pants as a symbol of chastity; "Kara," a steel bracelet worn as a token of allegiance to a guru; "Kirpan," a short sword to symbolize an unconquerable spirit.

17. Why can Mohandas K. Gandhi be called a Hindu social reformer?

    Gandhi spoke out against the inequities of the caste system and advocated tolerance of other faiths in India.

18. Why are both Catholics and Hindus accused of worshipping idols?

    Both Catholics and Hindus say prayers, bring flowers, and honor "holy ones" at shrines and special altars. Catholics pay special respect to statues and images of Mary and the saints, believing that these saints can intercede for those in need on earth.

19. List and give examples of three reasons for the use of religious imagery.

    Religious images have a value as ornamental and artistic pieces. They are also used to instruct people in matters of faith. Thirdly, they are objects of veneration and prayer.

20. What was the lesson that Svetaketu's father was trying to teach him?

    Svetaketu's father told him to put salt in water and then to retrieve it. When the boy told his father that the salt was completely dissolved in the water, his father explained that it was like this with Brahman and atman. There is no separation between atman and Brahman. Stories such as this one were often used to explain spiritual matters.

21. How does the Catholic vision of the afterlife differ from Hindu belief?

    Hindus believe in reincarnation or the cyclical movement of the soul from one body into another being, perhaps even into an animal or insect. This belief in samsara is very different than the Catholic and Christian view that each human being has an immortal soul that separates from the body at death to go to eternal reward or punishment.

22. What are other major differences between Hinduism and Catholicism?

    Another principal difference between these two major religions is that Hindus believe in many gods and goddesses. Images of hundreds of these deities are found and venerated everywhere—in Hindu temples, along the roadside, in businesses, and in homes. Catholics venerate statues and pictures of God, Jesus, Mary, and the saints—primarily historical figures.

Hindu Crossword Puzzle Answers

Across		*Down*		
5. satyagraha	11. shruti	1. moksha	4. brahmin	9. smriti
8. ahimsa	13. karma	2. yoga	6. atman	11. samskaras
10. murti	14. samsara	3. puja	7. dharma	12. maya
			8. avatar	

Chapter 5 Test Answers

Multiple Choice (3 points each)

1. b, 2. b, 3. d, 4. a, 5. c, 6. d, 7. b, 8. a, 9. c, 10. a, 11. d, 12. b, 13. d, 14. a, 15. a, 16. d, 17. b, 18 . b, 19. d, 20. a

Short Answer (10 points each)

1. The four stages of life for a Hindu male are Brahmancarin, Grihastha, Vanaprastha, and Sannyasin. Brahmancarin is the student stage where one learns about the Hindu tradition, usually at the feet of a guru. Grihastha is the stage of the householder when he marries, raises a family, and contributes to society. Vanaprastha is the stage when a man begins to move away from ordinary life to life as a hermit in order to pursue more otherworldly desires. Sannyasin is a spiritual pilgrim who renounces absolutely everything in this world for the purpose of pursuing moksha. In this stage the man abandons family and even family name and lives as if with no memory of his previous life.

2. The four life goals for a Hindu male in the first three castes are to be dutiful; to pursue material and political wealth; to pursue artistic, recreational, and sensual pleasures; and to obtain liberation from the cycle of rebirth.

3. The three paths of liberation are the Path of Action, the Path of Knowledge, and the Path of Devotion. The Path of Action is karma yoga where selfless service to others brings liberation from the endless cycle of rebirth. In this path the devotee resolves that his or her right actions and deeds will be performed not for personal gain, but for the sake of Brahman. Even the person's desire for liberation must be purged, for Brahman is more powerful than the noblest desire. The Path of Knowledge is known as the jnana yoga. There are three steps involved in this path: learning, thinking, and viewing oneself in the third person. Learning is the information the person receives from outside oneself. Thinking is the internal reflection on what one learned. Viewing oneself in the third person is like seeing from God's point of view. Meditation is the most common instrument in jnana yoga. Through meditation a person can see the truth in how he or she is attached to this world. The Path of Devotion, known as bhakti yoga, is the Path followed by most Hindus. A pure, long devotion to Brahman can bring liberation. Devotees of bhakti yoga perceive that Brahman is more immanent than transcendent.

4. Although Sikhs would disagree, many who study world religions maintain that Sikhism is a blending of Hinduism and Islam. Sikhs believe that God was revealed in a special way to Guru Nanak in 1459 in an area which is now part of Pakistan. Nine other gurus believed to be reincarnations of Nanak succeeded him. Sikhs are like Muslims in that they are monotheistic. But, like Hindus, Sikhs believe that God is transcendent and can be realized through nature or experience. Other Hindu components in Sikh practice are beliefs in karma, samsara, and moksha.

On The Experience

This poem reflects Kabir's perennial themes of humility and compassion.

When I was, Hari was not,

now Hari is and I am no more:

All darkness vanished,

When I saw the Lamp within my heart

The effulgence of the Supreme Being

is beyond the imagination:

Ineffable is His beauty,

to see it is the only "proof"

It was a good thing the hail fell to ground,

for it lost its own selfhood:

Melting, it turned into water

and rolled down to the pond

Him whom I went out to seek,

I found just where I was:

He now has become myself

whom before I called "Another!"

From *Kabir*, introduction and translation from Hindi and notes by Charlotte Vaudeville (Oxford: Clarendon Press, 1974).

Questions

1. What kinds of feelings are reflected in this poem?

2. What is the message Kabir wants to impart to his readers?

3. What does this poem say about the relationship between Brahman and atman? Cite the line in the poem as examples for your answer.

4. Write your own devotional poem about God, humility, or compassion.

Bhagavad Gita

In this selection of the *Bhagavada Gita*, Arjuna is caught between protecting his clan from bloodshed through violent or nonviolent means. This moral dilemma prompts Arjuna to seek help from the avatar Lord Krishna. In the course of this dialogue, Arjuna's devotion toward Krishna grows in intensity. Devotion to Krishna brings freedom from attachment to one's actions. Lord Krishna is speaking.

I deem most disciplined
men of enduring discipline
who worship me with true faith,
entrusting their minds to me . . .

Mastering their senses,
with equanimity toward everything,
they reach me, rejoicing
in the welfare of all creatures.

It is more arduous when their reason
clings to my unmanifest nature;
for men constrained by bodies,
the unmanifest way is hard to attain.

But men intent on me
renounce all actions to me
and worship me, meditating
with singular discipline.

When they entrust reason to me,
Arjuna, I soon arise
to rescue them from the ocean
of death and rebirth.

Focus your mind on me,
let your understanding enter me;
then you will dwell
in me without doubt . . .

One who bears hate for no creature
is friendly, compassionate, unselfish,
free of individuality, patient,
the same in suffering and joy.

Content always, disciplined,
self-controlled, firm in his resolve,
his mind and understanding dedicated to me,
devoted to me, he is dear to me.

The world does not flee from him,
nor does he flee from the world;
free of delight, rage, fear,
and disgust, he is dear to me.

Disinterested, pure, skilled,
indifferent, untroubled,
relinquishing all involvements,
devoted to me, he is dear to me.

He does not rejoice or hate,
grieve or feel desire;
relinquishing fortune and misfortune,
the man of devotion is dear to me.

Impartial to foe and friend,
honor and contempt,
cold and heat, joy and suffering,
he is free from attachment.

Neutral to blame and praise,
silent, content with his fate,
unsheltered, firm in thought,
the man of devotion is dear to me.

From the Twelfth Teaching in *The Bhagavad-Gita: Krishna's Counsel in Time of War*, translated by Barbara Stoler (New York: Bantam Books, 1986).

Name _____

Hinduism Crossword Puzzle

Across

5. nonviolent action advocated by Gandhi

8. nonviolence

10. a statue, image, or other picture of a Hindu deity

11. Hindu scripture believed to be written by Hindu seers

13. moral law of cause and effect

14. cycle of rebirth

Down

1. liberation from cycle of rebirth

2. "disciplines"

3. Hindu worship service

4. Hindu priest

6. "real self"

7. duties in life

8. incarnation on earth of Hindu deity

9. popular Hindu scripture category

11. various celebrations of events in Hindu life cycle

12. "illusion"

Chapter 5 Test

Name _____

Multiple Choice. *Write the letter of the best choice in the space provided.* (3 points each)

_____ 1. Hinduism
   a. was founded by Vivakananda.
   b. is a combination of a number of religious traditions in India.
   c. is not very tolerant of those who believe in only one God.
   d. has exactly 330 million gods.

_____ 2. According to Hinduism, our true self is
   a. maya.
   b. Brahman.
   c. samsara.
   d. Brahma.

_____ 3. Jainism and Buddhism
   a. are both derived from Hinduism.
   b. were both founded as reactions to Hinduism.
   c. both advocate nonviolence.
   d. all of the above

_____ 4. The Classical Period of Hinduism
   a. was the era when Hinduism became distinguished as a religion.
   b. was full of reformers like Ramakrishna.
   c. was a backwards period for Hinduism.
   d. all of the above

_____ 5. Dharma is
   a. the second of the stages of Hinduism.
   b. the lowest caste in Hinduism.
   c. the ethical duties of a person.
   d. another name for heaven in Hinduism.

_____ 6. The stage of life where one renounces family, name, and any memories of the past is called
   a. samsara.
   b. ahimsa.
   c. brahmin.
   d. sannyasin.

_____ 7. Which of the following is *not* a universal belief in Hinduism?
   a. karma
   b. gurdwara
   c. moksha
   d. samsara

_____ 8. The Hindu Creator god is
    a. Brahma.
    b. Brahman.
    c. Krishna.
    d. Shiva.

_____ 9. Krishna is the avatar of
    a. Brahman.
    b. Shiva.
    c. Vishnu.
    d. Arjuna.

_____ 10. The _Bhagavad Gita_ is in the _____ category of Hindu scripture.
    a. smriti
    b. shruti
    c. Vedic
    d. poetic

_____ 11. Sikhism
    a. has roots in Hinduism.
    b. was founded by Guru Nank.
    c. is a synthesis of Hinduism and Islam.
    d. all of the above

_____ 12. The path to moksha most followed is
    a. action.
    b. devotion.
    c. righteousness.
    d. knowledge.

_____ 13. This design is used by some in Hindu meditation.
    a. mantra
    b. maya
    c. murti
    d. mandala

_____ 14. The following would _not_ be found at a home puja
    a. brahmin
    b. murti
    c. flowers
    d. food

_____ 15. Hindu life cycles
    a. are more universal than Hindu festivals.
    b. are repetitive.
    c. are for boys only.
    d. are all done in conjunction with the Hindu calendar.

_____ 16. The Destroyer god is
   a. Vishnu.
   b. Brahman.
   c. Brahma.
   d. Shiva.

_____ 17. Another name for "yoga" is
   a. exercise.
   b. discipline.
   c. path.
   d. breathing.

_____ 18. Hindu temples
   a. are all exactly alike.
   b. have puja performed by Brahmin
   c. are more numerous in villages.
   d. are round in shape.

_____ 19. The Hindu life cycle rites of passage are called:
   a. ashramas.
   b. satyagraha.
   c. Sanskrit.
   d. samskaras.

_____ 20. With regard to other religions, Hinduism is
   a. tolerant.
   b. intolerant.
   c. tolerant only at first.
   d. indifferent.

Short Answer. _Briefly answer the following questions._ (10 points each)

1. What are the four stages of life for a Hindu male?

2. What are the four life goals for a Hindu male?

3. What are the three paths of liberation?

4. Explain the similarities and distinctions between Hinduism and Sikhism.

Chapter 6: Buddhism

Introduction

Siddhartha Gautama, a Hindu of the warrior caste, founded Buddhism in the sixth century BCE. The sight of different forms of suffering prompted him to give up luxury for asceticism. Then, dissatisfied with both the ascetic and materialistic ways of life, Siddhartha Gautama discovered the Middle Way. For him, salvation was through the cessation of desires. Siddhartha Gautama articulated his teachings in the Four Noble Truths, the fourth of which is the Noble Eightfold Path.

Buddhism is divided into three main branches—Theravada, Mahayana, and Vajrayana. Theravada is the most traditional, focusing on the teachings of the Buddha and seeing the Buddha as a sage. Mahayana Buddhism is more elastic, placing emphasis on the laity and seeing the Buddha as in some way divine. Vajrayana Buddhism is more esoteric. The vast majority of Vajrayana Buddhists are Tibetan, though some adherents can be found in Japan. Meditation is very important in every branch of Buddhism. It is through meditation that nirvana can ultimately be attained.

Pilgrimage to sites related to the historical Buddha are most popular. The temple is the place for worship, though there is no set day for Buddhists to worship. Monasteries are connected with temples.

Buddhism has become popular in the United States since the 1950s. At that time D.T. Suzuki brought Zen Buddhism to prominence. In 1989, the Dalai Lama received the Noble Prize for Peace. He has been an outspoken advocate for his fellow Tibetans against Communist China. His forced exile and the exile of other Tibetans has brought international attention to the plight of Tibet.

Resources for Chapter 6

Books

Aung San Suu Kyi. *Freedom From Fear and Other Writings*. rev. ed. London: Penguin Books, 1996.

Brauen, Martin. *Mandala: Sacred Circle in Tibetan Buddhism*. New York: Random House, 1997.

Bstan-'dzin-rgya-mtsho. *Freedom in Exile: The Autobiography of the Dalai Lama*. New York: HarperCollins, 1990.

Ch'en, Kenneth K. S. *Buddhism in China: A Historical Survey*. Princeton: Princeton University Press, 1964.

Conze, Edward. *A Short History of Buddhism*. Boston: Allen and Unwin, 1980.

———. *Buddhism: Its Essence and Development*. Mineola, NY: Dover Publications, 2003.

———. *Buddhist Meditation*. Mineola, NY: Dover Publications, 2003.

Conze, Edward, I. B. Horner, David L. Snellgrove, and Arthur Waley. *Buddhist Texts Through the Ages*. New York: Random House, 1990.

Earhart, H. Byron. *Japanese Religion: Unity and Diversity*. 4th ed. Belmont, CA: Wadsworth Publishing, 2004.

Fernando, Antony, and Leonard J. Swidler. *Buddhism Made Plain: An Introduction for Christians and Jews.* rev. ed. Maryknoll, NY: Orbis Books, 1985.

Lopez, Donald S. and Steven C. Rockefeller. *Christ and the Bodhisattva.* New York: State University of New York Press, 1987.

Nagarjuna, and Jay L. Garfield, ed. *The Fundamental Wisdom of the Middle Way.* New York: Oxford University Press, 1995.

Nhat Hanh, Thich. *The Miracle of Mindfulness: A Manual on Meditation.* rev. ed. Boston: Beacon Press, 1987.

Raahula, Wapola. *What the Buddha Taught.* rev. ed. New York: Grove Press, 1994.

Robinson, Richard H. *The Buddhist Religion: A Historical Introduction.* 5th ed. Belmont, CA: Wadsworth Publishing, 2004.

Strong, John. *The Experience of Buddhism: Sources and Interpretations.* 2nd ed. Belmont, CA: Wadsworth Publishing, 2002.

Suzuki, Shunryu. *Zen Mind, Beginner's Mind.* Boston: Weatherhill, 2006.

Watson, Burton. *The Lotus Sutra.* Delhi: Sri Satguru Publications, 1999.

White, David Gordon. *Tantra in Practice.* Princeton: Princeton University Press, 2000.

Audio-visual Resources

Buddhism. Essentials of Faith Series. DVD/VHS. (Films Media Group, 2006, 24 minutes)

Buddhism. Religions of the World Video Series. DVD/VHS. (Schlessinger Media, 1996, 50 minutes)

Footprint of the Buddha. The Long Search Video Series. DVD/VHS. (Ambrose Video Publishing, 2001, 60 minutes)

Kundun. DVD/VHS. (Walt Disney Video, 1998, 135 minutes) "The destiny of a people lies in the heart of a boy"—The XIV Dalai Lama. A commercially released film.

Robert A. F. Thurman on Buddhism. DVD. (Wellsprings, 2002, 220 minutes) A Buddhist scholar speaks from his point of view on Tibetan Buddhism.

Seven Years in Tibet. DVD/VHS. (Sony Pictures, 1997, 131 minutes) A commercially released film based on the true story of Heinrich Harrer, an Austrian mountain climber who became friends with the XIV Dalai Lama at the time of the Chinese Communist takeover of Tibet.

Internet Resources

Pontifical Council for Interreligious Dialogue— www.vatican.va/roman_curia/pontifical_councils/interelg/documents/rc_pc_interelg_pro_20051996_en.html

Religion and Ethics, British Broadcasting Company— www.bbc.co.uk/religion/religions/buddhism

World Wide Web Virtual Library: Buddhist Studies— www.ciolek.com/WWWVL-Buddhism.html

www.buddhanet.net

A Human-Centered Religion (pages 233–235)

Using the Text

- "Wake up!" Ask students why being alert or paying attention—as opposed to simply being physically awake—could have anything to do with spirituality. (*Hopefully, students will answer that being spiritually "awake" means seeing what's most important in life—not getting caught up in trivial, mundane worries and distractions.*)
- Display a variety of images of Siddhartha Gautama, the Hindu warrior who founded Buddhism about 2,500 years ago in Nepal. In sculpture, in paintings, in mosaic, hundreds and thousands of artists have tried to convey the Buddha as a compassionate presence. Poll students for any other adjectives or descriptive phrases they would want to connect with these portraits of Buddha.

Extending the Text

- Show a brief segment of *Kundun*, a full-length commercial release about the current Dalai Lama. Show just enough of the film to stimulate questions about Buddhism among the students. Make a list of the questions and keep it posted.
- Have students read through the Buddhism timeline on page 234. Point out that Buddhism precedes Christianity by 500 years. On the other end of the timeline, link modern times events highlighted in *Kundun* to the 1949 Communist takeover of China and the forced exile of the Dalai Lama from Tibet in 1959.

1. A Brief History of Buddhism (pages 235–246)

Siddhartha Gautama and *The Four Councils* and *Buddhism in India* and *Buddhist Expansion Beyond India* and *Buddhism in Modern Times*

Objective

In this section the students will:

- learn about the life of Siddhartha Gautama;
- review the major outcomes of each of the first four Buddhist councils;
- study the way Buddhism expanded throughout the Far East;
- Learn how Buddhism emerged in modern times into a worldwide religion;
- Become familiar with the contributions and impact of the fourteenth Dalai Lama, Tenzin Gyatso;
- Trace the development of Buddhism into different strains as it took root in China, Japan, and other parts of Asia.

Preview

The given name of the founder of Buddhism was Siddhartha Gautama, a Hindu from the warrior caste in Nepal. Growing up, Siddhartha was shielded from all pain and suffering. At nineteen, however, he discovered an old man, a very sick man, a corpse, and a poor, homeless man. He gave up his privileged life and later reached enlightenment under a bodhi tree. Siddhartha then began to share his insights. The Four Councils were periodic gatherings of the successors of Siddhartha. They helped to shape Buddhism, which began to find adherents throughout Asia. Particularly in India, Buddhism flourished. In the Common Era, Buddhism was influenced and adapted when it was taken to China and Japan. In Tibet, Vajrayana Buddhism, a branch of Mahayana Buddhism emphasized rituals and mantras. There, the head of the Buddhist leaders had also become the ruler of Tibet. When the fourteenth Dalai Lama was forced out of Tibet by the Chinese in 1959, a Tibetan Buddhist government in exile was established in Dharamsala, India. The Dalai Lama won the 1989 Nobel Peace Prize, and the impact of Buddhism in the West has been growing dramatically in modern times.

Using the Text

- Draw some obvious parallels between the life of Siddhartha and St. Francis of Assisi—discarding expensive clothes and possessions, adopting an ascetic lifestyle, gathering followers, etc. Point out, however, that Siddhartha was "enlightened" simply through meditation; his new direction came from within himself. Francis, on the other hand, found his new direction from visions of Jesus in the church of San Damiano and in the leper he met on the road. The transformation (or conversion) of St. Francis came from Christ.
- Trace the life of Siddhartha Gautama by highlighting key events from the text on the board. Have the students copy these notes or highlight the text themselves in their notebooks.
- As a check, ask the students to name (1) the origins of and (2) the results of each of the Four Councils. Allow them to refer to the text before they answer.

- Show pictures of the bodhi tree or "sacred fig" at the Mahabodhi Temple at Bodh Gaya under which Siddhartha Gautama arrived at "Bodhi" or "enlightenment." This particular tree does not date back to the time of Siddhartha but is probably a direct descendant of that tree. Bodhi trees are also sacred to Hindus and Jains. The leaves of this tree are heart-shaped.
- Ask students why they think this tree and the stupas, or dome-shaped monuments, are so important to modern Buddhists.
- Spend some time talking about "bodhi" which means an "awakening" or "enlightenment" to Buddhists. "Bodhi" is attained only by the accomplishment of the Paramitas (perfections), when the Four Noble Truths are fully grasped, and when all karma has reached cessation. Skip ahead to Practices and Beliefs, (pages 252–253) to present the Four Noble Truths here. Essentially, Buddhism says that a person is enlightened when he or she can see that:

  life is filled with suffering;

  suffering is caused by desire;

  suffering ceases when desiring ceases;

  the path to the end of suffering is the Noble Eightfold Path.

Extending the Text

- Pose the Reflection Question on page 235 about Buddhism in popular culture. Can students identify any Buddhist ideas, approaches to life, and conflicts that have become more mainstream?
- Show the film *The Middle Way of Compassion*. If there's time, consider using questions and discussion starts from the teacher's guide.
- Call on students to help review the divisions in Buddhism and outline these on the board.
- Consider using the Reflection Question on page 238 about living life to the extreme as the starting point for a debate on the plusses and minuses for (1) life lived to the extreme and (2) life based on the Middle Way. Students could respond in writing after the debate.
- Hand out a pop quiz with ten multiple choice questions on Buddhist terms and major events presented so far. Later, read the correct answers, but tell students you are offering Buddhist compassion and won't count the quiz.
- Display a map of the world, and challenge students to put small colored circle stickers on nations and regions of the world where Buddhism spread during the 2,000 years of the Common Era. Have students double-check the text—if they need to—to list locations where circles should be added.
- Though Buddhism began in India, there were only a few Buddhists there until the second half of this century. Since then some Hindu "untouchables" have converted to Buddhism. In addition, a number of exiled Tibetan Buddhists now live in northern India.
- If possible, play recordings of Buddhist chants. (Several Buddhist websites feature chants of various types.) Ask students why they think that certain types of chant or music might help a person to meditate and pray in a focused way.
- Show more of the film *Kundun* that traces the selection of the fourteenth Dalai Lama and his eventual forced exile from Tibet by Chinese Communists.

- Divide the class into small groups of three or four. Provide copies of the 1989 Nobel Peace Prize acceptance speech given by the Dalai Lama that is available on the Internet. Also distribute poster boards, markers, and art supplies. Assign each group to choose three sentences or four phrases from the speech that would work well on popular posters or billboards advertising Buddhist thinking. Have the groups share their posters with the whole class and explain why they chose the phrase or sentence that they did from the Dalai Lama's speech.
- Refer students to the list of Buddhist Research and Activities on pages 275–276. Have students choose a topic and work individually or in pairs to prepare an oral or written report. Allow a week to ten days for completion of the projects.
- Direct students to the Summary Statements on pages 245–246 for review, and the Section Review Questions on page 246 to be done as a written assignment.

Section 1 Review Questions and Answers

1. Briefly summarize the main events in the life of Siddhartha Gautama.

   Siddhartha Gautama was born into the warrior caste in India during the sixth century BCE. He was raised a prince, but upon seeing suffering on an outing, he gave up his earthly wealth and family and became an ascetic. One day under a Bodhi tree, Siddhartha was tempted by Mara, but to no avail. It was there under the tree that Siddhartha was enlightened. It was the Middle Way between asceticism and indulgences that brought moksha. He articulated his enlightenment in the Four Noble Truths, of which the fourth is the Noble Eightfold Path, that is, practices necessary for enlightenment. He formed a monastic community called the sangha and preached enlightenment to all who would listen.

2. What were the main issues addressed by each of the four councils?

   Those attending the first council attempted to preserve the Buddha's teachings through oral recitation to one another. The second council dealt with questionable practices of some "liberal" monks who sought a relaxation of monastic discipline. The third council was called by King Ashoka to purify the sangha of its various irregularities. It was at the third council that the Tipitaka was compiled. King Kaniska of Ceylon (present-day Sri Lanka) called the fourth council to rectify the problem of the emergence of various interpretations of Buddhist scriptures. Monks were assigned to edit the Tipitaka, making references and remarks for clarification. This task took twelve years to complete; the final document is known today as the Pali Canon and is used by the Theravada branch of Buddhism.

3. What attracted King Ashoka to Buddhism?

   King Ashoka was attracted to the Buddhist ideal of pacifism.

4. Why were the Japanese attracted to Zen Buddhism?

   Japanese soldiers in particular were attracted to Zen Buddhism because they were interested in overcoming the fear of death.

5. List countries in Asia where Buddhism took hold, at least for some time.

   Buddhism, founded by Siddhartha Gautama in his native Nepal in about 530 BCE, spread to nearby India in the succeeding centuries. After flourishing in India, Buddhism was established in Ceylon, Tibet, China, Japan, Vietnam, Korea, Thailand, and beyond. After the twelfth century, Muslim influences in India stifled Buddhism. Only remnants of a Buddhist community remained in India until recent times. Now, Buddhism is gaining more adherents again in India.

6. Who is the Dalai Lama? Briefly recount the history of Tibetan Buddhism.

   The head of Tibetan Buddhist monastic leaders is known as the Dalai Lama. The Dalai Lamas ruled over Tibet until Communist Chinese forced the present Dalai Lama and thousands of his followers to leave Tibet in 1959. He and his followers fled to Northern India and Nepal where they set up an exiled Tibetan government in Dharamsala, India.

2. Sacred Stories and Sacred Scriptures (pages 246–251)

Scriptures of Theravada Buddhism and *Scriptures of Mahayana Buddhism* and *Scriptures of Vajrayana Buddhism*

Objective

In this section the students will:
- learn that Siddhartha wrote no texts and that his teachings were initially transmitted orally;
- discover that Buddhism's sacred texts have been added often and in a variety of languages and literary forms;
- explore the early Buddhist scriptures, the *Tripitaka;*
- review the unique sacred texts of Mahayana Buddhism, including *The Lotus of the True Law,* or the *Lotus Sutra.*

Preview

Since the Buddha (Siddhartha) wrote no sacred texts himself, his followers initially kept his words alive through oral transmission. Then, written texts began to be composed in many different languages and literary forms. There is still no definitive agreement over which texts are truly sacred and which are not. The earliest written scriptures included the *Tripitaka,* or "Three Baskets." Written in the Pali language, this collection of three main works is the primary scripture for Theravada Buddhism. The three pitakas include instructions for monks and nuns, the discourses of Siddhartha, and a collection of Buddha's psychological teachings. Mahayana Buddhists use their own version of the *Tripitaka* and *The Lotus of the True Law,* or *Lotus Sutra,* as their sacred texts. They believe that the *Lotus Sutra* contains the final teachings of Buddha. Vajrayana Buddhists rely on the same scriptures used by Mahayana Buddhists, but add some *tantric* texts borrowed from India and China. This group of Buddhists also uses the *Kanjur,* its own unique collection of sacred scriptures. Two *tantric* prayer forms that are found only among these Buddhists are the use of the mandala and the use of the mantra. The most popular scripture in Vajrayana Buddhism is the *Tibetan Book of the Dead.*

Using the Text

- Repeat the point made in the text that Buddhism originally had no written texts and later seemed to have too many. The authenticity of many of these translations seems questionable. However, the fact that there is no agreement about which texts are definitely sacred isn't a problem for Buddhists.
- Ask students to share what they have learned about Buddhism's scriptures and stories.
- If possible, show students copies of the *Tripitaka* in English, and have a few students read excerpts from it.
- Divide students into diads or triads to read and discuss the feature, "The Way to Happiness." Have the small groups identify four or five statements that they could agree with and live by. Are there statements about happiness that they disagree with or simply don't understand? Can students think of any happiness statements that could or should be added? Discuss.

Extending the Text

- Give students a short pop quiz with ten matching questions on terms used in this section, such as *Vinaya Pitaka, Tripitaka, Pali, Lotus Sutra*, etc. Read the answers, and let students correct their own quizzes.
- Show previewed segments of the long film *Robert A. F. Thurman on Buddhism*, an interview with a Buddhist scholar. Ask students to pay special attention to what Thurman says about sacred scriptures.
- For extra credit, invite students to do reports on the Buddhist mandala, the mantra or the *Tibetan Book of the Dead* and how these are both used in Buddhist practice.
- Direct students to the Reflection Question on page 251 about the possible advantages of being able to add sacred texts. Discuss in the light of the students own religious traditions—probably Christian or Catholic.
- Have students read through the Section Summary Statements and the Section Review Questions.

Section Review Questions and Answers

1. In English, what does the term Tripitaka mean?

   The term Tripitaka means "three baskets."

2. What is the most popular Mahayana sacred text?

   The Lotus of the True Law, or the Lotus Sutra, is the most popular sacred text for Mahayana Buddhists and was likely composed over several generations.

3. What is the most popular Vajrayana sacred text? Why?

   The most popular Vajrayana sacred text is the Kanjur which contains the Theravada and Mahayana scriptures as well as some unique scriptures.

3. Beliefs and Practices (pages 251–257)

Four Noble Truths and *The Noble Eightfold Path* and *Community*

Objective

In this section the students will:

- learn and study the Four Noble Truths that sum up Buddhism;
- become familiar with the Noble Eightfold Path that reminds a person to avoid extremes and to take everything in moderation;
- identify the distinctions between the three main branches of Buddhism;
- find that Buddhist community (monks, nuns, and lay people) is so important that it is called one of the three Buddhist "jewels."

Preview

The center of all Buddhist belief is the Four Noble Truths, initially announced by Siddhartha Gautama. Understanding these four truths, Buddhists learn, will lead to the Noble Eightfold Path that directs a person to live with Right Understanding, Right Thought, Right Speech, Right Conduct, Right Livelihood, and so forth. Moderation and the middle path help a person towards Nirvana. The Four Noble Truths teach about suffering, its causes, and remedies. The fourth Noble Truth is the Noble Eightfold Path. For Buddhists, the liberation from samsara, or the cycle of reincarnation and rebirth, comes when the flames of all desires, cravings, or passions are extinguished. This is called Nirvana. Buddhists do not believe in immortality because they do not concede the existence of the individual soul. Buddhist community, once thought to mean only monks, now includes all believers. Community is crucial and constitutes one of the three Jewels or the core of Buddhism.

Using the Text

- Call on individual students to define the Four Noble Truths. Encourage them to explain or interpret these key Buddhist truths in their own language or to give several examples.
- Focus in more closely on the second and third Noble Truths about desires. Survey students for a list of things that people desire. Then, refer to the Reflection Question about ceasing all desires on page 253 and engage students in a discussion about:

    1. Is suffering always caused by desire—by not being satisfied with what one has?
    2. Is it possible to desire something truly good?
    3. What would it be like if people quit desiring things?
    4. Does our culture tempt us to desire too much?

- Elaborate on the importance of community for Buddhism. Monks provide spiritual nourishment for the laity, but the laity provides the physical nourishment and support for monks who seek their daily food through begging.

Extending the Text

- Distribute the "Buddhism Word Search" from page 176 of the Teacher's Manual to students. Allow students fifteen to twenty minutes to complete it.

- Recap the fundamental Buddhist teaching that the cessation of suffering takes place through living out the Noble Eightfold Path. Point out to the students that these eight items fall into three categories—moral actions, meditation, and wisdom.
- Divide the class into small groups of three or four. Distribute poster board, markers, other art supplies, and magazines filled with color photos useful for collages. Have each group choose one of the Noble Eightfold Paths for poster presentation. Students are also free to use text to "tell the story."
- At the end of this subsection invite students to respond to the Reflection Question about knowing yourself on page 255. Related to the question, ask: Why is it important to know yourself? What are some ways to get to know yourself better? Ask them to consider—and if they want to—share the name of the person who knows them best.
- The sangha or community is one of the Three Jewels of Buddhism. The other two jewels are the Buddha and the Dharma, or Buddhist teachings. Ask students: What do you think it means to "take refuge" in each of these three Jewels? Ask: "In what 'jewels' do you 'take refuge?'"
- Mahayana Buddhists point to the virtuous ones called *bodhisattvas* who defer nirvana until everyone else has reached this blissful state. Lead students in a discussion about the "bodhisattva" notion of "waiting until last" to enter Nirvana on page 256. Remind the students of Jesus' words: "Whoever wishes to be great among you will be your servant; whoever wishes to be first among you will be the slave of all" (Mk 10:49).
- Have students read through the Section Summary Statements and the Review Questions on page 257, but don't require students to write out the answers.

Section Review Questions and Answers

1. Name and explain the Four Noble Truths.

    1) Life is filled with suffering. Suffering refers not only to physical suffering, but also mental suffering that comes with facing the various traumas of life. We begin this life with the birth trauma. Then there is physical, mental, and emotional pain, illness, injury, old age, and fear of death. Samsara is the endless cycle of suffering through death and rebirth, and karma is the cause of samsara. Suffering even goes beyond life's physical and mental pains. The reason for suffering includes concepts of impermanence, incompleteness, imperfections, and discontent.

    2) The cause of suffering is desire. Because people believe the individual self is real, they have cravings. People constantly want things. When they do not get them, they are frustrated or disappointed. Even if a person gets what he or she wants, the resulting happiness is impermanent. Ignorance of the nature of the not-self and thus, believing the self to be real (that is, permanent and unchanging) is the fundamental cause of suffering.

    3) To cease suffering one must cease desiring. To end suffering is to end samsara and achieve nirvana. That is what is real in Buddhism. Everything is suffering, impermanent, and incomplete. The only thing permanent, and thus, real, is the end of suffering. Suffering ceases when we free ourselves of the bondage of desires and cravings and stop believing that our individual self is real. This freedom brings people happiness and contentment. Nirvana is the "extinction" of that suffering through the endless cycles of rebirth.

    4) The path to the end of suffering is the Noble Eightfold Path. This is the Middle Path between indulgence and self-denial. The Noble Eightfold Path is the moral standard of Buddhism.

2. List the three major categories of the Noble Eightfold Path.

    The three major categories are morality, meditation, and wisdom. Moral actions bring about meditation, and completing the circle, wisdom gives rise to good actions.

3. What are the Three Jewels of Buddhism?

    The Three Jewels of Buddhism are: 1) "I take refuge in the Buddha," 2) "I take refuge in the Dharma," and 3) "I take refuge in the Sangha."

Buddhism Word Search Answers

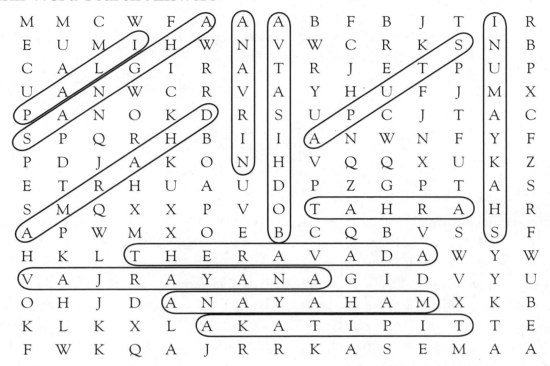

4. Sacred Time (pages 257–265)

Meditation and *Puja* and *Festivals* and *Celebrating the Buddha* and *Celebrating Sangha* and *Celebrating the Buddhist Life Cycle*

Objective

In this section the students will:

- become familiar with two types of Buddhist meditation;
- identify two categories of Buddhist festivals;
- learn more about the way that Buddhists celebrate the life cycle.

Preview

This section presents information about the sacred times of Buddhism as they are expressed in the three major branches of Buddhism. Generally, a Buddhist works to gain wisdom through meditation. There are no special days of the week for worship. So, Buddhists can make offerings at home. The ultimate goal is to follow the Eightfold Path and to become one who has achieved nirvana. During meditation, the Buddhist concentrates on the last three paths of the Noble Eightfold Path—right effort, right mindfulness, and right concentration. Two major types of meditation are the Mindfulness of Breathing and the Meditation of Loving-Kindness. In both types of meditation, the mind is cleared of worldly concerns in order to concentrate on God. Puja is part of the daily observance of a Buddhist. At home, Buddhists offer flowers, food, and lighted candles to offer reverence and gratitude to the Buddha. In Buddhist nations, images of the Buddha in all sizes and materials appear everywhere. Two kinds of festivals round out Buddhist worship—one sort based on the life of Buddha while the other is centered around sangha. Almost all Buddhists celebrate the birthday of Buddha, and focus on enlightenment. At the end of the three months of the monsoon season and the Sangha Retreat, Buddhist lay people host a festival and present the monks with new robes.

Using the Text

- Make the point that Buddhists do not have a "sacred day" on which they pray in a special way. Any hour and any day is a good time to pray. Emphasize that this is another aspect of the individualistic nature of Buddhism.
- Review the Buddhist approaches to meditation and the varieties of meditation—the Mindfulness of Breath and the Meditation of Loving-Kindness. Meditation is intended to bring new insights and wisdom, thus helping a Buddhist to move into the Noble Eightfold Path.
- Have a student read aloud the separate feature on meditation being taught to a juvenile offenders group in the California prison system. Invite students to react to this idea—teaching troubled youth how to meditate. Ask students if they think meditation would be therapeutic or helpful in their own lives.
- "Does holiness rub off?" Connect the question with the Reflection Question on page 263 and ask students to answer it with a written one page reflection.
- Redirect students to the Reflection Question on page 262 about home shrines in Hindu, Buddhist, and Catholic homes. Call on students to orally compare and contrast the shrines.

Then, have students quickly reread "Celebrating the Buddhist Life Cycle" on pages 263–264, and compare Buddhist and Catholic rituals relating to birth and death. How are they alike? How are they different?

Extending the Text

- Show the short overview film *Buddhism* from the Essentials of Faith Series to review concepts presented.
- Following the film, invite students to imagine what it is like to be a Buddhist monk. Point out that in some countries where Buddhism is the preeminent religious tradition, boys as young as twelve or thirteen are sent to monasteries to train as monks for a while.
- Share a *Mindfulness of Breath* meditation with the students.

  Allow approximately ten minutes for this exercise. It is helpful to play instrumental, reflective music during this time. Quiet the students. Then, say:

  "Sit up straight in your seat. Place your feet flat on the floor. For a straight back, imagine a string that starts in the base of your spine out through the top of your head. Breathe in deeply through your nose.

  "Hold your breath for four counts. Then breathe out slowly through your mouth, counting backwards from eight to one. (Repeat this several times.)

  "Allow your feet and ankles to relax. Relax your calves, thighs, and hips. As you relax, remain mindful of your breathing. Breathe in deeply through your nose. Hold your breath for four counts. Then breathe out slowly through your mouth, counting backwards from eight to one. Relax your stomach and chest. Relax your arms, letting them go limp. Relax your fingers, hands, and wrists. Remain mindful of your breathing. Relax your neck, your facial muscles, your jaw, and your eyes. Continue to be mindful of your breath. (Pause.) Once more, breathe in deeply, hold your breath, then breathe out slowly. When you are ready you may open your eyes."

- Invite students to share reactions to the meditation. Encourage students to try meditating again at home.
- Direct students to use the Section Summary Statements and the Section Review Questions to revisit information presented in this section.

Section Review Questions and Answers

1. Why is meditation important for Buddhists?

   Meditation is important for Buddhists because it is a means to enlightenment.

2. Briefly describe the Mindfulness of Breathing meditation.

   Mindfulness of Breathing is a meditation that focuses on one's breathing. This allows a person to gain power in concentration and calm oneself.

3. How do Theravada and Mahayana Buddhists celebrate the birth of the Buddha?

   Theravada Buddhists emphasize enlightenment during this festival. They celebrate by lighting colorful lanterns and candles around the monasteries where the celebrations occur. An image of the Buddha is decorated, and a monk gives a sermon on some aspect of the life of the Buddha. Mahayanas celebrate the life of Buddha on three separate days throughout the year. The celebration may entail a bathing of the sacred image followed by a procession. The bathing not only signifies great reverence for the Buddha, it is also a reminder that there are faults in everyone's life that need to be washed away.

4. What is the origin of the Rains Retreat?

    The Rains Retreat began as the three month period of the monsoon season when the monks could not go out and preach the dharma.

5. Sacred Places and Sacred Spaces (pages 265–268)

Temple and *Stupas* and *Places of Pilgrimage*

Objective
In this section the students will:
- learn the significance of temples as holy places for Buddhists;
- become familiar with the purpose and design of stupas;
- identify the important places in the life of Siddhartha Gautama that are now pilgrimage sites for Buddhists.

Preview
Catholic teens may be familiar with Christian monasticism. The opening to this section restates that there are Buddhist monks and that lay people share in their ministry. Monasteries, temples, and stupas are sacred places for Buddhists. Most holy pilgrimages in Buddhism are connected with the life of Buddha—his birthplace, the tree and garden connected with his enlightenment, the place where he preached his first sermon, and the place of his death. Have the students examine the photos in this section prior to assigning the text for reading.

Using the Text
- Remind students about the role of a Hindu temple (pages 214–215 of the Student Text). Ask the students to point out similarities and differences between the temples from both of these religious traditions.
- Show students pictures of a variety of stupas and present them as places where relics of Buddha or some of his most enlightened followers are preserved. Remind them that in the Catholic tradition, relics are objects, sometimes body parts or clothing of a departed saint. In many churches and shrines, relics of Christian saints are honored.
- Places where Buddhists like to pilgrimage most are those places connected with the life of the historical Buddha. Assign the students (individually or in small groups) to one place of pilgrimage to do further research and present their findings to the class. The research should include: what event(s) took place in the Buddha's life at this place; a description of the place today; the significance of the place for modern pilgrims; and the kinds of rituals (if any) that take place at this holy site. Students may want to create posters to accompany their presentations.

Extending the Text
- Draw student attention to the Reflection Question about "relics" on page 266 and to the question about holy places or shrines on page 267. Discuss student experience with these religious experiences and invite them to compare them with the way Buddhists seem to reverence relics and holy places.
- Make sure to have the students review the Section Summary Statements and do the Section Review Questions at the end of the section on page 268.

Section Summary Questions and Answers

1. Name a difference between a Theravada temple and a Mahayana temple.

   Theravada temples usually have images of the Buddha and stories about the life of the Buddha depicted in paintings or statues. Mahayana temples are likely to have a number of enshrined images of many people from the past who have become enlightened and thus are also called buddhas, but with a lower case "b."

2. How does a pagoda differ from an ordinary stupa?

   A pagoda is a large stupa. While an ordinary stupa is a simple, small mound, pagodas are large, elaborately decorated domes.

3. Name the four major sites of pilgrimage related to the life of Siddhartha. Why are these significant?

   The four major sites of pilgrimage are significant because they are related to the life of Siddhartha. They are Lumbini Gardens, the traditional site of the birth of Siddhartha, Bodhi Gaya, the site of the Bodhi Tree, Sarnath, the Deer Park where the Buddha gave his first sermon, and Kushinara, the traditional place of the death of Siddhartha.

6. Buddhism through a Catholic Lens (pages 268–272)

Jesus Christ and Siddhartha the Buddha and *Suffering*

Objective

In this section the students will:

- reexamine Buddhism in the light of Catholic teaching and practice;
- compare the lives and teaching of Siddhartha Gautama and Jesus Christ;
- analyze the way Buddhists and Catholics see the meaning of human suffering.

Preview

Buddhism and Christianity share common ground in several important areas. Both preach the importance of compassion, charity, and peace. Both religions also feature long monastic traditions that foster meditation and prayer. Dialogue between Catholics and Buddhists grew after the Second Vatican Council. Trappist monk and author Thomas Merton was deeply involved in this ongoing dialogue until his sudden death in Thailand in 1968. Merton and other Catholics had found many similarities in the lives and teaching of Jesus Christ and Siddhartha Gautama. Buddhists and Catholics had also begun to compare their respective approaches to suffering. These views are very different. Buddhists believe that all who have not yet reached Enlightenment and Nirvana are bound to suffer. Negative events and destructive traits in a previous life produce an endless cycle of birth, death, and rebirth, Buddhist teaching says. For Catholics, suffering is a fruit of original sin and suffering endured in the name of Christ is redemptive.

Using the Text

- Show students a photo of Thomas Merton and the Dalai Lama, and read some of Merton's reactions to this encounter and to Buddhism as he recorded them in *The Asian Journal of Thomas Merton.*
- Call on students to ask them to name five similarities between Siddhartha and Jesus. Write the best answers on the board. Then solicit five differences between Jesus and Siddhartha, or between their teachings. Record those responses for all to see. (*Clearly, students should point out that Jesus was divine and the Son of God; Siddhartha was an inspired spiritual teacher.*)
- Follow the same procedure to compare Catholic and Buddhist teachings about suffering. Have students create five statements to describe Buddhist teaching about suffering. Then, five statements to represent Catholic teaching about suffering. (*Catholic teaching suggests that suffering can be meritoriously linked to the redemptive suffering of Christ.*)

Extending the Text

- Divide the class into six groups and cluster them in places where they can read and write without distractions. Assign each small group one section of the chapter. The sections are: A Human-Centered Religion; A Brief History of Buddhism; Sacred Stories and Sacred Scriptures; Beliefs and Practices; Sacred Time; Sacred Places and Sacred Spaces; and Buddhism Through a Catholic Lens. Have each group create ten *Jeopardy*-style review questions from their section. The questions (and answers in parentheses) should then be reviewed by the whole group, and written on small index cards.

- Offer extra credit to students who read and do a written response to the worksheet, "A Bodhisattva" on page 175 of the Teacher's Manual.
- Read aloud the Conclusion statement on pages 272–273.
- Collect the *Jeopardy* review questions and use them to initiate a chapter review. Also use the Summary Statement, Review Questions, Vocabulary Terms and any student questions that have emerged during the study of Buddhism. Make sure that students know when the chapter test will be given. Have a brief prayer service after the chapter review that makes use of the Buddhist prayer "With Every Breath." Finish by having a student or students direct the class in the meditative recitation of the "Our Father." Remind students to remain conscious of their breathing while trying to focus only on the prayer's directives.

Section Review Questions and Answers

1. Name two similarities and two differences between Jesus and Siddhartha.

   Jesus and Siddhartha both had miracles linked to their births and later faced temptations before beginning their teaching missions. One difference between the two was that Jesus claimed to be divine while Siddhartha did not. Another difference was in their origins. Jesus was born in poverty; Siddhartha's family was wealthy and powerful.

2. How is compassion manifested?

   Buddhists maintain that suffering is inevitable for those who have not yet reached Nirvana or Enlightenment. Buddhist compassion—or the response to that suffering—is tempered by the belief that the end of suffering requires the end of desires and cravings. Christians see suffering differently. It is, they believe, the result of Original Sin. They show compassion and try to relieve the suffering of others in the name of Jesus. He healed the sick, gave hope and joy to the downtrodden, and fed the hungry.

3. Why would Buddhists say that there is no such thing as pure pleasure?

   Buddhists say that even within pleasure, there is pain because of the impermanence of things. We suffer even in the midst of pleasure because the pleasure is truly illusory and not real.

4. What is an occasion of dialogue between Catholic and Buddhist monastics?

   While the content in Catholic meditation and Buddhist meditation are different, it is a fundamental prayer practice in both traditions, and some experiences are quite similar.

Chapter 6 Review Questions and Answers

1. Briefly summarize the life of Siddhartha Gautama.

   Siddhartha Gautama was born into the warrior caste in modern-day Nepal during the sixth century BCE. He was raised a prince, but upon seeing suffering on an outing, he gave up his earthy wealth and family and became an ascetic. One day under a bodhi tree, Siddhartha was tempted by Mara, but to no avail. It was there under the tree that Siddhartha was enlightened. It was the Middle Way between asceticism and indulgence that brought him moksha. He articulated his enlightenment in the Four Noble Truths, of which the fourth is the Noble Eightfold Path, that is, practices necessary for enlightenment. He formed a monastic community called the Sangha and preached enlightenment to all who would listen.

2. What is the Middle Way?

   The Middle Way is a life in the middle of the spectrum between indulgence and asceticism.

3. Highlight the accomplishments of the Four Councils.

   At the first council, the followers of Siddhartha attempted to preserve the Buddha's teachings through oral recitation to one another. The second council dealt with questionable practices of some "liberal" monks who sought a relaxation of monastic discipline. The third council was called by King Ashoka to purify the Sangha of its various irregularities and the Tipitaka was compiled. King Kaniska of Ceylon (present-day Sri Lanka) called the fourth council to rectify problems associated with the emergence of various interpretations of Buddhist scriptures. Monks were assigned to edit the Tipitaka, making references and remarks for clarification. This task took twelve years to complete; the final document is known today as the Pali Canon and is used by the Theravada branch of Buddhism.

4. Outline the expansion of Buddhism beyond India.

   Buddhism expanded beyond India to China, Tibet, Korea, Vietnam, and Japan. In the modern era, Buddhism continued its expansion to Western countries.

5. Compare the role of monks to lay people in Buddhism.

   Traditionally, the laity provides physical nourishment to monks who seek their daily food through begging at the households of Buddhist devotees.

6. Briefly compare and contrast Theravada, Mahayana, and Vajrayana Buddhism.

   Theravada Buddhism is the only original sect that survives today. Theravada means "School of Elders." Mahayana Buddhism emphasizes lay participation. Mahayana means "Great Vehicle." Vajrayana Buddhism is a branch of Mahayana Buddhism. This is the prominent form of Buddhism in Tibet. It literally means "Diamond Vehicle."

7. What are the Three Jewels of Buddhism? When are they recited?

    The Three Jewels of Buddhism are: 1) "I take refuge in the Buddha," 2) "I take refuge in the Dharma," and 3) "I take refuge in the Sangha." The Jewels are recited often once a person becomes a Buddhist.

8. What is the meaning of atman to Buddhists?

    While Hindus taught that self or soul was God (atman), Gautama taught that if the soul was purely God then it is not a soul at all. Buddhists believe that a permanent, unchangeable, totally dependent self does not exist, though people act as if it does.

9. Name some of the benefits of meditation.

    Meditation helps people cultivate the awareness of their dreams, goals, and self-identities, and the means to engage in good karma.

10. Define stupa.

    A stupa is a dome-shaped monument used to house Buddhist relics.

11. What is Zen Buddhism?

    Zen Buddhism is a sect of Buddhism begun in China under the name of Ch'an Buddhism. It was originally a combination of Mahayana Buddhism and Taoism.

12. What is the difference between the way that Catholics and Buddhists look at suffering?

    Buddhists define suffering as the result of not having yet reached Enlightenment and Nirvana. Since they believe in the endless cycle of life, death, and reincarnation, suffering is linked to negative or destructive activities in previous lives. The end of suffering means the end of the life-death-rebirth cycle. For Catholics, suffering is part of the human condition and is the result of Original Sin. Enduring suffering in the name of Jesus Christ, who suffered greatly, is redemptive and helps us to feel compassion for brothers and sisters in the midst of great suffering.

Chapter 6 Test Answers

True or False (3 points each)

1. F, 2. T, 3. F, 4. F, 5. T, 6. T, 7. F, 8. T, 9. T, 10. F

Multiple Choice (3 points each)

1. d, 2. b, 3. a, 4. c, 5. b, 6. c, 7. c, 8. c, 9. c, 10. c

Short Answers (8 points each)

1.
   1) Life is filled with suffering. Suffering refers to not only physical suffering, but also mental suffering that comes with facing the various traumas of life.

   2) The cause of suffering is desire. Because people believe the individual self is real, they have cravings. Even if a person gets what he or she wants, the resulting happiness is impermanent. Ignorance of the nature of the not-self and thus, believing the self to be real (that is, permanent and unchanging) is the fundamental cause of suffering.

   3) To cease suffering one must cease desiring. To end suffering is to end samsara and achieve nirvana.

   4) The path to the end of suffering is the Noble Eightfold Path. This is the Middle Path between indulgence and self-denial. The Noble Eightfold Path is the moral standard of Buddhism.

2.
   1) Right Understanding: Right understanding is the understanding of the causes of suffering, the end of suffering, and the way one endures suffering.

   2) Right Thought: Right thought is not just getting rid of wrong thoughts. It is replacing wrong thoughts, like hatred and desire, with right thoughts, like loving kindness and renunciation.

   3) Right Speech: All forms of lying, slandering, gossiping, and using harsh words must be eliminated. Instead, a person must speak truthfully and kindly about others.

   4) Right Conduct: Right conduct calls on people not to cheat, steal, murder, or engage in any kind of sexual misconduct.

   5) Right Livelihood: This path calls upon people not to earn a living through actions that would harm other living things.

   6) Right Effort: This path has to do with a person's thoughts. He or she is to be diligent in getting rid of bad or delusional thoughts, while cultivating good, wholesome thoughts.

   7) Right Mindfulness: A person is to be aware of everything he or she is thinking and doing. Right mindfulness is being aware of one's thoughts, feelings, and actions at all times.

   8) Right Concentration: This final path is a form of meditation in which a person concentrates on one object in order to give full attention to the object, dispel distractions, see things as they really are, and thus, gain enlightenment.

3. There are three documents in this collection. Vinaya Pitaka is the code of monastic discipline for monks and nuns. Sutra Pitaka is the primary discourse of Siddhartha Gautama. Abidharma Pitaka examines Buddha's psychological teachings.

4. Temples are especially sacred to Theravada Buddhists. Monks live there and perform certain rites. Lay people come there for devotion, meditation, and instruction in Buddha's teachings.

5. One is centered in the life of Buddha, the other in the Sangha.

A Bodhisattva

A Bodhisattva resolves: I take upon myself the burden of all suffering. . . . I do not turn or run away, do not tremble, am not terrified. . . . Do not turn back or despond.

And why? . . . I have made the vow to save all beings. . . . The whole world of living beings I must rescue, from the terrors of birth-and-death, from the jungle of false views. . . . My endeavors do not merely aim at my own deliverance. . . . I must rescue all these beings from the stream of Samsara. . . . And I must not cheat beings out of my store of merit. I am resolved to abide in each single state of woe for numberless aeons; and so I will help all, to freedom, in all the states of woe that may be found in any world system whatsoever.

And why? Because it is surely better that I alone should be in pain than that all these beings should fall into states of woe.

Quoted from *The World's Wisdom: Sacred Texts of the World's Religions*, edited by Philip Novak (San Francisco: HarperSanFrancisco, 1994).

Questions

1. What does this passage mean?

2. What do you find appealing about a bodhisattva?

3. What is the difference between a bodhisattva and a buddha?

4. What are ways you can manifest compassion in your own life?

Buddhism Word Search

Test your skills on Buddhist terms by completing this word search. Words can be found horizontally, vertically, or diagonally. Words may be spelled from left to right or right to left, from top to bottom, or from bottom to top. Letters may overlap between two words.

```
M  M  C  W  F  A  A  A  B  F  B  J  T  I  R
E  U  M  I  H  W  N  V  W  C  R  K  S  N  B
C  A  L  G  I  R  A  T  R  J  E  T  P  U  P
U  A  N  W  C  R  V  A  Y  H  U  F  J  M  X
P  A  N  O  K  D  R  S  U  P  C  J  T  A  C
S  P  Q  R  H  B  I  I  A  N  W  N  F  Y  F
P  D  J  A  K  O  N  H  V  Q  Q  X  U  K  Z
E  T  R  H  U  A  U  D  P  Q  G  P  T  A  S
S  M  Q  X  X  P  V  O  T  A  H  R  A  H  R
A  P  W  M  X  O  E  B  C  Q  B  V  S  S  F
H  K  L  T  H  E  R  A  V  A  D  A  W  Y  W
V  A  J  R  A  Y  A  N  A  G  I  D  V  Y  U
O  H  J  D  A  N  A  Y  A  H  A  M  X  K  B
K  K  K  X  L  A  K  A  T  I  P  I  T  T  E
F  W  K  Q  A  J  R  R  K  A  S  E  M  A  A
```

1. "worthy one"
2. one who delays enlightenment out of compassion for others
3. Buddhist teachings
4. "The Greater Vehicle"
5. the ultimate goal of a Buddhist
6. the original language of the Tipitaka

7. the Buddhist community
8. "sage of the Shakyas"
9. a mound used to house Buddhist relics
10. "school of Elders"
11. main scripture of the Theravada Buddhists
12. "Diamond Vehicle"

Chapter 6 Test

Name _____

True or False. *Mark "T" if a statement is true. Mark "F" if a statement is false. Explain why the false answers are false.* (3 points each)

1. _____ Siddhartha Gautama was raised a Hindu in the princely caste.

2. _____ As Buddhism spread into the Far East, it broke up into sects.

3. _____ Throughout its history, Buddhism has remained an influential religion in India.

4. _____ Mahayana and Vajrayana Buddhism use none of the scriptures Theravada Buddhists use.

5. _____ Buddhists make offerings in the temple to gain merit.

6. _____ Buddhist pilgrimage sites in India and Nepal are connected with the historical Buddha.

7. _____ Not all branches of Buddhism find meditation important.

8. _____ Funeral rites are very important for Buddhists.

9. _____ Like Hindus, most Buddhist festivals are local or regional events.

10. _____ The Three Jewels once belonged to the Buddha.

Multiple Choice. *Write the letter of the best choice in the space provided.* (3 points each)

_____ 1. Buddhism is derived from the _____ religious tradition.
  a. Indian
  b. Jain
  c. Aryan
  d. Hindu

_____ 2. The Middle Way refers to
  a. living a life that is somewhere in the middle between rich and poor.
  b. the half way point between asceticism and indulgence.
  c. a Buddhist that falls somewhere between a Mahayanan and Vajrayanan.
  d. none of the above

_____ 3. The Four Councils of Buddhism
  a. were instrumental in determining the direction of Buddhism after the death of Siddhartha Gautama.
  b. remained Theravada in nature.
  c. acted on behalf of Buddhism in a dignified manner.
  d. took place outside of India.

_____ 4. A pagoda is a large
  a. sutra.
  b. arhat.
  c. stupa.
  d. dharma.

_____ 5. Funerals are important to Buddhists because
      a. it is the only life cycle rite that Buddhist's celebrate.
      b. of their strong interest in the afterlife.
      c. Buddhists were the first to develop them.
      d. that is the only place they can touch relics.

_____ 6. Siddhartha Gautama attained enlightenment
      a. when he discovered the Middle Way.
      b. when he was giving his first sermon at Deer Park.
      c. when he realized the importance of understanding suffering as articulated in the Four Noble Truths.
      d. when he renounced his Hindu faith.

_____ 7. Nirvana is attained through
      a. good works.
      b. great wisdom.
      c. meditation.
      d. renunciation.

_____ 8. Siddhartha Gautama believed that suffering
      a. will never end.
      b. is not what one thinks it is.
      c. will cease when one ceases desiring.
      d. can only end with the end of arhats.

_____ 9. Another name for the _Tipitaka_ is the
      a. Three Baskets.
      b. Three Jewels.
      c. Pali Cañon.
      d. both _a_ and _c_

_____ 10. Which of the following is _not_ one of the Three Jewels?
      a. Buddha.
      b. Sangha.
      c. Tipitaka.
      d. Dharma.

Short Answers. _Briefly answer the following questions._ (8 points each)

1. List and explain the Four Noble Truths.

2. List and explain the Noble Eightfold Path.

3. List and explain the collections that make up the _Tipitaka._

4. Why is the temple sacred to Buddhism?

5. Name two categories of Buddhist festivals.

Chapter 7: Chinese Religions

Introduction

Chinese religion, for the most part, is indigenous to China. It is a combination of folk religion, Confucianism, Taoism, and Buddhism. Only Buddhism originated outside of China. Because Chapter 6 is dedicated to Buddhism, this chapter will focus on Confucianism and Taoism.

Though in common parlance Confucius is the founder of Confucianism and Lao-tzu is the founder of Taoism, neither man claimed himself to be the founder of a religion. Further, there is some question whether Lao-tzu was truly a historical figure. Nevertheless, the origins of Confucianism and Taoism both date from the sixth century BCE in China. It was a time of great social upheaval. Confucius's answer to the social unrest was to return to the wisdom of the ancients. Meanwhile, Lao-tzu sought harmony with all of nature. While Confucianism was more social, Taoism was more individualistic. The teaching of Confucius was more action-oriented while that of Lao-tzu was interested in action without action, or a "letting go."

Neither Confucius nor Lao-tzu ever claimed to be the founder of a religious tradition, nor did they claim that their scriptures were of divine origin. Much of the scriptures used by Confucius and his followers were those of "the ancients." Confucius simply reintroduced his society to those great documents. Other Confucian scriptures are sayings of Confucius and of his disciples. The *Tao Te Ching*—the Tao scriptures—is a relatively small manuscript. Though legend says Lao-tzu wrote it, there is clear evidence that it was written over a number of centuries following his death and that it is based on documents written before he was born.

Buddhism was introduced into China in the first century of the Common Era, but it was of little influence for several centuries. Gradually, however, the Buddhists gained some political power and much land ownership due to their numerous temples and monasteries. Buddhism had a great influence on Taoism. It was not uncommon to find statues of both Siddhartha Gautama and Lao-tzu in the same temple.

Ancestors are of particular importance to all Chinese. It is vital to maintain ancestor shrines in temples and in homes. People were also taught to carefully tend to the graves of their ancestors. Like living people, ancestors were thought to be a mix of benevolent and malevolent personalities. Reverence for ancestors was not taken lightly.

Though not strictly religious in nature, Chinese people mark sacred times through seasonal festivals. The greatest is the Chinese New Year. Birth, marriage, and death are the major rites of passage celebrated in the life cycle. Since the Communist revolution in 1949, religion in China has been persecuted, forced underground, banished, or ruthlessly limited by the government. Since 1979, there has been some relaxation of the government's anti-religious policies, but human rights groups call for full religious freedom in China.

Tibetan Buddhists remain in exile in India, and there are still some Christians in Chinese jails. Fortunately, the limitations on religious freedom in mainland China are not reported in places like Taiwan and Hong Kong. Obviously, Chinese immigrants in western countries also enjoy religious freedoms denied to their relatives and friends in China. Many of the teachings and customs discussed in this chapter are derived from Chinese living outside of mainland China.

Resources for Chapter 7

Books

Confucius. *The Analects*. Trans. Arthur Waley. New York: Alfred A. Knopf, 2000.

Jordan, David K. *Gods, Ghosts, and Ancestors*. Berkeley: University of California Press, 1972.

Lao-tzu. *Tao-Te Ching*. Trans. Gia-Fu Feng and Jane English. New York: Alfred A. Knopf, 1972.

Maspero, Henri. *Taoism and Chinese Religion*. Amherst: University of Massachusetts Press, 1981.

Sommer, Deborah. *Chinese Religion: An Anthology of Sources*. New York: Oxford University Press, 1995.

Thompson, Laurence G. *Chinese Religion: An Introduction*. 5th ed. Belmont, CA: Wadsworth Publishing, 1996.

Tu, Weiming. *Confucian Thought: Selfhood as Creative Transformation*. Albany: State University of New York Press, 1985.

Van Norden, Bryan W. *Confucius and the Analects: New Essays*. New York: Oxford University Press, 2002.

Welch, Holmes, and Anna K. Seidel. *Facets of Taoism: Essays in Chinese Religion*. New Haven, CT: Yale University Press, 1979.

Yu, David C., and Laurence G. Thompson. *Guide to Chinese Religion*. Boston: G.K. Hall, 1985.

Audio-visual Resources

Believing. Heart of the Dragon series. VHS. (Ambrose Video, 1984, 57 minutes) Looks at that which shaped the Chinese people—Confucianism, Taoism, and Buddhism—as well as Maoism and Marxism.

Confucianism and Taoism. Religions of the World Video Series. VHS. (Schlessinger Media, 1996, 50 minutes)

Confucius: Words of Wisdom. DVD. (A&E Biography, 1996, 50 minutes)

Religions of China. DVD/VHS. (Films Media Group, 1999, 57 minutes)

Taoism: A Question of Balance. The Long Search Video Series. DVD/VHS. (Ambrose Video Publishing, 2001, 60 minutes) Study Guide available for separate purchase.

Internet Resources

Chinese Religions and Culture on the Internet— www.uh.edu/~fyang/china.htm

Internet Guide for Chinese Studies— www.sino.uni-heidelberg.de/igcs/igphil.htm#confucianism

Many Forms and Practices (pages 279–280)

1. A Brief History of Chinese Religion (pages 281–293)

Ancient Folk Religion and *Confucius and Confucianism* and *Lao-tzu and Taoism* and *Buddhism in China*

Objective

In this section the students will:

- learn about ancient Chinese folk religion;
- become familiar with the life of Confucius;
- study the life of Lao-tzu and Taoism, the religion he is associated with;
- recognize the influence of Buddhism in China.

Preview

Explain that unlike the monotheistic religions of Judaism, Christianity, and Islam, Chinese religion is a combination of indigenous religions of China such as folk religion, Confucianism, and Taoism, as well as the importation of Buddhism into China. Both Confucianism and Taoism developed from ancient folk religions that were common at that time. Folk religion refers to non-institutional religious beliefs and practices of a culture or group of people. For example, reading tea leaves, lighting candles, and using prayer beads are all forms of folk religion because they do not necessarily involve the services of a professional religious person. Rather, these are practices that the "folk" do.

Since the Communist Revolution of 1949, however, all religions in China have suffered greatly. Peoples of various religious persuasions were persecuted, and the Chinese government has regulated religion. Although there has been some relaxation of anti-religion sentiments, full religious freedom has not yet been realized. On the other hand, it is difficult to study adherents to Chinese religions since these religions do not require strict membership. Individuals may embrace practices of more than one religious tradition.

Using the Text

- Direct students to briefly scan the 3,000 plus years of Chinese history in the timeline. Point out that the influences of Confucius and Lao-tzu were several hundred years old before Buddhism began to take root there. The intermingling and blending of the three religious traditions took place for almost nine centuries. Then, political forces began to diminish the popular impact of religion.
- Have students scan the chapter to survey the timeline, photos, sub-headings, vocabulary terms, etc.
- Once students have read this section thoroughly, challenge two or three students to sum up this section with one carefully chosen statement. (For instance: 1) *Chinese religion isn't just one religion, but a blend of several religions—ancient folk religions, Confucianism, Taoism, and Buddhism* or 2) *After almost 3,000 years of persecutions, political change and the introduction of*

new religions, Chinese religion is a composite of diverse religious ideas and practices.) Let the class vote for the sentence that best sums up the material.

- Ask students: When did the Chinese veneration of ancestors begin? *(With the Shang dynasty that ruled China from the sixteenth to the eleventh centuries BCE.)* Were they monotheistic? *(No, they believed in many gods, but the principle and most powerful god was Ti).* What was divination? *(The belief that one could predict the future by accurately interpreting natural signs such as a cloud formation, cracks in a tortoise's shell, the stars, etc.)*

- Select two students to sit "on the hot seat" at the front of the class to talk collaboratively about ancestor veneration in the Chinese culture. Remind them to include such facts as: *Why it was done? Who did it? How was it done? What were the expected consequences if it wasn't done? When was it done?*

- Ask the students to describe how Chinese people during the Shang dynasty pictured the afterlife? Add that even today, Chinese people venerate their deceased relatives with visits to their graves where they leave items commonly used during life—a toothbrush, comb, towel, slippers, etc. Paper reproductions of valued objects such as a car or TV are also burned as offerings. The living view ancestors as "guardian angels" who protect them from serious accidents or guide them in life.

- Show portions of the film *Believing*, Heart of the Dragon series, that traces the strands of religious belief in China.

- Talk about the major gods worshipped during the Shang and then the Chou dynasties. During the Shang dynasty, the "highest" god was called "Ti." During the Chou era, the major god was called "T'ien." Ancestors were seen as intermediaries between T'ien and people on earth. The ancestors had power to grant good fortune. Because of their power and influence, ancient Chinese people were concerned about doing sacrificial rituals very carefully.

Extending the Text

- Read and discuss the "Words of Confucius" feature on page 292. What does he say about changes in his attitudes toward life and responsibility?

- Call on several students to explain the "Mandate of Heaven," a concept about responsible government and leadership that became popular during the Chou Dynasty. Ask students if they are impressed by such a concept—the belief that those who rule have a divine responsibility to do so fairly.

- A major belief of the ancient Chinese was known as *yin and yang*, that is the harmonious play of pairs of opposites. Yin and yang are complementary forces in nature. Yin and yang also point to the great value Chinese put on harmony and balance. One needs the other. They are not in conflict with each other. They are opposite and complementary.

- To further illustrate the idea of yin and yang, have the students suggest pairs of opposites (such as success and failure, infants and the elderly, freedom and constraints, etc.) Write them on the board. Next, have the students share ways these pairs of opposites could suggest balance and harmony.

- You can also illustrate yin and yang by distributing copies of the handout, "Who Knows What's Good or Bad?" It can be found on page 199 of the Teacher's Manual. This illustrates the Chinese concept of what is good and what is bad may not be fixed or unchanging. Make it clear that in this context "good and bad" do not refer to moral judgments; they describe whether an event is "lucky" or "unlucky." Assign the story for individual reading. Then have the students discuss the follow-up questions with a partner.

- Refer to the Reflection Questions about thinking your ideas would be a remedy to a problem on page 285. Start with an example in your own life, but invite students to share their own experiences or respond to the question about self-esteem. Point out that for Confucius, the answer to the problems of his society was to return to the wisdom of the ancients, to learn to be a *chun-tzu*, a "superior man." A *chun-tzu* was not one who lorded over another human person. Rather, a "superior man" was one of virtuous character whose person and behaviors influenced family and society for the good.

- Provide students with a collection of the sayings of Confucius from the *Analects*. Have students pick two or three related sayings and write a sixty-second public service style radio ad about the way these sayings can still provide practical advice today. Have students read their ads in class and submit a half dozen or more to the local public radio station for consideration.

- Conclude this section by tying in the history and development of Buddhism in China. With the influence of folk religion, Taoism, Confucianism, and Buddhism, the Chinese religious vision is really like a quilt—colorful and pieced together from many different materials.

Section Review Questions and Answers

1. Briefly describe these elements of Chinese religion: ancestor worship, divination, astrology, and yin and yang.

   Ancestor worship refers to various ways of showing respect and reverence for family members after their deaths. Worshippers bring offerings to their ancestors in order to obtain protection and guidance. Divination is the attempt to discover what underlies a present situation or what the future holds through the use of spiritual practices like Tarot card reading or the casting of bones. Astrology is a common form of divination. The configuration of the stars and planets were omens for either good or evil. Solar eclipses were usually particularly bad signs since the covering of the sun created darkness, an evil omen. Literally, yin and yang means "shaded" and "sunny" respectively. Yin is the female, dark, negative force in the universe while yang is the male, bright, positive force in the universe. Yin and yang are opposite, but complementary extremes in Chinese culture.

2. What was the Confucian ideal of education?

   The Confucian ideal of education was not merely an accumulation of knowledge, but an important means to build character.

3. What did the celestial masters of Taoism emphasize for temporal and spiritual matters?

   The celestial masters of Taoism emphasized for temporal and spiritual matters both political renewal and self-perfection.

4. How is Buddhism linked with Taoism?

   Buddhism was closely tied with Taoism with its various ascetical practices, the use of magic, and the emphasis on the attainment of immortality.

2. Sacred Stories and Sacred Scriptures (pages 293–297)

Confucian Classics and *Tao Te Ching*

Objective

In this section the students will:

- learn that the *Tao Te Ching*, the most widely read piece of Chinese literature, was likely written by followers of Lao-tzu in the first few centuries after his death;
- recognize that the sacred writings of Confucianism can be divided into the Five Classics and the Four Books;
- realize that neither Confucius nor Lao-tzu created any of the writings connected with their religious traditions.

Preview

Neither Confucius nor Lao-tzu claimed to begin a new religion. Nor did they claim any divine revelation with regard to either scripture or beliefs. Confucian teachings are found not only in his writings, but also in popular culture with the phrase, "Confucius says . . ." The sacred writings of Confucianism are called the Confucian Classics. They are divided into two main groups of writings: the *Five Classics* and the *Four Books*. The Five Classics are *The Shu Ching* ("Classic of History"), *The Shih Ching* ("Classic of Poetry"), *The Li* ("Classic of Rituals"), *The Ch'un Ch'iu* ("Spring and Autumn Annals"), and *The I Ching* ("Classic of Changes"). The great writings attributed to Lao-tzu, the *Tao Te Ching*, have been passed on primarily in written form with its translations in many languages.

Using the Test

- Display some popular images of Confucius and briefly recap the history of Confucianism from the Han Dynasty which fell from power in the third century CE. There are many reasons why Confucius is known as the "father of Chinese culture."
- Display and pass around some English translations of the writings of Confucius that are typically available in most public libraries. His writings included historical documents, poems, instruction about divination, works on the principles of "li," or proper conduct.
- Remind students that the *Five Classics*, though attributed to Confucius, predate him. He built on these older traditions and used them as the foundation for his own teaching. Ask students to suggest some teachings about life and relationships that "will never be out of date."
- Let students know that whether Lao-tzu was really a historical figure is questionable. Clearly, the foundational work of Taoism, the *Tao Te Ching*, was written over a period of time rather than at one period of time by a single person. Taoism also overlaps both religion and philosophy.

Extending the Text

- Show a selected portion of the film, *Taoism: A Question of Balance* from the Long Search Video Series to review what students have read about Lao-tzu and Taoism.
- Share this passage from the *Tao Te Ching*: "To remain whole, be twisted. To become stagnant, let yourself be bent. To become full, be hollow." Ask the students how it represents *wu-wei*, a

Tao concept that means "without action," referring to the way that nature evolves best without human interference.

- Have students individually read the feature, "The Story of Tung Yung" on pages 296–297 as an example of Confucian values. Then assign the Reflection Question about sacrifices made for families on page 297. Suggest that students write a half-page or more about what they would be willing to do to support their family in need.

- Have the students individually review the Section Summary Statements and the Section Review Questions on their own.

Section Review Questions and Answers

1. What are the two main categories within the *Confucian Classics*?

   The two main categories of the Confucian Classics are the Five Classics and the Four Books.

2. What is Tao?

   Tao refers to the nature of things. Those who live in harmony with Tao learn to live a life of simplicity.

3. What makes up the *Analects*?

   The Analects are the sayings of Confucius.

4. Who likely authored the *Tao Te Ching*?

   It's likely that the followers of Lao-tzu, rather than Lao-tzu himself, drew on ancient writings as well as his own work to create the Tao Te Ching.

3. Beliefs and Practices (pages 297–304)

Confucianism and *Taoism* and *Chinese Living*

Objective

In this section the students will:

- familiarize themselves with the teachings of Confucius;
- learn about the tenets of Taoism;
- review how the scriptures of Confucianism and Taoism developed;
- become acquainted with some of the applications of the teachings of Confucianism and Taoism.

Preview

Confucianism put its greatest stress on proper relationships in Chinese society. Confucius maintained that since the high god "Heaven" was perfect, people should strive for personal relationships that were perfect. The person who attained perfection was called *chun-tzu* or "the superior one." Confucius thought it was important to teach any interested male about proper relationships and character building. Two principles—the principles of li and jen—were thought to provide guidelines to living out Chinese culture. Li called for courtesy, etiquette, and respect and flowed from the basic goodness of the person. It guided people towards proper behavior in the five common relationships in Chinese society. Jen had to do with benevolence and a person's heart rather than relationships. Confucius taught that if a person combined and lived out li with jen, he or she was in position to be a *chun-tzu*, a superior one. Taoism, on the other hand, was more difficult to define. Taoism studies the nature of things and instructs its practitioners to "go with the flow." Taoism stresses simplicity and harmony with all creation.

Using the Text

- Reemphasize that Confucius lived in a world that was very chaotic, and he sought to return Chinese society to moral greatness. He taught that developing one's moral character—and not accumulating knowledge or power—was the mark of a superior person. A superior person was able to live out the principles of li and jen.
- Review the meaning of li with students. Enlist the input from students to imagine what li, proper behavior, would have meant in ancient China. Li was to be used in five common relationships in Chinese society.
- Have students role-play short scenarios in which li is demonstrated between an emperor and subject; father and son; husband and wife; elder brother and younger brother; and between two male friends. Remind students to "play" these roles as contemporaries of Confucius although the use of a little twenty-first century humor is okay if the point is made.
- In the spirit of li, assign students to write several modern rules of courtesy and respect for other common relationships they know of. For example, how should a teacher and student relate? What about an employer and employee? Coach and player? Boyfriend and girlfriend?
- Present some basic principles of Taoism, contrasting them with Confucianism. Suggest that students take notes to put important points about each religious tradition on paper.

Extending the Text

- Ask students to imagine a modern figure called "Reverend Jackson Confucius." He is a contemporary spiritual leader and writer who is trying to spread the message about the importance of personal character. Invite pairs of interested students to create a five minute dialogue between a television talk show host and Confucius. Discussion should include the way people need to act and treat each other, how the "superior one" is not the powerful, popular, or glamorous individual, etc.

- Distribute copies of the "Chinese Religion Word Search" from page 200 of the Teacher's Manual. Students should complete these on their own as a preliminary chapter review of Chinese terms.

- Read or summarize the text, pointing out that Taoism advocates wu-wei, action without action. Wu-wei is not passive. Rather, it is people acting in harmony with nature, a "go with the flow" or "letting go" attitude. However, while Confucianism sought harmony in the social order, Taoism believes that to live in harmony with nature is the goal. While Confucius pressed his students to action, Lao-tzu invited his followers to "action without action."

- Direct students to the Watts article, *Experiencing Taoism*. Ask students if the article gives a better picture of what is meant by the mysterious wu-wei.

- Brainstorm with students to create a list of two-faced actions taken by their peers. Then create a list of honest and sincere actions done by their peers. Have students write or discuss the Reflection Question about being phony or "two faced" on page 299.

- Show portions of the film *Confucius: Words of Wisdom*.

- To check student understanding, ask: What is wu-wei? (*action without action*) What do Taoists believe about immortality? (*physical immortality is possible*) Who do Taoists worship as gods? (*hsiens, Buddha, bodhisattvas, and other Chinese gods*)

- Share some additional information about Buddhism's influence on Chinese religions with students. Let them know that several centuries after the *Tao Te Ching* was written, Buddhism became more and more influential in China. Buddhist influences can be found in Taoism, especially the belief in immortality. Taoists believed that physical immortality could be achieved through maintaining a perfect balance with nature. Another Buddhist influence that made its way into Taoism was the establishment of temples where the Buddha and bodhisattvas were worshipped.

- Make sure students can give examples of how various religious traditions have blended into American culture.

- Have students read through the Section Summary Statements and the Section Review Questions.

Section Review Questions and Answers

1. Explain the meaning of li and jen. How do they compliment one another?

   Li has to do with the proper way to live. Li calls for courtesy, etiquette, formality, and respect. Li also calls for sincerity in these gestures, teaching that they should flow from the basic goodness of the person. Li focuses on an ideal way of behaving for five common relationships in Chinese society. Jen refers to "humanity" or "benevolence." While li points outward toward behavior, jen points inward to one's heart. A person who combines li with jen is in position to be a chun-tzu, a "superior one."

2. Define Tao.

    Tao literally means "the way;" it is considered the driving force of the universe.

3. Explain wu-wei by giving at least one example.

    Wu-wei means "without action"; it centers on allowing nature to evolve without human action. For example, the emotions a painting can evoke just by hanging in a gallery are a form of wu-wei.

4. How do Taoists picture immortality?

    Taoists believe that physical immortality is attainable. Life, they believe is a delicate balance between yin and yang, and if that balance could be maintained, death could be avoided and immortality achieved. To achieve that balance, Taoists engage in breath control, good hygiene, certain elixirs, meditation, and proper rituals. Taoists might also refrain from eating certain foods like grain and meat.

5. How does the saying "Chinese are Confucian in public, Taoists in private, and Buddhist with regard to death" help to describe the Chinese integration of religion?

    The saying helps to describe the Chinese integration of religion in that the Chinese have a broad spectrum of beliefs and practices that are woven so tightly into Chinese culture that the only way to make distinctions is to take the threads out piece by piece. However, systematically removing the threads would weaken the fabric of society.

4. Sacred Time (pages 304–309)

Festivals and *Life Cycles*

Objective

In this section the students will:

- become familiar with the arrangement of the Chinese calendar, a lunar calendar;
- explore the Chinese festivals of the New Year, Ching Ming, Tin Hau, Tuen Ng, and Mid Autumn;
- learn how key events in the Chinese life cycle are celebrated.

Preview

Although the Gregorian calendar was adopted in China in 1912, the Chinese still generally regard the date prescribed in the 354-day Chinese lunar calendar as the beginning of their New Year. The Chinese New Year takes place sometime between late January and late February and is the most important Chinese festival. In order to make the months of the lunar calendar correspond with the sun, a thirteenth month is added every two or three years. The text section examines the Chinese calendar, festivals, and life cycle events. Besides the Chinese New Year, a fifteen-day event, the Chinese celebrate Ching Ming or "Remembrance of Ancestors Day," Tin Hau, a celebration of the legendary eleventh-century girl who rescued her brothers from drowning, the Tuen Ng (Dragon Boat) Festival, and the Mid Autumn Festival. Life cycle events profiled in this section include those related to birth, the coming of age, marriage, and death.

Using the Text

- Assign five groups of students to read, research, and prepare oral reports on the five different festivals covered in this section. Each group should also create and present a visual display of their festival—probably a poster with festival photos and descriptions. A recommended site for Internet research is www.uh.edu/~fyang/china.htm.
- Alternatively, assign several other groups to research and present short reports on food served at Chinese festivals, Chinese music, Chinese games and pastimes, etc. Perhaps these groups can also cook and share some festival foods with the class.
- Provide more information on China's official family planning policy that grew out of China's desire for more aggressive national economic growth. The policy consisted of encouraging late marriages, family planning, late child-bearing, and fewer births. Single-child families were strongly encouraged and even mandated. Rural couples were permitted to have two children if they kept four years between births. For cultural reasons, boys were preferred over girls. Question students to make sure they understand the cultural reasons for the emphasis on boys.
- There are several websites with information on traditional Chinese weddings. Ask the students (individually or in small groups) to research and share more information about the various stages of Chinese weddings.

Extending the Text

- Invite a guest speaker to share with the class about his or her own experience of Chinese lifestyles and celebrations.
- Direct students wanting extra credit opportunities to the Research and Activities listing on page 319. Allow ten days to two weeks for completion of the projects.
- Show portions of the film *Confucius: Words of Wisdom.* DVD. (A&E Biography, 1996, 50 minutes)
- Use the Section Summary Statements and the Section Review Questions to orally review the material covered in this section with the students.

Section Review Questions and Answers

1. Describe the Chinese New Year's celebration.

   The Chinese celebrate the Chinese New Year with family members exchanging small gifts, often money wrapped in a red packet. Another traditional part of the festival is "Kai Nien" or "Squabble Day," so called because it is believed that if you argue on this day, many arguments will follow during the rest of the year. On the fourth day of the festival Tso Kwan ("Slave Master") is welcomed back, and a new picture is hung in the kitchen. On the fifteenth day of the festival, a three day lantern celebration begins. Lanterns are hung in homes promoting good fortune, health, and happiness. The celebration of lanterns ends the New Year's festivities.

2. Why is the birth of a boy preferred over the birth of a girl in Chinese culture?

   In the Chinese culture, it is a boy who carries on the family name, takes care of the parents in old age, and sees to it that ancestors are cared for.

3. Name the six stages of a typical Chinese marriage.

   The six stages of a typical Chinese marriage are proposal, engagement, dowry, procession, wedding, and morning after.

5. Sacred Places and Sacred Spaces (pages 309–311)

Temples and *Shrines of Ancestors* and *Ancestor Gravesites*

Objective

In this section the students will:

- become familiar with how temples play a part in Chinese religion;
- learn about the importance of ancestor shrines and graves.

Preview

China's sacred places and spaces have suffered greatly since 1949. In that year, the Communist government took power and began its policy of trying to eradicate the rich and ancient religious traditions that were thousands of years old. Some temples were destroyed while others became government facilities. The government tightly controlled religious practices at the remaining Taoist, Buddhist, and even some Confucian temples. At these local temples, at ancestor shrines, and at gravesites, Chinese people who remained faithful to religious traditions continued to make offerings to the gods and their ancestors. Feng-shui, the art of divining a place or date with a fortunate spiritual aura, guided choices for gravesites and many other daily decisions people made.

Using the Text

Show photos of a variety of Chinese temples and perhaps some that have been converted into government facilities. Share some information about architectural design, how they were constructed, which ones were frequented by Chinese emperors, etc.

Extending the Text

- Invite several students to demonstrate the principles of feng-shui as its principles are currently applied to interior design, etc. There are many popular books available on this topic.
- Have students share their responses to the Reflection Question on Chinese religious freedom on page 310.
- Remind students to read through the Section Summary Statements and the Review Questions on page 311.

Section Review Questions and Answers

1. Why are there fewer Confucian temples in China now than there were prior to 1949?

   There are fewer Confucian temples in China now than there were prior to 1949 because that was the year of the Communist revolution in China. That take-over introduced many anti-religious sentiments and policies, including the destruction and closing of many religious buildings.

2. Define *feng-shui*.

   Feng-shui is the art of divining a place or date that has a positive spiritual aura.

6. Chinese Religions through a Catholic Lens (pages 311–317)

Ancestor Veneration in Chinese Religions and *Catholic Belief in the Communion of Saints* and *Ancestor Veneration in Catholic Ritual*

Objective

In this section the students will:

- see that Chinese death rituals show the influence of Confucianism, Taoism, Buddhism, and folk religions;
- become familiar with feng-shui rituals related to the selection of grave site, time of funeral, position of the body being buried;
- learn about the spirit tablet and the annual Ching Ming Festival traditions;
- recognize similarities between Chinese reverence of the dead and Catholic beliefs related to the communion of the saints;
- review the Chinese Rites Controversy and the Christian response that allows *inculturation*, which means blending religious and cultural traditions that don't contradict Christian teaching.

Preview

In this last section of the chapter, students will have a final chance to compare and contrast Chinese religions with Catholicism. Though these two religious traditions are fundamentally different in many respects, Chinese remembrance and reverence of the dead has significant place in Catholic practice as well. Chinese families invoke the principles of feng-shui to determine the grave location and time of funerals. They believe that such considerations will bring better fortune to the living and the dead. Catholic thinking would likely see such concerns as superstitious. Attention to the grave and family altar is also precisely detailed for Chinese families. Most of this responsibility falls to the oldest son and his family. In Catholic thinking, all the people of God are encouraged to honor their deceased loved ones and all the saints. They believe in the community or communion of saints. These saints can intercede with God, Catholics believe. For several centuries, Catholic missionaries thought that Chinese customs of ancestor veneration were problematic. The issue was known as the Chinese Rites Controversy. But since Chinese practices were deeply rooted, and didn't fundamentally contradict Catholic teaching, converts began to blend Chinese and Catholic practices. Bringing the Gospel to native peoples and incorporating rich indigenous cultures into the life of the Church is called inculturation.

Using the Text

- Recap this section which compares and contrasts Chinese and Catholic practices related to honoring the dead.
- Call on students to explain and give context for terms such as: spirit tablet, Ching Ming Festival, communion of saints, intercession, Chinese Rites Controversy, inculturation.

Extending the Text

- Call on a student to read aloud the Conclusion on page 317.
- Have students provide written answers to the Section Review Questions on pages 316–317 and the Chapter Review Questions on pages 318–319.

- Direct all the students briefly to the prayer from Lao-tzu on page 320. Read the prayer aloud together. Encourage students to offer spontaneous prayers for growing religious freedom for China.

- Show all or part of the video *A Question of Balance*. Though changes in China have been made since the time of the filming in 1977, it is still quite accurate with regard to Chinese religion.

- Save most of the last day of class spent on this chapter for review. Distribute copies of the "Chinese Religions Word Search" handout to each student. Have them quickly complete it to review the vocabulary words in this chapter. Continue reviewing with the class by asking questions based on the summary statements, vocabulary words, and review questions. Announce the test date for this chapter test.

Section Review Questions and Answers

1. Why are feng-shui masters used by families upon the death of a loved one?

   It is believed that feng-shui principles will assure a favorable or auspicious placement of the grave and a fortuitous time for the deceased's funeral. It is commonly believed that if the burial environment or time is not proper, misfortune will befall the family and its descendants.

2. Why can it be said that Chinese people do not worship their ancestors?

   The Chinese venerate but do not worship their ancestors. They believe that their ancestors are the "living dead" and are still part of the family. It is thought that the ancestors can have an influence over the good or bad fortune of a family or community.

3. What is the Ching Ming Festival?

   The Ching Ming Festival is an annual celebration for the ancestors. Families take special care to decorate and care for the graves of loved ones. They bring flowers, light candles, and gather to honor and remember their deceased family members.

4. In what creed is the belief in the "communion of saints" professed?

   In the Apostles' Creed, Catholics profess their belief in the "communion of saints," the belief that both the living and the dead are bound together as children of God and brothers and sisters in faith.

5. Why do the bishops of Asia wish to acknowledge and even incorporate some ancestor veneration rites into Catholic practices?

   After centuries of concern about the Chinese Rites Controversy, Catholic bishops in Asia now see that ancestor veneration traditions that were deeply rooted in the Chinese really didn't conflict with Catholic teachings at all. In fact, Asian bishops began to see that these practices provided common ground for Chinese Catholics and people who still practiced traditional Chinese religion.

Chinese Religion Word Search Answers

```
J  Q  I  E  Z  Y  Q  A  Y  U  H  N  R  L  D
Z  S  E  T  L  J  P  E  C  B  O  Y  D  I  Y
N  D  W  U  N  Y  Q  L  K  I  U  Q  V  X  A
Z  L  U  V  K  P  R  E  G  J  Z  I  Z  W  N
M  A  W  S  O  H  K  I  M  S  N  O  U  E  G
K  H  C  T  I  Y  L  E  P  A  V  S  N  C  B
L  E  I  D  R  E  G  F  T  B  P  W  G  H  Q
E  I  K  Q  R  C  A  I  E  I  E  V  A  U  B
G  D  O  K  B  K  O  J  I  N  V  J  W  N  S
G  L  L  V  S  N  U  M  H  Y  G  V  H  T  T
J  O  S  T  C  E  L  A  N  A  I  S  D  Z  S
F  O  W  Y  O  M  Y  J  U  Q  J  N  H  U  D
G  B  E  Q  N  A  G  X  N  Y  E  A  G  U  S
G  N  I  H  C  E  T  O  A  T  N  S  Y  B  I
S  V  N  W  K  Z  V  Y  K  M  X  C  W  I  X
```

Chapter 7 Review Questions and Answers

1. Why are ancestors so important to the Chinese?

   Ancestors are important to the Chinese because they are considered older, wiser members of the family unit. The older a person was at the time of death, the more honored.

2. Explain wu-wei.

   Wu-wei means "action without action." For example, an adult looking at an infant evokes a smile on the face of the adult, but the infant did nothing to solicit that reaction.

3. What are two common relationships on which li is focused?

   Two examples are the relationship between emperor and subject or the relationship between father and son.

4. How has Buddhism influenced Chinese religion?

   Buddhist temples, monasteries, and the monastic lifestyle have influenced Chinese religion. In addition, the Buddhist notion of immortality has greatly influenced Taoism.

5. What would a person who kept a balance between yin and yang achieve?

   According to Taoists, a person who kept a balance between yin and yang could avoid death and achieve immortality.

6. How does the ultimate goal for a Confucian compare with the ultimate goal of a Taoist?

   While the ultimate goal of a Confucian was to be a chun-tzu, the goal of a Taoist is immortality.

7. What are some steps a Taoist might take to achieve immortality?

   Taoists believe that physical immortality is an achievable goal. It is achieved through union with Tao. Taoists engage in special practices such as breath control, good hygiene, certain elixirs, meditation, and rituals that contribute to immortality. They also often refrain from eating certain foods such as grains and meat.

8. How do li and jen complement each other?

   Li is the proper way to conduct relationships. It calls for courtesy, etiquette, formality, and respect. Jen points one inward to the ways of the heart. They complement each other because li orders relationships with others while jen directs our attention inward, towards the heart.

9. Why is it believed that Taoism predates Confucianism?

   It is believed that Taoism predates Confucianism because the Tao Te Ching, the Taoist sacred writings, is drawn from writings that were in existence centuries before Confucianism.

10. What is the *Tao Te Ching*?

   The Tao Te Ching, meaning the "Book of the Way," is the main body of sacred writings of the Taoists. The Tao Te Ching is the source of the Taoist beliefs, that is, that Tao is the nature of things, that all that emanates from Tao returns to Tao, the power of wu-wei (non-action), and the call to live a life of simplicity in harmony with Tao.

11. Explain why most Chinese may not be able to explain the origins of their religion or the differences between it and another religion.

   Many Chinese may not be able to explain the origins of their religion or the differences between it and another religion because there is great integration in Chinese religion, especially among Confucianism, Taoism, and Buddhism. The integration of these three religious traditions is so interwoven that the average Chinese could not distinguish one from another, for all are part of the tapestry of their lives.

12. Briefly describe these elements of Chinese religion: ancestor veneration, divination, astrology, and yin and yang.

   Ancestor veneration is the honoring of deceased family members with prescribed rituals such as decorating the graves with flowers, lit candles, and items needed by these "living dead" in the afterlife. Divination is the attempt to gather knowledge by the interpretation of omens or supernatural events such as reading Tarot cards or interpreting the casting of bones. Astrology is the attempt to interpret the stars and their formations. The forces of yin and yang refer to the complementary and harmonious interaction of opposites such as good and evil, light and dark, cold and hot, male and female.

13. List similarities and differences between Chinese ancestor veneration and Catholic veneration of saints.

   The Chinese veneration of ancestors is similar to the Catholic veneration of saints in many ways. Both often honor the remembered person by decorating the burial site with flowers and lit candles. Veneration also typically involves prayer. Catholics, however, ask saints to intercede for them to God. Chinese tradition assumes that ancestors have some independent power to affect their fortunes— negatively or positively. The Chinese also believe that the violent or sudden death of an ancestor can bring misfortune to the family and community.

Chapter 7 Test Answers

Multiple Choice (3 points each)

1. b, 2. c, 3. b, 4. a, 5. d, 6. a, 7. a, 8. d, 9. a, 10. b, 11. b, 12. d, 13. d, 14. a, 15. b, 16. b, 17. a, 18. c, 19. d, 20. b

Short Answer (8 points each)

1. The five relationships of li are emperor to subject, father to son, husband to wife, elder brother to younger brother, and friend to friend (males).

2. Tao translates as "the way, path, or course," though any definition falls short.

3. The Chinese honor ancestors at local temples, home shrines, and graves.

4. Divination is an ancient Chinese practice of discovering what underlies a present situation or what the future holds through the use of spiritual practices like Tarot card reading or the casting of bones.

5. Lao-tzu is known as a Chinese philosopher who lived in the fifth century BCE and is credited as the founder of Taoism.

Who Knows What's Good or Bad?

Once upon a time there was a farmer whose horse ran away. A neighbor came to console him, since it was the farmer's only horse. The farmer replied, "Who knows what is good or bad?"

The next day the horse returned with a herd of wild horses close behind. Hearing the thunderous noise of the horses' hoofs, the neighbor returned to the farmer gleefully rejoicing. The farmer only said, "Who knows what is good or bad?"

The third day the farmer's son went into the coral to break one of the horses. But the horse threw the son off so fiercely that the son broke his leg. Again the neighbor came by to give the farmer his condolences. The farmer replied, "Who knows what is good or bad?"

Several months later some government officials came to the property of the farmer seeking to draft his son. However, because of the son's broken leg, his draft was deferred. Once more the neighbor came by to congratulate the farmer on his good fortune. The farmer again replied, "Who knows what is good or bad?"

- What is the point of the farmer's words, "Who knows what is good or bad?"
- What does this story say about harmony and balance?
- Tell about a time something that at first seemed to be bad turned out to be good.
- Tell about a time something that at first seemed to be good turned out to be bad.

Chinese Religions Word Search

Test your skills on terms associated with Chinese religions by completing this word search. Words can be found horizontally, vertically, or diagonally. Words may be spelled from left to right or right to left, from top to bottom, or from bottom to top. Letters may overlap between two words.

```
J  Q  I  E  Z  Y  Q  A  Y  U  H  N  R  L  D
Z  S  E  T  L  J  P  E  C  B  O  Y  D  I  Y
N  D  W  U  N  Y  Q  L  K  I  U  Q  V  X  A
Z  L  U  V  K  P  R  E  G  J  Z  I  Z  W  N
M  A  W  S  O  H  K  I  M  S  N  O  U  E  G
K  H  C  T  I  Y  L  E  P  A  V  S  N  C  B
L  E  I  D  R  E  G  F  T  B  P  W  G  H  Q
E  I  K  Q  R  C  A  I  E  I  E  V  A  U  B
G  D  O  K  B  K  O  J  I  N  V  J  W  N  S
G  L  L  V  S  N  U  M  H  Y  G  V  H  T  T
J  O  S  T  C  E  L  A  N  A  I  S  D  Z  S
F  O  W  Y  O  M  Y  J  U  Q  J  N  H  U  D
G  B  E  Q  N  A  G  X  N  Y  E  A  G  U  S
G  N  I  H  C  E  T  O  A  T  N  S  Y  B  I
S  V  N  W  K  Z  V  Y  K  M  X  C  W  I  X
```

1. contains the sayings of Confucius

2. "superior one"

3. the attempt to discover what underlies a present situation or what the future holds through the use of spiritual practices like Tarot card reading or the casting of bones

4. the art of divining a place or date that has a positive spiritual aura

5. non-institutional religious beliefs and practices of a culture or a group of people

6. the highest virtue in Confucianism

7. authorship of this attributed to Lao-tzu

8. action without action

9. "shady," the female, dark, negative force in the universe

10. "sunny," the male, bright, positive force in the universe

Chapter 7 Test

Name _____

Multiple Choice. *Write the letter of the best choice in the space provided.* (3 points each)

_____ 1. Chinese religion is
  a. mono-religious.
  b. multi-religious.
  c. panthe-religious.
  d. none of the above

_____ 2. Through much of the history of China, Chinese religion and the Chinese government
  a. exercised the separation of church and state.
  b. were constantly in conflict with each other.
  c. were closely connected.
  d. had little to do with each other.

_____ 3. For Taoism, the call to "let go"
  a. is seen as irresponsible.
  b. is the only way to be in harmony with nature.
  c. means to leave nature alone.
  d. happens only if one is a Taoist.

_____ 4. For Confucius the greatest virtue is
  a. benevolence.
  b. courtesy.
  c. proper behavior.
  d. social etiquette.

_____ 5. Which of the following is *not* an example of wu-wei:
  a. seeing a very good friend from a distance
  b. admiring a beautiful statue
  c. a sleeping puppy
  d. chairing a committee

_____ 6. Reverence for ancestors is important for the living because
  a. ancestors are still part of the family.
  b. the living do not want the ghosts of the ancestors to haunt them.
  c. when a family member dies, they become deities.
  d. ancestors demand to be reverenced.

_____ 7. All the Chinese festivals have something to do with
  a. appeasing the gods, spirits, or ancestors.
  b. the position of the moon.
  c. the Chinese New Year.
  d. local deities.

_____ 8. All are an example of feng-shui except
    a. securing a wedding date.
    b. the position of furniture in a room.
    c. flowers in front of a statue.
    d. watching television.

_____ 9. The funeral rite for the majority of Chinese
    a. is Buddhist in nature.
    b. is Taoist in nature.
    c. is Confucian in nature.
    d. is a ceremony of divination.

_____ 10. According to Taoists, this element of a human person is used the most:
    a. intellect
    b. intuition
    c. attitude
    d. senses

_____ 11. Wu-wei
    a. requires people to do nothing.
    b. requires a "letting go."
    c. is passive.
    d. is laissez-faire.

_____ 12. Confucius's great desire in life was to be a
    a. teacher.
    b. pupil.
    c. sage.
    d. public official.

_____ 13. Which of the following is _not_ an example of divination?
    a. throwing odd shaped bones in a temple
    b. astrology
    c. fortune telling
    d. ancestor worship

_____ 14. In Confucianism, a chun-tzu
    a. has authority by way of character.
    b. has authority by way of birth.
    c. has no authority.
    d. does not want authority.

_____ 15. A traditional Chinese marriage has _____ stages.
    a. five
    b. six
    c. seven
    d. eight

_____ 16. Which of the following is a Taoist virtue:
   a. patience
   b. simplicity
   c. honor
   d. courage

_____ 17. For Confucius, jen is the highest virtue for
   a. relationships.
   b. ancestor worship.
   c. appeasing the gods.
   d. building character.

_____ 18. The Chinese communist revolution
   a. was indifferent toward religion.
   b. denied the existence of religion.
   c. was quite hostile toward religion.
   d. was lukewarm toward religion.

_____ 19. Boys are important in Chinese culture because
   a. they carry on the family name.
   b. they are considered gods.
   c. they are responsible for arranging marriages for all siblings.
   d. both *a* and *c*

_____ 20. Confucianism puts great stress on
   a. the political climate.
   b. tradition.
   c. nature.
   d. society.

Short Answers. *Briefly answer the following questions.* (8 points each)

1. List the five relationships of li.

2. What is the meaning of Tao?

3. How do the Chinese honor their ancestors?

4. Define divination.

5. Who was Lao-tzu?

Chapter 8: Japanese Religions

Introduction

Like Chinese religion, Japanese religion is a combination of both indigenous and imported religious traditions. Indigenous Japanese religious traditions of folk religion and Shinto are combined with Chinese religions (Confucianism, Taoism, and Buddhism) to create the unique Japanese religion. Because Confucianism, Taoism, and Buddhism have been discussed in previous chapters, this chapter will emphasize the indigenous religion of Japan, Shinto. However, the other religious traditions are not to be pushed to the background. They take on a distinctively Japanese flavor.

Shinto had its origins before the writing of Japanese history. In fact, both the name and written word Shinto were brought to Japan from China via Korea. Shinto is from the Chinese word *shin tao* meaning "way of the kami." (Kami translates as spirits or deities). The Japanese believe kami are found in all of nature. Kami are also known to be found in exemplary people. In general, it can be said that kami are the life force and blessing to the Japanese people.

Shinto has no formalized doctrine, ethical code, or scripture. Rather, rituals and festivals are the chief religious actions in Shinto. Rituals can take place either at a home or a public shrine. Purity before approaching kami is essential.

Though Shinto has no divinely inspired scriptures, there are two documents that chronicle the ancient story of Japan in myth and history. The *Kojiki* (*Record of Ancient Matters)* and the *Nihonshoki* (*Chronicles of Japan*) were written in the eighth century BCE, and each includes the Japanese creation myth that defined Japan as a nation and people of divine origin. In fact, until Japan's defeat in World War II, the emperor of Japan was considered to be divine.

The second major religious influence in Japan is Buddhism. Again, imported from China via Korea, Ch'an Buddhism in China became Zen Buddhism in Japan. With its unique form of monasticism and its important role in Japanese funerals, Buddhism has had a major influence in Japan.

Like the Chinese, the Japanese see no conflict in engaging in several religious traditions at the same time. It may be a Shinto prayer at a shrine, a Buddhist funeral, and memorial services for ancestors at the family home, a Confucian social structure, or a Christian wedding. Japanese festivals ("matsuri") are prime examples of Japanese religion as an amalgamation of several religious traditions.

This chapter focuses on Shinto and how it intersects with other religions of Chinese origin.

Resources for Chapter 8

Books

Anesaki, Masaharu. *History of Japanese Religion with Special Reference to the Social and Moral Life of the Nation.* New York: Columbia University Press, 1995.

Bocking, Brian. A *Popular Dictionary of Shinto.* Lincolnwood, IL: NTC Group, 1997.

Breen, John, and Mark Teeuwen. *Shinto in History: Ways of the Kami.* Honolulu: University of Hawaii Press, 2000.

Earhart, H. Byron. *Japanese Religion: Unity and Diversity.* 4th ed. Belmont, CA: Wadsworth Publishing, 2004.

Havens, Norman. *Kami.* Tokyo: Institute for Japanese Culture and Classics, Kokugakuin University, 1998.

Holtom, Daniel Clarence. *The National Faith of Japan: A Study of Modern Shinto.* New York: Columbia University Press, 1995.

Kasahara, Kazuo. *A History of Japanese Religion.* Tokyo: Kosei Publishing Company, 2001.

Kitagawa, Joseph Mitsuo. *On Understanding Japanese Religion.* Princeton: Princeton University Press, 1987.

Nelson, John K. *A Year in the Life of a Shinto Shrine.* Seattle: University of Washington Press, 1996.

Sullivan, Lawrence Eugene. *Nature and Rite in Shinto.* Philadelphia: Chelsea House Publishers, 2001.

Audio-visual Resources

Spirits of the State: Japan's Yasukuni Shrine. DVD/VHS. (Films Media Group, 2004, 28 minutes)

The Land of the Disappearing Buddha—Japan. The Long Search Video Series. DVD/VHS (Ambrose Video Publishing, 2001, 60 minutes). Study Guide available for separate purchase.

Internet Resources

Contemporary Papers on Japanese Religion— www2.kokugakuin.ac.jp/ijcc/wp/cpjr/index.html

Shinto Documents— www.sacred-texts.com/shi/index.htm

Shinto Online Network Association— www.jinja.or.jp/english/s-0.html

Shinto: The Way of the Gods— www.trincoll.edu/zines/tj/tj4.4.96/articles/cover.html

Heavenly Origins (pages 323–325)

1. A Brief History of Japanese Religions (pages 325–335)

The Chinese Influence and *The Expansion of Buddhism* and *The Modern Period*

Objective

In this section the students will:

- discuss the Japanese creation myth and the role it plays in Japanese identity;
- review the timeline of Japanese religious history;
- become familiar with animism and its pervasive impact on Japanese culture.
- sort out and explore the threads of Japanese religion—Zen Buddhism, Confucianism, Taoism, folk religion, and Shinto.
- explore the introduction and rejection of Christianity in the sixteenth century and the reasons for it.

Preview

The opening text in "Heavenly Origins" presents the primary Japanese creation myth. Traditionally this myth has been the source for explaining Japan's identity as a people. It tells us that even the land itself was created by the deities and is, therefore, the center of the world. The leaders of the people—and the imperial throne—were also divine, according to this myth. The divine nature of the land has also been played out in Japanese religion with the stress on the importance of nature and natural settings for worship space. In the timeline and in A Brief History of Japanese Religions, students will see that many other religious and cultural influences helped to shape Japanese religion. Japan was always fascinated with China, and was eager to welcome Chinese religious traditions to the island. The Japanese adopted Confucian education and li, but they were most interested in Buddhism. Ch'an (a combination of Buddhism and Taoism) in China became Zen in Japan. For several centuries Buddhism was the state religion of Japan. However, folk religion and Shinto never disappeared.

Using the Text

- After students have read "Heavenly Origins" and up to "The Chinese Influence" on page 327, ask them to respond to the Reflection Question about what they've learned about God from nature on page 331, and the question on page 327 about a national myth for their own country. (If the weather is accommodating, take the students outside for a closer look at nature around them.) Both of these questions dig below the surface; support students attempting to answer. Sum up some of the material presented about Japan's creation myth and its major historical events.
- Read some short American myths such as the story of Paul Bunyan and Babe the Blue Ox, and Johnny Appleseed. Invite students to comment on these myths (or other American myths) and how they may have helped Americans to describe the courage needed to tame the American wilderness or to explain the abundance and rich productivity of this new world.

- Tell students they may explore the book before they answer the following questions. *1) How are "kami" the major source of Japanese religion? 2) What does the creation myth say about Japan's national identity? 3) Why did the Japanese become interested in Chinese religions—Confucianism and Taoism?*
- Trace the origins and rise of Zen Buddhism in Japan. Though meditation is the heart of Zen Buddhism, manual labor and artistic creativity are also integral parts of a Zen monk's life. Of particular interest is the artistic work of Zen Buddhists (both lay and monastic). Zen Buddhist artistry exclusively has nature as its topic.
- Have students count off by threes, and assign each group to one of the three subsections: "The Chinese Influence," "The Expansion of Buddhism" and "The Modern Period." Have each student in these groups write five fill-in-the-blank questions from their subsection. Answers should be in parentheses beneath each question. Collect the questions and assign a team of four students to create a fill-in-the blank test of the best 25 questions. Have the team offer the test as a reviewing tool.

Extending the Text

- Show all or parts of the twenty-eight-minute film *Spirits of the State: Japan's Yasukuni Shrine*. Ask students if they see evidence of the deep Japanese reverence for nature. Can they pinpoint any elements of Buddhist influence, any Confucian practices, etc.?
- Present a more extensive explanation of koans and their role in motivating students of Zen to break through logic and intellectual thinking to intuitive insights or satoris. Give plenty of koan examples. Now, let students have some fun with this topic. Ask them to be quiet for a time in order to reflect and create koans. Let the class choose the best one. Ask them to answer the Reflection Question about koans on page 330.
- Invite several students to earn extra credit by presenting brief oral reports about the mission of St. Francis Xavier in Japan, Christian outreach there and the eventual backlash against Christianity in the late sixteenth century. Make sure that the students don't duplicate topics though they will certainly overlap. As an alternative, suggest that students consider giving a brief persuasive talk related to the Reflection Question on page 333 about living in a system that separates church from state.
- Relate the Japanese rejection of Christian and foreign influences to your local area. Are there any ways that students can identify a similar conflict when outside groups infiltrate a neighborhood or region and try to change it? Wrap this discussion into the Reflection Question on page 332 that discusses what it would be like to try to remove one culture's influence from a neighborhood.
- Read aloud the Section Summary statements on page 334.
- Have students write responses to the Section Review Questions and also answer the Reflection Question about a government system that separates church from state on page 333.

Section Review Questions and Answers

1. What role does the Japanese creation myth play in Japanese identity?

   The Japanese creation myth places Japan as the center of the world and its rulers as direct descendants of Amaterasu, the sun god. In short, the myth holds that Japan is of a divine origin.

2. Why might *kami* be a better word to describe Japanese religion than Shinto?

   Kami relates to any spiritual or sacred power. Kami permeates Japanese religion. There are thought to be eight million Kami divided into gods of the sky or gods of the soil.

3. What was the traditional role of the emperor in Japanese religion?

   The traditional role of the emperor in Japanese religion was that of a kami. The emperor was believed to be a direct descendant of the sun goddess, Amartasu.

4. Describe the differences between Soto Zen Buddhism and Rinzai Zen Buddhism.

   While Rinzai Zen believes a person can gain immediate enlightenment, Soto Zen believes enlightenment is a gradual process. While Soto Zen emphasizes a method of zazen, or sitting meditation, Rinzai places more emphasis on the koan.

5. What did the Meiji government restore?

   The Meiji government restored some of the imperial power that had been lost to the shogunates.

6. What happened to the Emperor Hirohito after World War II?

   Due to the defeat of the Japanese in World War II, Emperor Hirohito was forced to renounce his divinity.

7. What are "new religions" among Japanese religions?

   The "new religions" were really only resurfacing surges in the interest in Shinto and Buddhism at the beginning of the twentieth century. These movements shuffled and reintegrated elements of the older religious traditions into new movements or society. One of these so-called "new religions" was Soka Gakkai.

2. Sacred Stories and Sacred Scriptures (pages 335–336)

3. Beliefs and Practices (pages 336–340)

Kami and *Buddhism in Japan* and *Japanese Living*

Objective

In these sections the students will:

- learn about the origins, content, and use of the Shinto texts, the Kojiki and the Nihonshoki;
- become more familiar with kamis;
- recognize that Shinto does not have any divinely inspired texts;
- become aware of the special importance of the two virtues—harmony and loyalty;
- further explore how the Japanese understand themselves to be a divine people.

Preview

An important reality and unique trait to share with students about Japanese religions is that Shinto lacks formal doctrine, scripture, and ethical code. As students will discover, the one belief that permeates Japanese religion is kami. Kami are any kind of spiritual or sacred power found in animate and inanimate objects, as well as any kind of spiritual force or power. Thus things both human and divine are kami. Things of nature are also kami. Kami can be either a positive or negative force. For example, kami can protect or destroy a village due to volcanic eruption. This section not only covers kami in more detail, but offers a brief look at significant Shinto texts and the unique blending of religion, politics, and nature in Japan. Students will also become aware that unity and the values of harmony and loyalty are particularly important in Japanese society.

Using the Text

- Have students carefully read Sacred Stories and Sacred Scriptures and Beliefs and Practices through the feature on Mount Fuji (pages 337–338).
- Show some slides or hold up some pictures of natural scenes—including Mount Fuji—and ask, "In the Japanese view, is this (waterfall, mountain, pond, field, deer, etc.) 'sacred' or 'holy'? Why or why not? How does the Japanese culture and religious vision define 'holiness'?" (*Students will likely respond that Japanese religion sees the natural world as intrinsically good and holy. The kami "inhabit" the world in trees, mountains, people, etc.*) Add that some kami are also destructive—such as a tsunami or an earthquake.
- Point out that though the average American's image of the Japanese people focuses on their economic prowess and skill, in fact, the Japanese are truly a very religious people. While Americans tend to separate their religious and secular lives, the Japanese make no such distinctions. Hence, even daily rituals like drinking a cup of tea take on religious overtones to the Japanese.
- If possible, display some copies of the Shinto texts the *Kojiki* and the *Nihonshoki*. (See the Internet resource listing at the beginning of this chapter.) Elaborate on how these texts were used in the past and how they are used today.

Extending the Text

- Display a map of Japan, a nation made up of over 3,000 islands. Ask: "What role do you think geography plays in the Japanese self-understanding as a divine people? How do you think Japan's island status affects their self-understanding? Could this self-understanding have contributed to Japan's sense of destiny in shaping world events and its imperial outreach before and during World War II?"*(Remind students that Japan attacked Pearl Harbor, a U.S. Naval base in 1941, an act which forced the U.S. to declare war on Japan.)*

- Back up and refer students once again to the quotation from Professor Ninian Smart on page 339. Ask students how the virtues of loyalty and harmony made the Japanese formidable opponents for the U. S. during the war. (*Some students may have seen the Academy Award-winning films* Flags of Our Fathers (2006) *and* Letters from Iwo Jima (2007) *about the 1944–45 battle between the U.S. and Japan for control of the island of Iwo Jima.*)

- Point out that there have been many major cultural changes in Japanese society since the end of World War II. However, as a people, the Japanese still find it important to be in harmony with nature, politics, the kami, and each other. This emphasis on harmony with each other is manifested in the Confucian influence of li. The five relationships Confucius outlined ideally are to include loyalty to one another. For example, the subject is to be loyal to the superior. But the superior, in turn, must be loyal to his or her subjects.

- Engage students in discussion focused on the Reflection Question on page 340 about being preordained to accomplish something in life. Remind students that the Japanese people believed that they were a divine people with the emperor as their divine head. Ask: "What would be the implications for you, personally, and your nation if your fellow citizens believed themselves to have a divine origin? Would you see American foreign policy goals as divinely ordained? What about your own goals?"

- Assign students to research and write an essay on one of topics suggested in the Research and Activities feature 1 on page 353. Allow a week or more for completion of the topic and allow the substitution of other topics related to Japanese religion.

- Read through the Section Summary statements for both Sections 2 and 3. Ask students to answer the Review Questions for these sections.

Section Review Questions and Answers

Section 2

1. Name the two texts that contain the national myth of Japan.

   The two texts are the Kojiki (Record of Ancient Matters) and Nihonshoki (Chronicles of Japan).

2. For whom were the texts written?

   These texts were not written for the common people. They were addressed to the elite classes and to the imperial government.

Section 3

1. Besides being a name of Shinto gods, what does kami refer to?

   Kami also refers to whatever is sacred or powerful. Nature, such as mountains, rivers, trees, or rocks, can be kami. Human beings can be kami. The emperor, as representative of sun goddess Amaterasu, great warriors, poets, scholars, and wise ancestors are also kami.

2. Why are harmony and loyalty valued virtues in Japanese religion?

   Harmony describes how kami and people live together. Loyalty is the state that holds the five relationships of li together.

4. Sacred Time (pages 341–344)

Japanese Festivals and *Life Cycle*

Objective

In this section the students will:

- learn about a number of different Japanese festivals, called matsuri;
- become acquainted with the eclectic rites of passage that celebrate the Japanese life cycle;
- discover that the Japanese now use the Western or Gregorian calendar.

Preview

Prior to visiting a Shinto shrine a person washes, symbolizing purification from an impure world. This cleansing, called misogi, is one of the most important rituals in Shinto. Misogi is in stark contrast to matsuri, the name for Japanese festivals which emphasize the celebratory nature of Shinto worship. This section describes five festivals. Like festivals of many religious traditions, most matsuri are generally local. The festivals described in the student textbook have a more universal appeal. Begin by reading the opening paragraph, mentioning that although the Japanese once used a lunar calendar similar to the Chinese, Japanese now generally follow the Gregorian calendar.

Using the Text

- After students have finished reading this section, recap and elaborate on the major themes. Note that Japan's use of the Gregorian or Western calendar has undoubtedly strengthened its ability to develop as an economic power in Asia and in the world. Despite its relative lack of indigenous natural resources, Japan became an industrial nation second to none. State that this native flexibility and creativity probably also explains the eclectic nature of Japanese religion. This is best illustrated in rites of passage for the Japanese life cycle. Birth is generally a Shinto event. Weddings traditionally were a Shinto event, but more and more Japanese hold Christian weddings, even if neither the bride nor groom is Christian. Most funerals are Buddhist events, though some are Christian.
- Ask students to describe some of the matsuri they have read about. Are these festivals similar to other holidays or festivals they can think of? Tap student views about what makes a good holiday or feast.

Extending the Text

- Assign individuals or small groups to research more information about each of the festivals described in the text. Groups should find photos of the festival, and present additional information to the class about how they are celebrated.
- Suggest alternative research projects to students. Some may wish to report on and cook some typical matsuri foods. Another group might wish to create carp kites and demonstrate the art of flying them. Students interested in music could describe Japanese musical instruments and play some recorded examples to give students a feel for Japanese music. Some students may also want to report on and perhaps display traditional Japanese costumes such as the kimona. (Students could also simply display photos of the traditional costumes.)

- Give students copies of the "Japanese Religion Crossword Puzzle" from page 222 of the Teacher's Manual as a preliminary review of the chapter.
- Assign the Section Summary statements and the Section Review Questions on page 344.

Japanese Religions Crossword Puzzle Answers

Across

5. kamidana

7. shogunate

8. torii

9. hara kiri

Down

1. matsuri

2. koan

3. satori

4. zazen

6. kami

7. samurai

Section Review Questions and Answers

1. Why did Japan move to the Gregorian calendar?

   Japan moved to the Gregorian calendar because of its interest in competing with the Western world.

2. Describe what takes place on the Girls' Day festival.

   On the Girls' Day festival, parents arrange dolls that have been dressed in traditional Japanese court costumes on a tier to symbolize a princess wedding. The prince and princess are placed on the top of the tier and the dolls go down in rank to the court musicians at the bottom. Offerings of rice cakes, peach blossoms, and sweet white sake are set before this tier. The daughters themselves dress in kimonos and the families celebrate, wishing the girls health and happiness.

3. What happens on the fiftieth anniversary of a Japanese person's death?

   On the fiftieth anniversary of a Japanese person's death the deceased is considered to be truly an ancestor in the Japanese tradition.

5. Sacred Places and Sacred Spaces (pages 344–347)

Shinto Shrines and *The Grand Shrine at Ise*

Objective

In this section the students will:

- learn that the sacred places of Japanese religion are temples, shrines, and monasteries;
- view pictures of a variety of temples and shrines;
- review the history of the Grand Shrine at Ise.

Preview

The first Shinto shrines were built in places where it was believed the kami dwelt, especially around or near mountains, rivers, and waterfronts. Later, these shrines became connected with political concerns. This section looks at some of those shrines, as well as the home shrines prevalent in the rural areas of Japan. Students will also learn about torii, entrance gates made of two timber posts and two timber crossbeams that symbolically divide sacred space near the shrine from the profane world outside. The design and format for worship at local shrines, and the origins and history of the national shrine, the Grand Shrine at Ise, is also presented.

Using the Text

- Address an important characteristic of Japanese religion that students must understand. Since Shinto lacks formal scripture, doctrine, and ethical code great emphasis has been placed on ritual. Rituals takes place in shrines—home, local, or national.
- Call on students to describe how they would conduct prayer rituals if they were Japanese. How would home rituals be done? What about rituals done at the local shrine?
- Show and share images of a variety of Japanese shrines and temples. See if students can identify a kami body, the torii, the area in the shrine where devotees perform purification rituals, etc. Then share pictures of Japan's most glorious shrine, the Grand Shrine at Ise.

Extending the Text

- Discuss the tradition of the Japanese home shrine—a place to pray at home. What do they think of having a prayer place in their own homes?
- Ask the students to consider the entrances to their own churches. Can they describe the architectural features that symbolically separate the profane (secular) from the sacred (doorways, baptismal fonts, holy water, etc.).
- Ask the students to name the main or "grand" shrine, church, temple, or synagogue from other religious traditions they are familiar with. You may want to make this a research project for students to not only locate such places, but to write an essay and provide photos of these sites.
- Invite any interested students to earn extra credit by creating and displaying a visual (poster, collage, etc.) report on the mirror in Japanese religious tradition. Another topic might be the recent history (from the twentieth century) of the royal or imperial family. Students might also prefer to choose a project from Research and Activities 2 or 3.

Section Review Questions and Answers

1. Why do many Japanese homes have both Shinto and Buddhist shrines?

   The Shinto tradition emphasizes things of life such as birth, marriage, agriculture, or even a new job; the Buddhist emphasis is on the end of life and the afterlife. Offerings made by the head of the family to kami or a Buddhist deity seek blessings and protection for the family.

2. What is the significance of a torii at a shrine or temple?

   Symbolically, the torii separates the profane world outside from the sacred residence of the kami inside.

3. Name the typical elements in a Shinto worship service.

   The typical elements or procedures in a Shinto worship service are the rite of purification, the offering, and the prayer.

4. Why is the Grand Shrine at Ise significant for Japanese religion?

   The Grand Shrine at Ise is significant for Japanese religion because it was the location of the shrine for the imperial family in ancient Japan. At one time, the emperor acted as priest of that shrine.

6. Japanese Religions through a Catholic Lens (pages 347–350)

Sacred Time in Japanese Religions and *Sacred Time in Catholicism*

Objective

In this section the students will:

- learn that Japanese religion uses three calendars to set its events—the lunar calendar, the Gregorian solar calendar, and the complex Chinese calendar;
- compare the way Japanese religion creates and organizes sacred time with the way Catholicism organizes and uses sacred time.

Preview

A useful way to compare Japanese religions with Catholicism is to compare the way both religious traditions organize sacred time. In the Japanese tradition, three calendars are used to organize and set dates for the numerous Japanese festivals. The lunar calendar, the Gregorian (or Western) calendar, and the Chinese calendar are all consulted to schedule Shinto or Buddhist events. Since Shinto spirituality focuses on kami and ancestor worship, Shinto feasts stress purification before the first day of the new year. So, New Year's Day is a special Shinto occasion. Catholic sacred time, on the other hand, focuses on the death and resurrection of Jesus Christ, and adds many feasts that commemorate the lives of Mary and the Christian saints.

Using the Text

- Revisit the central point made in this section—that sacred time is organized very differently in Japanese religions as compared to Catholicism. Elaborate on this by listing the dates of some Shinto or Buddhist feasts or festivals celebrated in Japan. Ask students to compare these to Catholic feasts.
- Show portions of the film *Land of the Disappearing Buddha—Japan* to give students a visual summary of Japanese religious practice. Have students write down several facts they have learned from the film. Later, have students share their facts with the whole class.
- Ask a student to read the "Shinto Prayer for Peace" on page 354. Invite students to "extend" this prayer for peace and harmony by adding additional prayers for harmony between other people in the world.

Extending the Text

- Show students a liturgical calendar for Catholic feasts. Call on students to point out the beginning of this year and then its most important feasts. When is the Japanese New Year? What are the central feasts of the Japanese calendar?
- Divide the group up into small groups of three or four. Have the small groups briefly discuss the Reflection Question about Christian celebrations and secularism on page 350. After ten to fifteen minutes, call on the groups to share their answers. Read the last paragraph of the Conclusion on page 351 about Japanese religious practice and extend the discussion about secularism. Is it possible that Americans are also more religious than we think?

- Have the small groups read through the Section Summary statements, the Conclusion and then answer the Review Questions on pages 351–353 to prepare for the chapter test. Notify students of the date for the chapter test. Have students break out of groups and finish the review with oral questions and comments. Conclude this review session with a brief prayer during which you could invite students to voice various prayers for unity—in the school, community, among religious groups, etc. Recite the Our Father together.

Section Review Questions and Answers

1. How many calendars do Japanese religions typically use to designate their sacred time?

   Japanese religions use three different calendars to set the dates for religious festivals and feasts—the 354-day lunar calendar, the 365-day Gregorian (or Western) calendar, and the complex Chinese calendar.

2. Why do Eastern and Western Christians use slightly different calendars?

   Christians of the Eastern churches and the Western churches typically set the date for Easter and other important liturgical feasts on different dates. That's because Western churches use the Gregorian calendar and the Eastern or Orthodox churches use the older Julian calendar.

3. Why are Mary and the saints honored and memorialized on the Catholic Christian calendar?

   Mary is seen as the preeminent saint and played an essential role in the saving work of her son Jesus. The Christian saints, men and women who also followed in the footsteps of Jesus, are also remembered and memorialized in the Catholic Christian calendar because their example encourages contemporary Catholics. Feast days also provide opportunities to build Christian community and solidarity in a world beset by consumerism.

Chapter 8 Review Questions and Answers

1. Define the term *Shinto*.

   The term Shinto means "the way of the gods."

2. Why is kami difficult to define?

   Kami is the Japanese name for any kind of spiritual force or power. For example, mountains, rivers, trees, or rocks can be kami. Human beings can be kami, too.

3. What is the significance of the Kojiki and the Nihongi?

   The Kojiki includes the creation myth of Japan and includes a genealogy of Japan's emperors from Emperor Temmu who commissioned the work. The Nihonshoki chronicles the history of Japan. Neither source is seen as a "sacred text," that is a text revealed by the gods. But, these two texts are authoritative resources for the historical heritage of the Japanese people.

4. Define and give one example of kami.

   A kami is not a god in the sense that a god is a transcendent and all-powerful entity. A kami is the essence of something sacred. A mountain, river, rock, tree, or even a person could be kami.

5. What is the role of the "kami body" in Shinto shrine worship?

   The "kami body" in Shinto shrine worship is the receptacle into which it is believed a kami descends during a Shinto worship service.

6. What is at the heart of Zen Buddhism?

   The heart of Zen Buddhism is meditation.

7. Give an example of a koan.

   One example of a koan is, "What is the sound of one hand clapping?"

8. What was the overall theme of Tokugawa reformers?

   The overall theme of Tokugawa reformers was the purification of Japan from all outside influences.

9. What is the purpose of a kamidana?

   A kamidana, which means "kami shelf," is the place where the kami of that household is honored.

10. Explain why harmony is an apt word to describe Japanese living.

    Harmony is an apt word to describe Japanese living because Japanese religion makes no distinction between religion and politics or between religion and nature. Further, people and kami dwell together.

11. What is the most important festival celebrated by adherents of Japanese religions?

The most important Japanese religious festival is the celebration of the New Year. This festival is called Shogatsu and is celebrated on January 1, 2, and 3.

12. Why is the Grand Shrine at Ise so important to Shinto?

The Grand Shrine at Ise was the family shrine of the imperial family of Japan. Dedicated to the sun goddess Amaterasu, this shrine became significant nationally because the emperor made offerings there on behalf of the entire nation. Today, this shrine has many pilgrims.

13. What is the purpose of torii?

A torii is a gateway of two timber posts and two timber cross beams which is set up at Shinto shrines. The torii symbolically separates the profane world from the sacred space inside where the kami resides.

14. Why is ancestor veneration so important?

In Japan, the clan or extended family is the most important social structure. Family loyalty is very important. Because of Buddhist influences, Japanese culture and religious practice includes Buddhist rituals that honor the dead and ancestors. Shinto beliefs suggest that ancestors can help protect their living descendants and relatives.

15. What are the core beliefs of Japanese calendars?

Core tenets of Japanese religious practice include belief in the kami, and in ancestor worship. Approaching the deities requires purification in the home, shrine, and at burial sites. Many festivals on the Japanese calendar are related to purification. The largest is the celebration of New Year's Day. The days preceding this feast are dedicated to cleaning and purification rituals.

16. What is at the core of the Catholic Christian calendar?

Catholic Christian calendars reflect a core belief that Jesus Christ was the Son of God and that he suffered, died, and then rose again from the dead. The Catholic calendar is organized to celebrate events in the life of Jesus.

Chapter 8 Test Answers

Multiple Choice (3 points each)

1. b, 2. d, 3. d, 4. c, 5. a, 6. b, 7. d, 8. b, 9. b, 10. d, 11. c, 12. b, 13. d, 14. b, 15. c, 16. b, 17. a, 18. d, 19. a, 20. b

Short Answer (8 points each)

1. The written history begins when Japanese culture meets with Chinese and Korean culture at the beginning of the Common Era.

2. Loyalty is still exhibited in corporate Japan where loyalty to the clan until death has been replaced with loyalty to the corporation until retirement.

3. The occasion for opening the chamber at a Shinto shrine is usually a festival in which the kami is invited to participate.

4. Matsuri is the name for Japanese festivals.

5. An increasing number of Japanese weddings are taking place at Christian churches, even if the couple is not Christian.

Name _____

Japanese Religion Crossword Puzzle

Across

5. kami shelf

7. military-type ruler

8. always found at Japanese shrine entrance

9. Japanese name for sacrificial suicide

Down

1. Japanese festival

2. a puzzle with illogical solution

3. name for enlightenment in Zen Buddhism

4. sitting meditation

6. any kind of spiritual force or power

7. exemplar of loyalty toward superior

Chapter 8 Test

Name _____

Multiple Choice. *Write the letter of the best choice in the space provided.* (3 points each)

_____ 1. The Japanese creation myth
   a. is to say God created the earth.
   b. provides Japanese identity.
   c. shows Japanese belief in kami.
   d. tells how Japan was created before all other countries.

_____ 2. Japanese religion contains all of the following *except*
   a. Taoism.
   b. Confucianism.
   c. Buddhism.
   d. Hinduism.

_____ 3. Japanese emperors
   a. were considered divine.
   b. were considered kami.
   c. presided at the national shrine.
   d. all of the above

_____ 4. All of the following are considered kami except
   a. some human beings.
   b. gods.
   c. ritual.
   d. hurricanes.

_____ 5. In Shinto, which of the following is highly formalized?
   a. ritual
   b. scripture
   c. ethical code
   d. doctrine

_____ 6. Shinto shrines are placed in natural settings because
   a. the urban noise keeps the kami away.
   b. nature is sacred.
   c. of the strong sense of beauty.
   d. it is the purest of all settings.

_____ 7. Which of the following is not a traditional kami body?
   a. jewel
   b. mirror
   c. sword
   d. scripture

_____ 8. The life cycle rituals of Japanese religion include
   a. a coming of age ceremony.
   b. parts of a number of religious traditions.
   c. the presence of a political leader.
   d. an emphasis on purity.

_____ 9. Japanese festivals
   a. are generally more local than universal.
   b. exclude the other religious traditions.
   c. are more Shinto in nature than anything else.
   d. seldom involve kami.

_____ 10. Samurai
   a. were willing to commit _hara kiri_ rather than bring shame upon the ruler.
   b. were exemplars of the virtue of loyalty.
   c. rose during the 1200s.
   d. all of the above

_____ 11. Japanese social structures were highly influenced by
   a. Shinto.
   b. Taoism.
   c. Confucianism.
   d. Buddhism.

_____ 12. The two most valued virtues in Japanese religion are
   a. purity and harmony.
   b. harmony and loyalty.
   c. loyalty and spontaneity.
   d. spontaneity and harmony.

_____ 13. Which type of Shinto is the most institutionalized?
   a. Folk
   b. Sect
   c. Soto
   d. Shrine

_____ 14. The symbol for Shinto is the
   a. mirror.
   b. torii.
   c. sword.
   d. jewel.

_____ 15. The sound of one hand clapping is an example of a
   a. kami.
   b. kamidana.
   c. koan.
   d. kami body.

_____ 16. The Tokugawa shogunate
     a. allowed Western influence in his country.
     b. believed Christian missionaries had a political rather than a religious agenda.
     c. rejected the notion that Japan was of divine origin.
     d. believed salvation was through Shinto alone.

_____ 17. The Meiji Period of Japanese history
     a. accommodated Western influence in Japan.
     b. held that Christian missionaries had a political rather than a religious agenda.
     c. rejected the notion that Japan was of divine origin.
     d. believed salvation was through Shinto alone.

_____ 18. Shinto scriptures
     a. are considered gifts from the kami.
     b. are of divine origin like the Japanese land and people.
     c. do not contain the Japanese creation myth.
     d. are more accurately described as documents of ancient history.

_____ 19. The religious tradition _most_ likely to conduct funeral services in Japan is
     a. Buddhism.
     b. Christianity.
     c. Shinto.
     d. Taoism.

_____ 20. Soto Zen
     a. is a sect of Theravada Buddhism.
     b. believes enlightenment is a gradual process.
     c. is another name for Rinzai Zen.
     d. none of the above

Short Answer. *Briefly answer the following questions.* (8 points each)

1. When did the written history of Japanese religion begin?

2. How is the virtue of loyalty still exhibited in Japanese society?

3. When is the occasion for opening the chamber at a Shinto shrine?

4. What is matsuri?

5. In which religious tradition are an increasing number of Japanese weddings taking place?

Appendix: Religions with Christian and American Roots

Close to Home (pages 361–385)

High school students often have questions about the religious traditions found in this Appendix. They may have friends or relatives who are adherents, or perhaps they are members of these religious groups themselves. Sometimes, these religions are categorized as Protestant. But really, these traditions are not included among those traditions that accept the Christian Bible as the sole scriptural source for authority. Hence, religious traditions that use other texts in place of the Bible, use other texts in addition to the Bible, alter the traditional Christian Bible in some way, or simply choose to deny some parts of the Bible cannot be considered Christian or part of mainstream Protestantism. Nevertheless, these traditions do have a place in our study of the world's religions because of their popular acceptance in North American culture.

Objective

In this Appendix, the students will:

- see the special importance of learning about smaller American religious traditions outside mainline Protestant Christianity or Catholicism;
- briefly review the history of the Church of Jesus Christ of Latter-day Saints, Seventh-day Adventists, Watchtower Bible and Tract Society, Church of Christ, Scientist, and the Unitarian Universalist communities;
- become acquainted with the main beliefs and practices of these five religious traditions.

Preview

Religious traditions studied thus far have taken us all around the world. However, it is just as important to be familiar with smaller religious groups that are indigenous to America. This Appendix encourages students to answer in a more informed way the question, "Who is my neighbor?" Who are the people who live next door, down the block, or across town who have religious beliefs and practices that are quite different from ours?

Using the Text

- Before assigning the reading, poll the students about the religions to be covered. Ask the class how many of them personally know any Mormons? Seventh-day Adventists? Jehovah's Witnesses? Christian Scientists? Unitarian Universalists?
- Assign the opening text, "Close to Home," on page 361 for reading.

Extending the Text

- Distribute half a dozen copies of the local phone book that include "yellow pages" and a subject directory in the back. Write down the names of the five religious traditions being studied in this epilogue—Mormon, Seventh-day Adventist, Jehovah's Witnesses, Christian Scientist, and Unitarian Universalist. Have students raise their hands as soon as they locate local contact information for any one of these religions. Assign one student to keep a record of the address-es and phone numbers of any local branches of these five churches.

- Divide the class up into five groups, one for each religious tradition in this Appendix. Assign each group to read their respective religious traditions and then plan a way to present their material to the class in a creative way. Dedicate one day's lesson for each religious tradition. The following may be a part of each lesson:
  - Student presentations on the text material. (Assign the entire class the text to be covered one day prior to the presentation.)
  - Reflection Questions (see below).
  - Summary Statements (in the student text) and Review Questions (see below).
  - Student sharing of any Research and Activities assignments (see student text on page 385) completed in conjunction with their assigned religious tradition.

Reflection Questions

The reflection questions in the Appendix can be used in a number of ways. For example:

- Assign some or all of the questions for personal journaling.
- Facilitate and extend class discussion after student presentations for a particular section.
- Use the reflection question(s) as part of a short quiz for a particular section. Include the re-view questions as part of the quiz.

Review Questions

The review questions in the Appendix can be used after student presentations to check the class's com-prehension of the material. Assign the questions as a written quiz or as part of a formal or informal discussion.

Chapter Test

An Appendix Chapter Test is included on pages 233–234 of this Teacher's Manual. It may be given as an in-class or take home test.

The Reflection Questions, Review Questions, and Review Questions Answers are listed under the following sections.

Church of Jesus Christ of Latter-day Saints

Reflection Questions

- If members of a new religion descended on a rural town today, what do you think would be the reaction of the local people?
- Why do you think the Church of Jesus Christ of Latter-day Saints is one of the world's fast-est growing religions?

Section Review Questions and Answers

1. Where does the term "Mormon" come from?

   The term "Mormon" comes from the sacred text of the Church of Jesus Christ of Latter-day Saints, the Book of Mormon.

2. Why is the Church of Jesus Christ of Latter-day Saints not considered a Protestant church?

   Mormons do not consider themselves Protestants, but Christians in the most pure form as founded by Jesus. However, they do not view Jesus as God.

3. Why were Mormons persecuted in Illinois?

   Mormons were persecuted in Illinois for practicing polygamy. A more practical reason for opposition was that the Mormons had established a powerful voting bloc in Nauvoo through which they took political control away from the locals.

4. Why do Mormons allow baptisms of the dead?

   Mormons believe such baptisms bring salvation to their ancestors.

5. What is one essential difference between Catholicism and Mormonism?

   The most important difference between Catholics and Mormons is that Mormons do not believe that Jesus was divine. Because of this, Mormons are really not Christians.

Seventh-day Adventists

Reflection Question
- Why do you think some Christians wish to forecast the exact date of Jesus' Second Coming?

Section Review Questions and Answers
1. Summarize the origins of the Adventist movement.

   The Adventist movement was a nineteenth century movement arising from the beliefs of William Miller, who was very specific about the date of the Second Coming of Jesus. When it did not occur as planned, some Adventists modified the teaching, leading to the founding of the Seventh-day Adventist Church.

2. What was the Great Disappointment?

   William Miller had calculated the Second Coming of Jesus. When it did not happen the first time, he recalculated the event for seven months later. When the Second Coming did not happen a second time, it became known as the Great Disappointment.

3. Why do Seventh-day Adventists worship on Saturday rather than Sunday?

   Seventh-day Adventists worship on Saturday rather than Sunday because the Jewish Sabbath is Saturday. Early Christians also observed Saturday as the seventh day. Thus, the Seventh-day Adventists restored the Sabbath to Saturday.

4. Why does the Catholic Church hold that Sunday is the proper day of worship?

   Catholics and other Christians celebrate Sunday as the fulfillment of the Sabbath and as the proper day for worship. It was on Sunday, the first day of the week that Christ rose from the dead.

Watchtower Bible and Tract Society

Reflection Question

- In your opinion have Christian holidays become too secularized?

Section Review Questions and Answers

1. What is the significance of the name "Jehovah's Witness"?

   The significance of the name Jehovah's Witness was to emphasize Jehovah (another name for Yahweh), the God of the Hebrew Scriptures, as the one true God. Those who witnessed in the name of Jehovah were the true followers of the one God.

2. What is the goal of Jehovah's Witnesses' teaching and practice?

   The goal of Jehovah's Witnesses' teaching and practice is to establish a theocracy on earth. Jehovah's Witnesses hope to purify the earth of all evil before Christ sets up his earthly kingdom.

3. Why do Jehovah's Witnesses not celebrate holidays and birthdays?

   Jehovah's Witnesses do not celebrate holidays and birthdays because Jehovah did not command it and because "false" Christians and pagans celebrate them. The only day they celebrate is the memorial of Christ's death because Christ mandated this in the Bible.

The Church of Christ, Scientist

Section Review Questions and Answers

1. What did Mary Baker Eddy discover about healing?

   Mary Baker Eddy discovered that healing is accomplished through spiritual means alone.

2. Why is it incorrect to say Christian Scientists are hostile to the medical profession?

   It is incorrect to say Christian Scientists are hostile to the medical profession because they encourage their members to adhere to public health laws including immunization requirements. They also seek medical help for the delivery of babies. They visit dentists and eye doctors as well.

3. What is the role of registered practitioners?

   The role of registered practitioners is to devote their full-time employment to assisting the healing of other church members through prayer.

4. Name a Christian Scientist belief that contradicts Catholic doctrine.

   Christian Science contradicts the existence of a Creator God, the divinity of Christ, the Redemption, free will, Original Sin, and many other Catholic teachings.

Unitarian Universalist

Reflection Question

- What would it be like being a part of a religion with no formal creed?

Section Review Questions and Answers

1. Why are Unitarian Universalists not considered a Christian church?

   Unitarian Universalists do not consider themselves a Christian church since they do not believe in the divinity of Jesus Christ. They do believe that spiritual wisdom can be found in all the religions of the world.

2. What are some sources Unitarian Universalists draw on for worship?

   Some sources Unitarian Universalists draw on for worship are direct experience, words, and deeds of prophetic women and men, wisdom from the world's religions, Jewish and Christian teachings, humanist teachings, and spiritual teachings of earth-centered traditions.

Appendix Test Answers

Identification (3 points each)

1. JW
2. CS
3. LDS
4. LDS
5. JW
6. CS
7. LDS
8. UU
9. SA
10. JW
11. SA
12. SA
13. JW
14. CS
15. LDS
16. JW
17. SA
18. UU
19. JW
20. CS

Short Answer (25 points)

21. There are two reasons why religious traditions studied in this chapter are not considered Protestant Christians. One reason is because in some way what they accept as authoritative scripture is different than what Protestant Christians accept. A second reason they are not Protestant Christians is because they do not claim to be so.

Essay (15 points)

22. Answers will vary.

Appendix Test

Name _____

Identification. *For each of the following statements, identify the correct religious tradition by placing the following initials* (3 points each):

LDS—Church of Jesus Christ of Latter-day Saints
CS—Church of Christ, Scientist
JW—Jehovah's Witnesses
SA—Seventh-day Adventists
UU—Unitarian Universalist

_____ 1. Charles Russell was their founder.

_____ 2. Mary Baker Eddy was their founder.

_____ 3. Joseph Smith was their founder.

_____ 4. Brigham Young led this group to Salt Lake City, Utah.

_____ 5. Joseph Rutherford coined the popular name of this group.

_____ 6. *Science and Health* is one of their authoritative texts.

_____ 7. The *Book of Mormon* is one of their authoritative texts.

_____ 8. They draw inspiration from various religious traditions.

_____ 9. They believed the Second Coming of Jesus would be in 1844.

_____ 10. They believed the Second Coming of Jesus would be in 1914.

_____ 11. Their founder calculated the Second Coming of Jesus twice. When it did not happen, they experienced the Great Disappointment.

_____ 12. They believe the Second Coming of Jesus will be preceded by an Investigative Judgment.

_____ 13. Their goal is to establish a theocracy.

_____ 14. Contrary to popular opinion, they are not hostile to the medical profession.

_____ 15. They believe in baptizing the dead through a proxy.

_____ 16. They do not celebrate holidays.

_____ 17. They worship on Saturdays.

_____ 18. They believe authority comes from the individual.

_____ 19. The official name for this group is Watch Tower Bible and Tract Society.

_____ 20. They believe physical healing comes from spiritual, and not natural laws.

Short Answer. *Briefly answer the following question.* (25 points)

21. Why are the religious traditions studied in this chapter not considered Protestant Christian?

Essay. *Write a short essay for the following topic. Use a separate sheet of paper.* (15 points)

22. Several religious traditions in this chapter are in some way seeking the Second Coming of Jesus. What groups are these? What is their understanding of the Second Coming of Jesus? Note in your essay whether there was a change in understanding from one period of time to another. What was that change?

Afterword

Using the Text

- Invite a couple of good readers to read aloud the text on pages 357–359 to the class. Then have students write or share their final reflections on this world's religions course. Suggested questions:

1. How have I been most surprised by my study of other religions?

2. What feelings do I take away from this class about other religions?

3. How can I apply what I have learned in this class to the people and events around me?

4. How has my own faith been strengthened?

Catholic Handbook for Faith

Exploring the Religions of the World surveys several world religions while offering perspectives of each through the lens of Catholicism. It is expected that the text will be used as part of a course in a Catholic high school. The brief Catholic Handbook for Faith (pages 386–391) provides further resources on the history, Scripture, beliefs and practices, sacred time, and sacred places and spaces that are part of the Catholic faith.

Throughout the course you may use the pages of the Catholic Handbook for Faith as a reinforcement and starting point for further reflection on study on these and other themes important to Catholics. It is meant to be a supplemental resource that may be used whenever needed.